Advance Praise for
COUNTDOWN TO DALLAS

"Paul Brandus has produced a gem of a book, a completely up-to-date look at what led up to President Kennedy's assassination, a comprehensive tick-tock of Lee Oswald's dismal life, clarifying timelines of the events that awful day in November 1963, and a careful examination of the conspiracy theories and suspects that have been proposed in the six decades since. Brandus has also incorporated the findings from secret documents released in recent years, so **if you think you already know all of the story, think again—and read this well-written, fascinating volume."**

—**Dr. Larry J. Sabato**, Author, *The Kennedy Half-Century: The Presidency, Assassination, and Lasting Legacy of John F. Kennedy*; Director, Center for Politics, University of Virginia

COUNTDOWN TO DALLAS

ALSO BY PAUL BRANDUS

Jackie: Her Transformation from First Lady to Jackie O

Under This Roof: The White House and Presidency

This Day in Presidential History

This Day in U.S. Military History

COUNTDOWN TO DALLAS

The Incredible Coincidences, Routines, and Blind "Luck" that Brought John F. Kennedy and Lee Harvey Oswald Together on November 22, 1963

PAUL BRANDUS

A POST HILL PRESS BOOK

Countdown to Dallas:
The Incredible Coincidences, Routines, and Blind "Luck" that Brought John F. Kennedy and Lee Harvey Oswald Together on November 22, 1963

ISBN: 978-1-63758-194-0
ISBN (eBook): 978-1-63758-195-7

Cover design by Cody Corcoran
Interior design and composition by Greg Johnson, Textbook Perfect

This is a work of nonfiction. All people, locations, events, and situation are portrayed to the best of the author's memory.

Post Hill Press
New York • Nashville
posthillpress.com

Published in the United States of America

To Julia, Kathryn, and Rosemary

And in memory of Eugene, Jim, and Bobbie

CONTENTS

INTRODUCTION

Why Another Kennedy Book?

The midnight-blue Lincoln—a 1961 Continental, yellow DC plates GG 300—glided softly down the sunny, curving street. It was 12:30 in the afternoon; the car gleamed in the midday Texas sun. It was later determined that it was going 11.2 miles an hour, slow and steady, right down the middle lane. The vehicle had no roof attached because it was a beautiful November day, crisp and clear, the temperature sixty-five degrees.

That there was no roof that day—it wasn't bulletproof, by the way—has been the source of speculation ever since. But there is no reason for this. There was no roof because its principal occupant always wanted to be seen, always wanted people to get a good look at him. It had always been that way. This particular day even more so, because to his left sat his beautiful young wife in her chic pink suit and pillbox hat. She was ravishing.

Someone *was* getting a good look. From the sixth floor of a dingy book warehouse, peering through the 4x scope of a cheap but powerful Italian rifle, he tracked the car and its famous passengers as they waved to bystanders. His heart likely raced with nervousness and excitement as he waited for just the right moment to squeeze the trigger.

Of course, we know what happened next.

Don't we?

* * *

Why another book on the Kennedy assassination? After all, it's not like this is untrod ground. More than forty thousand books on JFK, his presidency, and its sudden end have been published over the decades. On the big fiftieth anniversary in 2013, there was a high tide of books, television programs, panels, and remembrances about that awful day.

But history is never static. It is always plodding forward as more details are uncovered. Even the murder of Abraham Lincoln nearly 160 years ago (or nearly eight score, to borrow from the great emancipator's vocabulary) continues to be the subject of new works. In 2020, for example, there were two excellent contributions: *What Really Happened: The Lincoln Assassination* by Robert J. Hutchinson (don't we know what happened?) and Brad Meltzer and Josh Mensch's *The Lincoln Conspiracy: The Secret Plot to Kill America's 16th President—and Why It Failed.*

And so it is with the death of JFK. The story of his assassination needs a freshening up because since that fiftieth anniversary, a great deal of new information has been made public. Most of it has come from the US government. Between July 2017 and December 2021, for instance, the National Archives and Records Administration (NARA) released, in several batches, some fifty-five thousand pages of documents, many from the Central Intelligence Agency and the Federal Bureau of Investigation.

What have we learned from all this? In chapter two, we'll hear from a variety of respected historians and journalists who have devoted significant chunks of their lives to studying the assassination and its aftermath. One has followed the Kennedy saga from the very beginning. Others have taken yearslong deep dives into the labyrinth of federal bureaucracy, particularly the CIA and FBI. Some have also explored every known facet of Lee Harvey Oswald's life, ranging from his violent and unstable childhood—including his teenaged threat to murder President Eisenhower—to his time in the Marines, defector to the Soviet Union, and final seventeen months in America, when his instability, violent behavior (he was a notorious wifebeater, for example), and other psychoses were on full display to those who knew him best: his wife Marina, obviously, and coworkers at the many jobs he drifted between. Conspiracy writers often ignore or, at best, downplay many of these things.

Of course, you can decide for yourself what the 2017–2021 revelations mean and whether they contain any—and I emphasize this word—*conclusive* evidence to contradict the central finding of the famous Warren Commission, which reported in September 1964 that Oswald, acting alone and without assistance from any other individual or group, killed President Kennedy. Doubtless, there will be some readers who will continue to believe that sinister forces, six decades later, are still busy obscuring the truth.

Why have fifty-five-thousand-plus pages been released since 2017, anyway? In 1991, the movie director Oliver Stone came out with a film—*JFK*—which implied that anyone and everyone, including Vice President Lyndon Johnson, the Central Intelligence Agency, the Federal Bureau of Investigation, the Pentagon, big business, anti-Castro Cubans, the Dallas police department, and a motley assortment of characters from New Orleans, were either co-conspirators or had some sort of motive to cover up the truth of the president's assassination. Stone called his movie a "counter-myth" to the Warren Commission's "fictional myth."

The great conceit of *JFK* is that in its accusation of a vast government conspiracy and cover-up, Stone engaged in a vast cover-up himself of undeniable truths about the assassination itself. As artistic expression—a 189-minute movie—it was a masterpiece. Critics praised Stone's cinematography, editing, and bravura storytelling (indeed, it went on to win Academy Awards for those first two categories). The *Chicago Tribune*'s Gene Siskel, for example, called it "thoroughly compelling." At the same time, Stone came under fire for playing fast and loose with the facts. Siskel also said that *JFK* was stuffed with "gross alterations of fact," while crosstown rival Richard Roeper of the *Chicago Sun-Times* said, "One can admire Stone's filmmaking skills and the performances, while denouncing the utter crapola presented as 'evidence' of a conspiracy to murder." And on Christmas Eve 1991, Bernard Weinraub in the *New York Times* quoted a "top Hollywood producer" who said, "Political and ethical questions about a film like *JFK* were simply dwarfed by money considerations."[1]

But the very next day, Christmas Day, Harvard Law professor Alan Dershowitz came to Stone's defense. *JFK* was "too conspiratorial for my tastes," he wrote in an op-ed for the *Los Angeles Times*, "but it is precisely what is to be expected when the government sets out on a deliberate policy of keeping its citizens from making up their own minds on the basis of all the available facts." He said Stone "takes full literary licenses not so much with the facts as we know them, but rather with the facts that have been kept from us by questionable claims of national security."

Dershowitz ended with this: "Until history comes forward with facts, art is entitled to paint with a broad brush." He had a point.

The film was so controversial that within a year, Congress passed the President John F. Kennedy Assassination Records Collection Act, which was signed into law by President George H. W. Bush on October 26, 1992. It mandated that all assassination records be released no later than twenty-five years from that date.

Fast forward to 2017. Here is what NARA released that year:

- July 24: 3,810 documents
- October 26: 2,891 documents
- November 3: 676 documents
- November 9: 13,213 documents
- November 17: 10,744 documents
- December 15: 3,539 documents

But the government missed its deadline to release everything in 2017. On April 26, 2018, another 19,045 documents were made public, bringing the total to 53,918. On December 15, 2021, another 1,491 pages were released.

But it's still not everything. An estimated 14,343 documents related to the assassination remain partially or completely classified, according to the National Archives. Most were created by the CIA and FBI and are said to include reports generated around the time of the president's murder, files of CIA officers who knew about accused assassin Lee Harvey Oswald, and interviews conducted by congressional investigators in the mid-1970s.

Why? The JFK Records Act mandated that, twenty-five years after its passage, all records should be released in their entirety, unless the president determined that "continued postponement is made necessary by an identifiable harm to the military defense, intelligence operations, law enforcement, or conduct of foreign relations" and "the identifiable harm is of such gravity that it outweighs the public interest in disclosure."

President Donald Trump made such a determination in the fall of 2017. On October 26 of that year, he issued an executive order saying: "I have no choice—today—but to accept those redactions rather than allow potentially irreversible harm to our Nation's security." He cited "national security, law enforcement, and foreign affairs concerns," that were raised during a conversation with then-CIA director Mike Pompeo.

On April 26, 2018, Trump issued another order setting a new date for remaining documents to be released: October 26, 2021. His 2020 election defeat meant the matter was now in the hands of President Joe Biden.

But four days before that deadline, Biden ordered yet another delay. The cause this time? The pandemic. In a White House memo, Biden cited the National Archives, the repository of JFK-related documents, which "require[s] additional time to engage with the agencies and to conduct research within the larger collection to maximize the amount of information released." Biden quoted the archivist further: "Making these decisions is a matter that requires a professional, scholarly, and orderly process; not decisions or releases made in haste." The archivist proposed one "interim release" of documents in late 2021 and "one more comprehensive release in late 2022." As mentioned, the archivist made good on the late 2021 release.

Will we see everything? Biden, in his October 22, 2021, statement, said that after all this time—three-fifths of a century—"the need to protect records concerning the assassination has only grown weaker," and yet "only in the rarest cases is there any legitimate need for continued protection of such records."

So we'll see.

This book will update the narrative of the assassination and events leading up to it, using all new documents released through December 2021. Beyond official documents, other material has also surfaced, and when relevant to the assassination's narrative, it will be included, too.

The new material, in chapter two—"What Have We Learned Since 2013?"—the fiftieth anniversary of the assassination—will be added to individual chapters as well, adding context and illumination to topics such as Lee Harvey Oswald's life, the activities of President Dwight D. Eisenhower, the Central Intelligence Agency, Secret Service procedures and traditions, Fidel Castro, and more.

This will all come together in chapter eight, when I'll count down the 365 days before the assassination, November 22, 1962, to November 21, 1963, and then the fateful day itself—November 22, 1963—up to the moment when President Kennedy's limo made its fateful left turn onto Elm Street.

But there's more to it than this. I've always thought that greater clarity concerning the assassination can be found by also examining the broader context in which it occurred. For example, many conspiracy proponents think that the security setup in Dallas—no top on the car, Secret Service agents well behind Kennedy—was unusual. It wasn't.

Prior to Dallas, it was quite normal for presidents to ride around in open cars. It was also quite normal for Secret Service agents to be near—*but not right by*—chief executives when they were driven about.

Even after nearly being assassinated as president-elect, Franklin D. Roosevelt rode around in an open car; Secret Service agents sometimes clung to the side of his vehicles, sometimes they did not. There were assassination scares involving Harry Truman and Dwight Eisenhower, also, but as we'll see, they too continued to ride about in the open for all to see—even in risky foreign lands. They were politicians. They wanted to stand up and wave. They were there to be seen.

John F. Kennedy was no different. All over the world, from Hawaii to West Berlin and everywhere in between, he preferred open cars. He admired his Secret Service agents, but generally preferred to keep them, again, close by, *but not right by*. It was a different era, "A More Innocent Era," as chapter three is called.

There is also this: we Americans love mysteries and conspiracies. Not just Kennedy's assassination. There are those among us who question everything from the moon landing to 9/11 to what's going on at Area 51, to name but three things. I'll discuss this too, in a chapter called "The Vast Conspiracy-Industrial Complex." Truth and perception, it seems, are often in the eye of the beholder.

In fact, let's start there, by venturing into the frigid dark waters of the North Atlantic.

CHAPTER ONE

The Vast Conspiracy-Industrial Complex

"To see what is in front of one's nose requires a constant struggle."

—GEORGE ORWELL

What happened when RMS *Titanic* sank on the night of April 14–15, 1912? That's an easy one, isn't it?

At the climax of James Cameron's spectacular 1997 movie, we see the great ship snapping in two moments before it plunges to the bottom of the icy North Atlantic. We hear a deep moan, terrifying and ghostly, as the hull strains, followed by a long and ear-splitting roar as it gives way.

Indeed, when famed explorer Robert Ballard found the remains of the *Titanic* a dozen years earlier, in 1985, it certainly appeared as if the ship had, in fact, broken in two. Incredible images, vivid and awe-inspiring, show the bow quite recognizable, but the stern, about one-third of a mile away, clearly suffered extensive damage during its 12,500-foot plunge (about 3.8 kilometers) and subsequent slamming into the ocean floor.

Yet many passengers and crew who survived that terrible night said nothing about the *Titanic* breaking in half before it went under.

One was the ship's second officer, Charles Herbert Lightoller.* During a US Senate inquiry into the maritime disaster—just a week after the doomed ship went down—he was questioned by Republican senator William Alden Smith of Michigan:

Senator SMITH: Was the vessel broken in two in any manner, or intact?

Mr. LIGHTOLLER: Absolutely intact.

Senator SMITH: On the decks?

Mr. LIGHTOLLER: Intact, sir.

Another survivor was Third Officer Herbert John Pitman.

Senator SMITH: Did you see the *Titanic* go down?

Mr. PITMAN: Yes, sir.

Senator SMITH: Describe, if you can, how she sank?

Mr. PITMAN: Judging by what I could see from a distance, she gradually disappeared until the forecastle head was submerged to the bridge. Then she turned right on end and went down perpendicularly.

Senator SMITH: Did she seem to be broken in two?

Mr. PITMAN: Oh, no.

And yet Alfred Olliver, quartermaster, had a different recollection. The questioner this time was Senator Theodore Elijah Burton (R-Ohio):

Senator BURTON: Did you see the boat sink?

Mr. OLLIVER: I cannot say that I saw it right plain; but to my imagination I did, because the lights went out before she went down.

Senator BURTON: How did she sink?

Mr. OLLIVER: She was well down at the head at first, when we got away from her at first, and to my idea she broke forward, and the afterpart righted itself and made another plunge and

* Lightoller, featured prominently in the 1997 movie, was second officer on board the *Titanic*. During the evacuation he was in charge of loading the lifeboats on the ship's port side. He was the most senior member of the crew to survive the sinking. He died in 1952, age seventy-eight.

> went right down. I fancied I saw her black form. It was dark, and I fancied I saw her black form going that way.

Hundreds of other survivors—there were 705 in all—in lifeboats at various distances from and on both sides of the ship, were also conflicted as to whether the *Titanic* sank in one or two pieces. Four decades later, a seminal book on that terrible night—Walter Lord's magnificent *A Night to Remember*, which was based on exhaustive research and interviews with some sixty survivors, said nothing about the great ship snapping in two.

The *Titanic* was 882.5 feet (269 meters) long. The seas were calm, the night clear. A ship the length of three football fields, *and yet people who were right there—up close eyewitnesses to one of the twentieth century's most shocking and unthinkable tragedies—tell very different stories about what they saw*. This, in turn, would influence how succeeding generations would study and interpret what happened that frigid night on the high seas.

How does this happen? In 2014, the National Academy of Sciences issued a comprehensive report on eyewitness evidence and how people can see, and recall, things quite differently. One key excerpt from its summary is of particular interest:

> Factors such as viewing conditions, duress, elevated emotions, and biases influence the visual perception experience. Perceptual experiences are stored by a system of memory that is highly malleable and continuously evolving, neither retaining nor divulging content in an informational vacuum. As such, the fidelity of our memories to actual events may be compromised by many factors at all stages of processing, from encoding to storage and retrieval. Unknown to the individual, memories are forgotten, reconstructed, updated, and distorted.

Here's the question: If hundreds of people saw with their own eyes the incredible sight of a huge ship one-sixth of a mile long sinking over some two and a half hours—but disagree on what happened—why should anyone be surprised that there is such variance in the stories told by those who saw or heard the *six-second* assassination of President Kennedy? There were as many as 178 eyewitnesses* (or just earwitnesses) in Dealey Plaza on November 22, 1963, and, as was the case with the *Titanic* in 1912, their accounts of what happened differ wildly. This in turn has helped fuel what I'll call the "vast conspiracy-industrial complex."

As mentioned, the assassination of JFK took just six seconds, and we've been discussing and debating it ever since. Six seconds, six decades. It has never ended, and long after you and I are gone, the twentieth century's most shocking assassination will continue to be the subject of debate, not to mention countless books and movies, not unlike the nineteenth century's most heartbreaking crime: the killing of Abraham Lincoln.

After all this time, a clear majority of Americans continue to believe that Kennedy's death was the result of a conspiracy. An Associated Press-GfK poll conducted in 2019 said 59 percent of Americans held this view, while 24 percent thought Oswald acted alone, with 16 percent being unsure. Yet in the absence, after all this time, of clear, verifiable, and irrefutable proof, the conspiracy crowd has been steadily shrinking. A 2003 Gallup poll, for example, had found that 75 percent of Americans thought there was a conspiracy.[2] Thus between 2003 and 2019, the conspiracy majority has been shrinking by one percentage point per year.

It's only fair to point out that the absence of that clear, verifiable, and irrefutable proof doesn't mean that there wasn't a conspiracy. But it's also fair to say that the various irregularities, shadows in photographs, and other alleged oddities certainly doesn't mean that one existed, either. In the end, as is the case with other great questions of history, we're left with only what can actually be proven.

This dynamic isn't unique to JFK's assassination. Similar doubt about other events has persisted for decades as well. A Scripps Howard/

* According to curator of the Sixth Floor Museum in Dallas, Stephen Fagin, the Warren Commission identified around 120 eyewitnesses. In the 1970s, the House Select Committee on Assassinations reviewed 178 witness statements (some more earwitnesses than eyewitnesses).

Ohio University survey in 1997, for instance, revealed that 42 percent of Americans thought it "very likely" or "somewhat likely" that President Franklin D. Roosevelt knew ahead of time that the Japanese were going to bomb Pearl Harbor, but did nothing because he wanted the United States to enter World War II. The same survey shows that one in five Americans—21 percent—believe that a UFO crashed Roswell, New Mexico, in 1947, and that it was covered up by the federal government. Meanwhile, 55 percent believe that the 1968 assassination of Dr. Martin Luther King Jr. was "part of a larger conspiracy."[3]

But wait: there's more. Going back in time, another Scripps Howard/Ohio University poll (July 2006), said that 16 percent of Americans believe that "people in the federal government either assisted in the 9/11 attacks or took no action to stop the attacks because they wanted the United States to go to war in the Middle East"; another 6 percent said "the collapse of the twin towers in New York was aided by explosives secretly planted in the two buildings," while the same percentage—6—think "the Pentagon was not struck by an airliner captured by terrorists but instead was hit by a cruise missile fired by the US military" (hopefully the same 6 percent). A CBS News survey in 2004 said that 26 percent of Americans thought that the car crash in Paris that killed Princess Diana in 1997 was "probably planned," 9 percent think it "might be true" that the US government bombed the Murrah Federal Building in Oklahoma City in 1995 (1995 CBS survey), and that 6 percent of Americans thought the moon landings, which first occurred in 1969, were faked (1999 Gallup survey).

It doesn't seem to matter whether they are major, history-altering events (Pearl Harbor, JFK, 9/11), lesser tragedies (Oklahoma City, Diana), or out-of-this-world events (UFOs and moon landings). Conspiracy theories, in fact, arc across recorded time, dating as far back as 68 AD, when Roman Emperor Nero is said to have committed suicide (or did he?). There will always be a chunk of the population that just doesn't buy the official version of events and is convinced that someone, somewhere is hiding the truth.

And yet the percentages of conspiracy theorists are far higher around Kennedy's murder than these other events. Here I bring in the late Vincent Bugliosi, the powerhouse prosecutor turned writer, who once estimated that of more than one thousand books written about the assassination, at least 90 percent of them claim that there was a conspiracy.[4]

But Bugliosi, the meticulous lawman—who lost just 1 of the 106 felony jury trials he prosecuted over the course of a long courtroom career*—tacked in a different direction, famously arguing that there was no conspiracy. It was hardly idle judgment. His conclusion was based on the same painstaking, granular approach that he used to such great effect as a prosecutor and is described in what is arguably the most important and impactful book ever written on the assassination and its aftermath: 2007's powerful *Reclaiming History: The Assassination of President John F. Kennedy*, a thorough, meticulous 1,648-page work, with a CD-ROM containing an additional 958 pages of endnotes and 170 pages of source notes.

It was Bugliosi's belief that the 90 percent of assassination books that play up an assortment of conspiracy theories have by sheer volume overshadowed any reasonable, unemotional analysis of November 22, 1963. He writes:

> Unless this fraud is finally exposed, the word *believe* will be forgotten by future generations and John F. Kennedy will have unquestionably become the victim of a conspiracy. Belief will have become unchallenged fact, and the faith of the American people in their institutions further eroded. If that is allowed to happen, Lee Harvey Oswald, a man who hated his country and everything for which it stands, will have triumphed even beyond his intent on that fateful day in November.[5]

* From 1964 to 1972, Bugliosi worked for the Los Angeles County District Attorney's Office and later in private practice. In addition to his 99 percent successful prosecution rate (winning 105 out of 106 felony jury trials), he had a 100 percent success rate representing criminal defendants, winning all three of the major cases he took on.

Bugliosi didn't set out to write a 1,648-page book. In 1986, a British television network decided to hold a mock trial of Lee Harvey Oswald. Determined to make it as realistic and fair as possible, it hired noted criminal defense attorney Gerry Spence to defend Oswald, and to prosecute the case against him, it hired Bugliosi.

As spectacular as Bugliosi's record as a criminal prosecutor was, Spence's was even better. Bugliosi lost 1 of his 106 cases. But according to American Bar Association records, Spence never lost a case, ever—neither as a prosecutor, nor in representing a criminal defendant.[6]

A member of the American Trial Lawyers Hall of Fame, he retired in 2008, age seventy-nine, with a perfect record. Thus, the "documentary-trial" of Oswald was, in legal terms, a mega-showdown between the best criminal prosecutor and best criminal defendant in the United States.

President Kennedy's assassination would have been tried under Texas law, because, if you can believe it, despite the assassinations of three presidents in thirty-six years—Abraham Lincoln (1865), James Garfield (1881), and William McKinley (1901), there was no federal statute against murdering a commander in chief. Thus producers followed Texas's criminal trial procedure as it existed at the time of Kennedy's murder. The jury consisted of citizens from the Dallas area—drawn from official court roles—who reviewed hundreds of exhibits and listened to testimony from twenty-four witnesses, including spectators, ballistics experts, pathologists, and Ruth Paine, with whom Oswald's wife Marina was living at the time of the assassination. Exhibits included the most important piece of assassination evidence: the home movie of the assassination taken by Dallas businessman Abraham Zapruder. Presiding over all this was a real judge, Lucius Bunton III of the Western District of Texas, who had been on the federal bench for seven years and was a former Texas district attorney.

It was just a television program, yet it was the first and only time that various—and contradictory—versions of the assassination have been subjected to legal cross-examining. And the fact that this was done by two of the most powerful and thorough trial attorneys in the United

States—men with impeccable reputations and records—conveyed extra gravitas. *Time* magazine called it the closest thing to a real prosecution that Oswald would ever have.

The trial lasted twenty-one hours. In his closing argument, Bugliosi maintained there was "not one microscopic speck of evidence that anyone other than Lee Harvey Oswald was responsible for the assassination of John F. Kennedy." He added: "As surely as I am standing here, as surely as night follows day, Lee Harvey Oswald was responsible for the murder."

Wrapping up his defense of Oswald (or as he called him "my client, Lee,") Spence said "There is only one truth in this case and that is the truth that nobody knows the truth....They won't tell us what's in the closet."

The bar for conviction was, of course, to show beyond any reasonable doubt that Oswald killed the president. The jury did so, finding him guilty. But it wasn't unanimous. Seven of the twelve jurors said Oswald acted alone, while three said he acted with others. The remaining two were undecided. As defense attorney Spence, suffering an unheard-of defeat, acknowledged, "No other lawyer in America could have done what Vince did in this case."[7]

And no other writer could (or has) written the kind of book that sprang from Bugliosi's typically exhaustive research. Here's what I mean by exhaustive: it took twenty years for Bugliosi to write the book, including eighty-to-one-hundred-hour weeks over the final seven years.

Of course, length doesn't necessarily correlate with quality, but with Bugliosi it does. "Reclaiming History" expands upon his successful prosecution in Oswald's "trial," but what makes it so delicious is his well-documented demolishing of assorted conspiracy theories that have existed since 1963. Those theories—fueled, more than anything, by Warren Commission inconsistencies and omissions, but also later books and movies like *JFK*, the 1991 Oliver Stone film that remains so much mother's milk for the conspiracists—continue to flourish today and will never go away.

CHAPTER TWO

What Have We Learned Since 2013?

"Incompetence is a better explanation than conspiracy in most human activity."

—PETER BERGEN

The thirtieth anniversary of President Kennedy's assassination—1993—coincided with the passing by Congress of the JFK Records Act, which mandated the full release of all government files relating to the murder. It also created a civilian Assassination Records Review Board (ARRB) to oversee this process. By the time the Board's work was completed in the late 1990s, some six million pages of documents had been made available to the public through the National Archives.

"People often forget that at the time the law was passed, 98 percent of all Warren commission documents had been released to the public," notes Gerald Posner, author of *Case Closed*, a 1993 book that makes the case for Oswald as a lone assassin. That 98 percent amounted to more than four million pages of documents.

Before disbanding in 1998, the ARRB also set a twenty-five-year schedule for the release of remaining documents, and then turned over control of those documents to the National Archives.

Then...nothing happened.

"Nobody did a thing," said Mark Zaid, a Washington lawyer who, aside from representing whistleblowers in their cases against the federal government, has been very active in the JFK assassination documents area for decades. "Congress dropped its oversight authority, didn't follow up and everybody was busy with other things. We had 9/11. We had the wars in Afghanistan and Iraq and elsewhere. So this all dropped to a point where only JFK geeks like Gerald and I, who were paying attention, were constantly saying, 'where are the records, where are the records.'"[1]

Which brings us to 2017–2021, and the release of those previously mentioned fifty-five thousand documents. Let's review and then see what a variety of historians/professors/researchers on both sides of this issue have to say.

July 24, 2017—Documents released: 3,810

This batch of documents has proven to be frustrating for assassination researchers. Much of the material was illegible. Much of it appeared to be duplicates of previously released and partially redacted documents. Some are in foreign languages and filled with various code words.

The most interesting part of the July 24 release concerned seventeen audio files of interviews with Yuri Nosenko. Nosenko, a KGB officer who defected to the United States in January 1964, claimed to have been the officer in charge of Oswald's file during parts of his time in the Soviet Union.

In the hours after the assassination, President Johnson feared that it was the prelude to an attack on the United States. Nosenko defected with a message: that the Soviet Union had nothing to do with Kennedy's murder. Oswald was never an agent of the KGB, he maintained, emphasizing that the Soviets considered him an oddball who was unstable and unfit for espionage work. The argument could be made that Oswald's own work record in the United States, bouncing from menial job to menial job, and the distinctly negative impression he left on practically everyone he came into contact with (we'll explore this later) would support this view.

But Nosenko wasn't believed, not at first. James Angleton, the CIA's legendary counterintelligence chief, suspected that Nosenko was a false defector, sent to America to muddy the waters and confuse the agency's Soviet division. Ironically, Angleton's distrust was fueled by a defector he did believe: Peter Deriabin, who'd been working for the CIA for years, and had provided it with extensive knowledge on the workings of Soviet intelligence. Angleton also had faith in another defector, Anatoliy Golitsyn, who had warned the CIA that someone just like Nosenko would defect and try to subvert its efforts.

"In the spring of 1964, after years of crushing failures, Angleton sought redemption," intelligence reporter Tim Weiner wrote in his 2007 book, *Legacy of Ashes: The History of the CIA* (Anchor Books). Angleton "believed that if the CIA could break Nosenko, the master plot might be revealed—and the Kennedy assassination solved."[2]

And so Deriabin was ordered to interrogate Nosenko to help determine whether he was a legitimate defector or, as Angleton suspected, a plant. Nosenko, who had been locked up in a safe house attic and then a cell at Camp Peary, a CIA facility near Williamsburg, Virginia, certainly understood that this was how he was viewed.

The transcripts from the July 24 release show that Nosenko didn't help his case when, over the course of his many drawn-out interrogations, he kept saying that he couldn't remember certain procedures or the ranks of specific officers within the Soviet intelligence and security service.

Deriabin was eventually pulled off the Nosenko case, but the interrogations would continue. It wouldn't be until 1967 that the CIA finally accepted that he was telling the truth. He was released, given $80,000 and a new name, and shipped off to live in anonymity in the southern US, with sporadic trips to Langley for consultations and to deliver lectures. A month prior to his death in 2008, he was visited by a group of CIA officers who presented him with a letter from then–CIA Director Michael Hayden, thanking him for his service to the United States. It can be considered an apology for his yearslong, often brutal treatment after his 1964 defection.

But to this day, Nosenko remains a controversial figure, with some assassination analysts insisting that he was a KGB plant, and that he was successful in helping to obscure alleged Soviet involvement in Kennedy's murder.

October 26, 2017—Documents released: 2,891

Upon first examination, this batch of documents was a mess, says Larry Sabato, founder and director of the Center for Politics at the University of Virginia, who assembled a team to review them. "Handwritten notes from the CIA and others are often illegible," he told the *New York Times* the evening of their release. "Think of this as an unassembled million-piece puzzle."

These million pieces are all rabbit holes that can take someone in any direction. As a skeptical Sabato asks: "Are they true? How do they augment our current knowledge, if at all? Do they somehow help us to answer the larger questions about the assassination? These are questions we should ask as we examine this treasure trove."[3]

But much has been found. Among the highlights:

The release gave new details on US efforts to bring down the Castro regime.

In a January 19, 1962, memo from Gen. Edward Lansdale—who ran the Kennedy administration's "Operation Mongoose" program against Cuban leader Fidel Castro—the Pentagon was asked to submit a plan to cripple Cuba's crucial sugar industry by targeting its workers with "non-lethal BW [biological warfare], insect-borne, introduced secretly to the target area by the Navy." If that wasn't sufficient, a September 6, 1962, memo suggested "agricultural sabotage...specifically the possibility of producing crop failures by the introduction of biological agents which would appear to be of natural origin." McGeorge Bundy, JFK's national-security adviser, said he had no worries about such a plan, but that "we must avoid external activities such as release of chemicals, etc., unless they could be completely covered up." Meanwhile, an August 6 memo that year floated the idea of an outright invasion using some 261,000 troops who could seize control of "key strategic areas" on the island within ten to fifteen days. "There may be a requirement for amphibious lift for rapid deployment and counterguerilla activity until order has been restored," the memo added.[4]

Mexican authorities worked closely with US officials in a variety of ways.

Long before the assassination, Mexican authorities helped wiretap the Soviet and Cuban embassies. They made thorough attempts to investigate Oswald's dealings in Mexico. One probe concerned a tip the CIA received that Oswald had deposited $5,000 in a Mexican bank during his September/October visit to Mexico City. After that tip was received on January 6, 1964, Alfonso Frias, the assistant chief of the Bank of Mexico—a man "who has furnished reliable information in the past"—investigated and traced all deposits in Mexican banks, looking for the money. No such Oswald transaction was found.[5]

The FBI kept tabs on Mark Lane, a conspiracy advocate who also happened to be an attorney who represented Oswald's mother Marguerite.

According to a January 20, 1964, document, an FBI source—"who has furnished reliable information in the past"—said that Lane met with a Polish journalist, and in the meeting, a series of wild conspiracy theories were tossed around, including one ridiculous claim that J. D. Tippit, the Dallas policeman killed by Oswald shortly after Oswald shot Kennedy, was the real presidential assassin—and that Jack Ruby had killed Tippit.[6]

A handwritten CIA document, dated June 16, 1964, alleges—despite a mountain of evidence to the contrary—that Oswald may have been accompanied on his mysterious September 1963 trip to Mexico City by "El Mexicano."

Yet another document claims that "El Mexicano" may have been a man named Francisco Rodriguez Tamayo, the captain of something called "Cuban Rebel Army 57" until he defected to the United States in June of 1959. Tamayo, the documents allege, was Rodriguez Tamayo, the head of an anti-Castro Training Camp at Pontchartrain, Louisiana.[7]

One of Richard Nixon's Watergate burglars claimed—in 1976—that "El Mexicano" and Jack Ruby met Castro in Havana months before the assassination.

The burglar, the convicted felon Frank Sturgis, phoned the CIA and claimed the president's assassination was discussed, as well as Castro supplying Ruby with drugs. Of course, there's no proof of any of this.[8]

The FBI worried, correctly, that the murder of Oswald would raise doubts about whether Oswald acted alone in killing Kennedy.

Calling the killing of Oswald "inexcusable" in light of "our warnings to the Dallas Police Department" about his safety, FBI Director J. Edgar Hoover said Ruby's mob connections (described by Hoover as "some rumors of underworld activity in Chicago") would open a pandora's box of speculation and doubt among Americans about the president's assassination and whether Oswald was silenced. "The thing I am concerned about, and so is Mr. Katzenbach (the deputy attorney general), is having something issued so that we can convince the public that Oswald is the real assassin."[9]

There was Soviet speculation that Lyndon Johnson was involved in the assassination.

Hoover—three long years after Kennedy's killing—sent the White House a memo summing up the Soviet reaction to Dallas. Kremlin officials were shocked by the assassination, Hoover said, and that church bells tolled in that atheistic country the weekend of the assassination. Hoover also reported that the view from Moscow was that the killing was the result of an "ultraright" conspiracy to "effect a 'coup.'"

None of this was news. It had all been reported the day after the assassination itself. Aline Mosby, a United Press International correspondent who interviewed Oswald after his defection to Moscow in 1959, wrote that "Soviet commentators blamed 'ultra conservatives' for the assassination. They made no mention of Lee Harvey Oswald, charged in Dallas with the murder of the president" (by the time of the assassination, Mosby had transferred to UPI's Paris bureau).

Johnson himself knew of the Soviet shock within hours of the assassination, having received heartfelt cables from Premier Nikita Khrushchev, who called Kennedy's murder "a heavy blow to all people who hold dear the cause of peace and Soviet-American cooperation," and Soviet president Leonid Brezhnev, who said "the Soviet people share the sorrow of the American people for their grave loss, the tragic death of this outstanding statesman in his prime."[10]

That Hoover considered this information relevant years later is bizarre, and the fact that the government sat on such a trivial memo for years seems equally inexplicable.

Khrushchev thought the Dallas police were inept—if not complicit.

A CIA report revealed that the Soviet leader thought that Big D's police had been an "accessory" to Kennedy's killing, on the grounds that something as momentous as a presidential assassination could not have occurred without a conspiracy.

False, alcohol-fueled dead ends.

The documents detail at least two instances of people who had been drinking and claiming, after the assassination, to have overheard fishy things. A Canadian man said he had been in a bar on the US side of the border in early November and heard three men talking about JFK's trip to Dallas and how "he would never leave there alive." The man, Henry Gourley, claims the three men were on their way to Cuba, and that one of them was Oswald. A drinking buddy later told the FBI that Gourley often let his inauguration get the best of him.

Also weeks before the assassination, a New Orleans man, Robert C. Rawls, claimed to have heard a man in a bar betting $100 that Kennedy would soon be dead. Reporting the incident to the Secret Service after Kennedy's murder, Rawls said that he (Rawls) was drunk and couldn't remember any other details.[11]

Isn't it funny how alleged conspirators, seeking to commit the crime of the century and cover their tracks, would blab in a bar?

November 3, 2017—Documents released: 676

The majority of these documents—553 of them—are from the CIA and are records that were previously denied in their entirety to the public, according to the Archives. The withholding seems little more than typical bureaucratic overreach, given that the documents released concern things that had been common knowledge since 1963–64, such as the fact that Oswald sought a visa from the Soviet embassy in Mexico City. Wow! What a revelation.

Another non-bombshell involves Thomas B. Casasin, who at the time of the assassination was said to be an officer in the CIA's "Soviet Russia Division." Reading about Oswald's return to the US in 1962, Casasin told subordinates that while he was interested in knowing more about the Minsk factory where Oswald had worked, that Oswald shouldn't be pushed "too hard...because this individual looks odd." Of course, there's no evidence that Oswald was "pushed" by anyone from the CIA about the factory.

There is one interesting tidbit, however: on the night of the assassination, CIA officer Paul Hartman was ordered by his superior to "make a thorough check within the Agency at Headquarters to determine whether Lee Harvey OSWALD had ever been used by the agency or connected with it in any conceivable way." In a memo dated September 18, 1975—nearly twelve years later—he said that any allegations of such connections "are totally unfounded." This included the Covert Action Staff, which, Hartman added, "also found no record on him." Of course, an absence of documentation doesn't necessarily mean that there wasn't any sort of official connection, beyond monitoring Oswald's comings and goings in Mexico City in September and October 1963.

November 9, 2017—Documents released: 13,213

CIA documents, nearly thirteen thousand of them, make up nearly the entire batch of this release. All were formerly withheld in part except for two. The release also includes more than two hundred documents from the National Security Agency, then as now the biggest of all American intelligence agencies.

In one document dated December 13, 1963—three weeks to the day after the assassination—John Moss Whitten, who had been the agency's covert operations chief for Mexico and Central America, was put in charge of the CIA's internal investigation concerning Kennedy's murder.

As officers were listening to assassination coverage on the radio on November 22, "When the name of Lee Oswald was heard, the effect was electric," Whitten wrote. "A phone message from the FBI came at about the same time, naming OSWALD as the possible assassin and asking for traces."

Whitten adds that in the wake of the assassination, a task force was assigned to review Oswald's Mexico trip and any other information it had on him. He notes that when Cuban officials in Mexico City learned of the assassination, the reaction was "sombre" [sic] and that "to date there is no credible information in CIA files which would appear to link Lee OSWALD with the Cuban government or the Cuban intelligence service." He adds: "The whole question of whether Lee OSWALD had any secret connection with the Soviets or Cubans in Mexico cannot yet be answered, but certain parts of the evidence indicate to the contrary."[12]

November 17, 2017—Documents released: 10,744

All but 144 of this batch of records released by the Archives had been made public before, but with various redactions. They were now released again and revealed code names that had been assigned to a group of informants that the FBI relied on for information about Soviet intelligence activities in the United States.

At least three, code-named "Nick Nack," "Gunson," and "Gleme," supported the claims of Yuri Nosenko, the defector mentioned previously. Nosenko, who defected to the US in 1964, claimed that the Soviets had nothing to do with Kennedy's assassination, but you'll recall that the CIA's longtime counter-espionage chief James Angleton didn't trust Nosenko and considered him a Kremlin plant.

The FBI's intelligence chief, William Sullivan, wrote in a January 6, 1965, memo that "Gleme" was "a woman Soviet agent," who was by then dead. He did not identify Nick Nack or Gleme other than to say they were back in the Soviet Union.

Meanwhile, another informer, code-named "Fedora," was also supplying information that corroborated Nosenko's. It would turn out that "Fedora" turned out to be one Aleksei Kulak, a KGB official working as a "science officer" at the Soviets' United Nations mission.[13]*

December 15, 2017—Documents released: 3,539

Writing about this release in the *Dallas Morning News*, reporters Todd Gilman and Charles Scudder note that "while assassinations buffs weren't likely to find any major revelations—no proof of a second gunman, a Cuban plot, or evidence the killer could have been stopped—they'll have plenty to chew on."[14]

For example, the records include FBI and CIA reports on Soviet spies, the assassination of the Rev. Martin Luther King Jr., and Oswald's trip to Mexico City just weeks before President Kennedy's murder.

One thing to note. In the run-up to the September 11, 2001, terror attacks on New York and Washington, various federal agencies, for reasons such as turf wars or sheer bureaucratic ineptitude, often communicated independently of one another, failing to share key information that might have helped prevent catastrophe.

The same argument can be made in the period before President Kennedy's assassination. For example, among the December 15, 2017, documents is a 1975 CIA memo marked "top secret," which shows that Oswald was on a watch list of people whose mail would be intercepted. In Oswald's case, it began on November 9, 1959—days after

* Kulak also told the FBI in 1962 that there was a Soviet mole inside the bureau, a man known only as "Dick." The FBI assigned that unknown suspect the code name UNSUB Dick. UNSUB means "unknown subject."

he stormed into the US Embassy in Moscow and said he wanted to renounce his American citizenship—and lasted until May 3, 1960. It would commence again on August 7, 1961, through May 28, 1962. There's no evident reason for these dates. The list also includes Francis Gary Powers, the U-2 pilot shot down on May 1, 1960.* But after Oswald returned to the US, Langley seems to have lost interest.

Of course, as I'll discuss in chapter seven ("Oswald Returns to America"), the FBI was interested in Oswald and had been since his 1959 defection. But coordination with the CIA was negligible.

Another tidbit: a July 1978 memo to the House Select Committee on Assassinations revealed that the FBI was unable to find the original fingerprints lifted from the rifle found at the sniper's perch on the sixth floor of the Texas School Book Depository. The prints, originally recovered by Dallas police on the day of the assassination, were turned over to the FBI but never returned. The FBI told the committee that finding them—among the most important pieces of evidence from one of the greatest crimes in American history—would take a "mammoth research effort." It's understandable that this could be red meat to conspiracy theorists, though inexcusable bureaucratic incompetence can never be ruled out.

"We don't pass judgment on the value of the information or draw any conclusions about the content. That's left for the American people—for journalists, researchers, historians, and the like," said Jay Bosanko, at the time the chief operating officer at the National Archives.[15]

April 26, 2018—Documents released: 19,045

The FBI's interest in Oswald, which dates back to his 1959 defection to the Soviet Union, is evident in this batch of documents. One concerns an April 1960 interview between John Fain, a Fort Worth–based agent, and Oswald's brother, Robert, and mother, Marguerite.

---

* The same memo indicates that at various points, the mail of some very prominent Americans was opened, including Richard Nixon, Hubert Humphrey, various members of the Rockefeller family, and "Harvard University."

Not unlike much of the material released by the National Archives during this period, the Fain interview isn't new. The agent who eventually took over the Oswald file, James Hosty—who we'll be hearing more of later—wrote of it in his 1996 book *Assignment Oswald*, for example, noting that Marguerite Oswald insisted that her son did not defect. She was convinced, in fact, that someone else was using her son's passport.[16]

Some of the redactions in this batch of documents—and others—makes little sense to one assassination researcher, Jefferson Morley. He points to a July 1961 document that refers to four confidential informants, code-named T-1, T-2, T-3, and T-4, but their names are blacked out.

"Why are the names still being withheld?" he asks.[17]

Withholding came at the direction of then-President Donald Trump. In a White House memo, Trump said he was ordering agencies to "re-review each of the redactions over the next three years," and set a deadline for further release of documents of October 26, 2021, citing "identifiable national security, law enforcement, and foreign affairs concerns." The order meant that future releases would be at the discretion of President Joe Biden.

December 15, 2021—Documents released: 1,491

A common thread concerning news coverage of the 2017–2021 document releases is that present-day journalists have often treated the releases as information that's being made public for the first time. Oswald went to Mexico City just before the assassination and visited the Soviet and Cuban embassies! What a blockbuster! Of course, these sorts of things have been known since 1963, but apparently seem shockingly new to younger journalists writing about the story for the first time.

In any case, this batch of documents includes CIA cables and memos discussing the Mexico City trip, as well as documents released after the assassination that speculated on the possibility of Cuban involvement.

One CIA cable describes how Oswald phoned the Soviet Embassy while in the Mexican capital to request a visa to return. He had just left the USSR sixteen months earlier, after living in Minsk, the capital of Soviet Byelorussia, for about two and a half years. Another memo, dated the day after JFK's death, said that according to an intercepted phone call in Mexico City, Oswald communicated with an identified KGB officer while at the Soviet Embassy that September. Again, none of that is new. Nor is it any kind of revelation that Oswald, while visiting the Cuban embassy, "professed to be a Communist and an admirer of Castro,"[18] according to one cable. One CIA document marked "Secret Eyes Only" discusses US government plots to assassinate Castro, including a 1960 plot "that involved the use of the criminal underworld with contacts inside Cuba." Of course, John F. Kennedy wasn't president in 1960, Dwight Eisenhower was. Another document speculates, while adding nothing more, whether Oswald, while living in New Orleans in the summer of 1963, may have been influenced by coverage of an Associated Press interview with Castro, in which Castro allegedly warned of retribution if the US were to kill Cuban leaders.

But again, some context is needed. Castro knew in 1963 that the Kennedy administration was actually trying to reach out to him, to discuss a possible lowering of tensions between Washington and Havana. Conceivably, Kennedy could have removed the Cuban leader in April 1961 during Operation Zapata—the "Bay of Pigs"—but instead chose to cut his losses when the invasion foundered. Conceivably, he also could have given in to his hardline advisors and removed Castro the following year during the Cuban Missile Crisis. But Kennedy, looking for a way to remove Soviet nuclear missiles without resorting to war, again allowed Castro to remain in power.

During the final year of his presidency, and his life, Kennedy was working back channels in hopes of achieving some sort of rapprochement with Castro. Castro, having communicated with assorted American cutouts, knew this, and his responses to them have been well documented. Any reasonable analysis of the situation by Castro would have led him—and his Soviet benefactors—to the reasonable thesis that Lyndon Johnson almost certainly would not have reached out to the degree that Kennedy did.

That's a summary of the 2017–2021 releases. In aggregate, there does not appear to be a great deal that is new, or that moves the needle away from central findings of four government-led investigations into President Kennedy's assassination. But what do the JFK researchers and historians think? I've conducted a series of interviews with them—on both sides of the issue—and share their views here. Chances are you'll find someone you both agree and disagree with.

Hancock, Larry

Background: Independent researcher in the area of intelligence and national security. Lifelong student of the Kennedy assassination. Winner of the Mary Ferrell Legacy Award for his contributions concerning documents released under the JFK Act. Books include *Tipping Point: The Conspiracy that Murdered President John Kennedy*, (2021), *NEXUS: The CIA and Political Assassination* (2011), and *Someone Would Have Talked* (2006). University of New Mexico: BA with honors, majoring in history, cultural anthropology, and education. Air Force veteran.

What he thinks today: Hancock has always believed, and continues to maintain, that President Kennedy's death was the result of a conspiracy (he thinks "anti-Castro Cuban CIA-associated paramilitary operatives" were involved), though he acknowledges that "anyone that would say 100 percent either way is wrong, because we can't know either way." He thinks that "most of the primary evidence from the crime scene is highly questionable," and that "probably the net of all the documents we've seen released over the decades shows how much doubt remains after the evidence was collected, even among individuals that participated in it being collected."

What of all the documents that have been released since 2017? "Probably the documents that are most significant are those that show how the official storyline that was given to the Warren Commission is questionable in certain areas, particularly in regard to Lee Oswald."

Hancock thinks Oswald's September–October 1963 trip to Mexico City offers one example. "We can now see documents where the Mexican government was telling the FBI things that the FBI chose not to put in their summary report. One of the things we quite see in a lot of the FBI documents is that the field reports don't match up to the report that was sent to the Warren Commission."

But does this reflect conspiratorial activity—or a federal bureaucracy (J. Edgar Hoover's FBI) seeking to protect its reputation in the aftermath of the president's murder?

Kosner, Edward

Background: As a young National Affairs writer for *Newsweek*, he covered the Kennedy assassination from the beginning. Later served as its top editor, followed by stints at *New York* and *Esquire* magazines and the *New York Daily News*. Currently a book reviewer for the *Wall Street Journal*.

What he thinks today: Oswald acted alone. Kosner thinks that bureaucratic ineptitude six decades ago is a major contributor to conspiracy theories today. "Take the FBI. People don't know how decentralized the FBI was back then. Different agents would submit 302s (forms used to report information collected during an interview), but I don't think there was ever much of an effort to synthesize all this material." There were no computers in those days, of course, no databases, just paper. And as was the case with the September 11, 2001, terror attacks, turf wars precluded the Bureau from sharing information with the CIA and vice versa. Not to mention lack of coordination between the FBI and Secret Service.

"If you study human activity, you'll always find anomalies, but it's not enough in this case to change the overall conclusion" that Oswald was responsible for the president's murder, Kosner says. "I worked on it for *Newsweek* from November 22, 1963 on, and haven't read anything that has changed my mind."

Morley, Jefferson

Background: Thirty-five years in journalism, including fifteen at the *Washington Post* and WashingtonPost.com, where he was world news editor. Editor of *JFK Facts*, a blog about the assassination of President Kennedy. Plaintiff in *Morley v. CIA*, a Freedom of Information Act lawsuit concerning certain JFK assassination files. Prior stints at the *New Republic*, *Nation*, *Slate*, *Salon*, and *Arms Control Today*.

What he thinks today: Conspiracist who believes "the case that Kennedy was killed by his enemies has gotten stronger in the last twenty years." And who might they have been? Like many conspiracists, Morley, after decades of probing, offers mere supposition: "I don't have a theory about what happened. I don't have proof beyond a reasonable doubt that any one individual was involved." But that's because, he claims, "in a good covert operation—a well-designed and executed covert operation—you would never be able to tell. That's the point of a covert operation. A secret from conception to eternity."

Unlike some conspiracy believers, he does eliminate Cuba and its then-leader, Fidel Castro. "There is simply no evidence that Castro had anything to with the assassination." In fact, upon learning the news, Castro was upset because Kennedy had been seeking ways to talk indirectly with him. Like fellow conspiracist Hancock, Morley also casts a suspicious eye towards the CIA, accusing it of an ongoing cover-up because it continues to withhold documents.

Again the question: Does a document cover-up reflect conspiratorial activity—or a federal bureaucracy seeking to protect its reputation, along with sources and/or methods in the aftermath of the president's murder?

Newman, John

Background: Twenty years in US military intelligence. Longtime professor (University of Maryland, James Madison University) of history, terrorism, counterterrorism, and intelligence. Consultant for Oliver

Stone's 1991 film, *JFK*. Books include *JFK and Vietnam: Deception, Intrigue, and the Struggle for Power* (1992) and *Oswald and the CIA* (1995).

What he thinks today: "You would think that this vast increase in access to documents and records would, at some point, maybe just narrow a little bit, the sheer breadth of all these views," Newman says. But he believes the opposite has occurred, and "what I think explains this widening breadth of diverse views on this subject [JFK's murder] is because over time, all the way up through, not just the Warren Commission but the House Select Committee and Senate committee, which threatened to do 'real' investigations [quotation marks added by me] and that scared people, and in order to get their arms around the narrative that was going to come out of the Senate and House, enormous misdirections were laid in our path—and had been all along. And so you keep getting more and more of these misdirections. No wonder we don't know what the hell's going on," Newman claims. "And it just gets worse."

What about the assassination itself? Like Morley, he doesn't have a theory. "I don't do the Dealey Plaza stuff," Newman says, before adding "but I know quite a bit about it and people who were 'doing stuff' [again, my quote marks]. That was a military ambush. There's a guy with an overview who can send the signals, and he had many shooters, [five or six, he thinks] but they don't all shoot. Only one or two of 'em."

Did Oswald shoot? "I don't know," Newman says. "There's evidence that looks like he was downstairs, or he came downstairs awfully fast, not out of breath, to buy a Coke in the machine and be standing there. I think he could have been the shooter," Newman says, "but probably not." But Newman—"I don't do Dealey Plaza stuff"—adds, "If Oswald was shooting, then someone else is shooting." He says Oswald's Mexico City trip "tied him to Castro and the KGB," meaning a plot to kill President Kennedy.

"That makes me a conspiracy theorist, right there," Newman says. "And I don't mind being called a conspiracy theorist."

Posner, Gerald

Background: Investigative journalist, author of thirteen books, including *Case Closed: Lee Harvey Oswald and the Assassination of JFK*—a finalist for the 1994 Pulitzer Prize in history—and *Killing the Dream: James Earl Ray and the Assassination of Martin Luther King, Jr.* His other books have focused on everything from the September 11, 2001, terror attacks, infamous Holocaust mass murderer Josef Mengele, the connection between the US government and the Saudi royal family, and more. Former corporate lawyer.

What he thinks today: "I haven't seen anything that changes the underlying conclusion," says Posner, whose *Case Closed* argued that Oswald killed Kennedy and did so alone without being involved in a conspiracy. "If anything, I'm disheartened in the sense that I thought that some of the little puzzles of Mexico City (where Oswald visited in late September to early October 1963) might be resolved. But it's not going to change my view of what happened on November 22. If the CIA really did have video surveillance of the Soviet and Cuban embassies of Oswald entering, and after the assassination, destroyed it because they wanted to be as far away from him as they could, they should be castigated for it and taken to task. I don't know if that's the case, but I wouldn't be surprised if that came out. That would be big news. But I'm disheartened that we don't even have the answers to those things."

Sidebar: In Bugliosi's *Reclaiming History*, he notes that the cameras only worked about 80 percent of the time. Tapes were only kept for about two weeks and recycled. At the time, they had no reason to think that Oswald was a threat to the president. No one knew about the Walker incident (Oswald's attempted murder of the far-right general Edwin Walker, which I'll discuss in chapter eight). They had no reason to think of him in terms of a threat to Kennedy.

But while agreeing with this, Posner adds that "They didn't often have an American show up, who turned out to have been a former defector to the Soviet Union, who visited both the Cuban and Soviet missions. We had some intelligence assets in the Cuban mission. At least we would have known that Oswald was trying to get to Cuba. And at the Soviet mission, I'm not sure about the extent to which they were able to have any audio surveillance of what was happening inside. Those rooms may have been secure from that. But if they had, they would've heard Oswald ranting on and even smashing his gun at the table at one point."

What might come out when (if) the final documents are released? Posner, like others, thinks it'll show things that today would be embarrassing. "As they did with the Warren commission, they didn't disclose that they were in league with the Mafia to try to kill Castro. Their first concern was the Cold War, what was going on, and they weren't going to provide information to the commission that was embarrassing toward the agency in any way. And some of that may still be, I'm not sure, if so I wouldn't be surprised."

As our chat wrapped up, Posner pointed out an inconsistency that applies to a lot more than conspiracist views of the assassination. "It's interesting that you read these surveys and there's so much distrust of the government. The federal government is just incompetent and can't do anything right. And yet, when it comes to the assassination, these conspiracy people think that all of a sudden they were just competent and highly organized and pulled it off. And yet today, of course, they can't. The government can't butter a slice of bread."

Priess, David

Background: Former CIA intelligence officer, a manager, and a daily intelligence briefer during the presidencies of Bill Clinton and George W. Bush. Author of two books: *The President's Book of Secrets* and *How to Get Rid of a President*. Currently chief operating officer of the Lawfare Institute, a term visiting professor at the Schar School, a senior fellow at the Michael V. Hayden Center, and a writer and speaker on the presidency, intelligence, and national security.

What he thinks today: Echoing Posner's view, Priess notes that while the CIA obviously knew that Oswald had been in Mexico City weeks before the assassination, its failure to inform the Warren Commission of this doesn't mean—as some conspiracists seem to think—that this somehow implicates the agency in the president's murder.

Here's an excerpt from a 2021 discussion he had with Posner and another guest, Mark Zaid (more on him below), on his "Lawfare" podcast: "The logic being of course, that these [documents concerning Oswald] were not directly related to the shooting itself and they were embarrassing to the agency. So someone in the agency, likely Angleton [a reference to counterintelligence chief James Angleton] made the choice in the Warren Commission era not to move these documents forward, but in the 1990s, those documents did come out, not necessarily shining light on the assassination itself, but certainly shining a negative light on the agencies and their behavior during the time of the Warren Commission."

Priess also expresses frustration with the way in which documents have been released since 2017.

"What struck me about them was really two things. One was that I was seeing documents that I swear I'd seen before." He offers an example: "There was an earlier version of the same document and it had one word redacted and now that word wasn't. And secondly, just how banal some of these things were." Must be that "competent and highly organized" federal bureaucracy that Posner referred to.

Why hasn't everything been released? "With some of these documents, there is a case to be made as to why they have been delayed," he says. "On the FBI side, they could contain names or other informants who are still alive—even if those informants weren't giving information directly related to the assassination. If they're mentioned in a document, that identity could be revealed. On the CIA side, what we'll generally call sources and methods could be revealed, or specific ways that information is collected, that either could still be going on in that country or could reveal something about people who worked with the United States up to and including assets of the United States intelligence agencies."

Sabato, Larry

Background: Political scientist and political analyst. Professor of Politics at the University of Virginia, where he is also the founder and director of the Center for Politics, which works to promote civic engagement and participation. Author or editor of two dozen books on American politics, including the *New York Times* bestseller *The Kennedy Half Century*, which examines the life, assassination, and lasting legacy of John F. Kennedy. Rhodes scholar, winner of four Emmys, recognized as one of the nation's most respected political analysts in the United States.

What he thinks today: "I haven't changed my fundamental view of the Kennedy assassination because the evidence is overwhelming that Lee Harvey Oswald was the lone assassin. It all fits together, when you look at the scientific evidence, the film evidence. You have to disregard some of the first-person interviews, the testimony of people who were actually there, because they were confused, or didn't have time to process it [see the story of how the *Titanic* sank in chapter one, which may contextualize this]."

Has anything stood out in the documentation that has been released since 2017? "Look, if there were anything that would completely revise our opinions about the assassination," he says, "either it would've come out long before now because too many people know about what's actually in there, or it would've been destroyed back in the sixties before you had any mandates to release it. In either case, I don't think that the changes would be significant enough to alter the basic storyline. So in what I have seen, I've learned more, a little bit more anyway, about the Mexico City trip. I've learned a bit more about the Oswalds themselves and their unusual life. But they're details, and they fill in some of the picture, and they'll add a stroke to the overall portrait. But if you're looking for fundamental change, you're not going to find it in these documents. And I'm holding to that, no matter what's released in the final bunch. The reason they haven't been released, primarily, as I've been told anyway, is because of the names of specific informants and agents and others."

Sabato also agrees that some documents probably haven't been released because "Even now, there could be retribution in foreign countries against the surviving relatives of those individuals." Thus it's perfectly understandable, after all this time, to withhold documents, or redact them. "It's perfectly reasonable. I think to the degree that they can, they should excise, as little as possible, making sure there's no hint in there as to who the individual might be, or where the information was coming from, but give people a general context of why this paragraph has to be redacted, give people a context."

Finally, Sabato pivots to something that never occurred to me previously, and it concerns Oswald's undeniable record as a wifebeater. As we'll see in succeeding chapters, Oswald beat his wife Marina repeatedly, often viciously. Had this Soviet immigrant—barely out of her teens when she arrived in Texas in June 1962—spoken English, known how the system worked, or had an inkling of the help and resources that might have been available had she been able to speak up, it's possible that the trajectory of Oswald, who bounced ineptly from one menial job to another, might have been quite different. Had she also mentioned Oswald's attempted murder of Walker in April 1963 to someone, perhaps Oswald might have gone to jail. It's one of those "what ifs" that make the study of history so fascinating.

"He shouldn't have been a free man prior to Dallas."

Shenon, Philip

Background: Author of the 2013 bestseller *A Cruel and Shocking Act*, and the 2008 bestseller *The Commission: The Uncensored History of the 9/11 Investigation*, Shenon spent more than twenty years as a Washington correspondent for the *New York Times*, covering the Pentagon, the Justice Department, and the State Department. As a foreign correspondent for the paper, he reported from more than sixty countries and several war zones.

What he thinks today: Shenon tells me he hasn't come across any "blockbuster" documents, and that the most controversial material is still being withheld. That being said, he emphasizes, as he noted in *A Cruel and Shocking Act*, that "the Warren Commission missed a lot and that Oswald may have told people what he was going to do, which might make them accomplices," though he adds "there wasn't a second gunman in Dealey Plaza." In other words, there could be "something like a conspiracy, but certainly not the sort of conspiracy that Oliver Stone would point to."

Asked about Oswald's Mexico City trip in September and October 1963, Shenon says "It's pretty clear that Oswald had lots of suspicious meetings with Russians and Cubans. He's trying to get a visa that would allow him to defect to Cuba," (as he did to the Soviet Union in 1959). "It's all very suspicious what's going on there," he says.

When Oswald was in Mexico he talked openly about killing Kennedy, and what happened after the assassination, Shenon thinks, was that "the CIA in particular knew from its surveillance of Oswald in Mexico that they missed a lot of clues that this guy might be dangerous."

In keeping with the finest Washington tradition of "CYA"—cover your ass—the CIA and FBI then "did their best to bury everything they had known about that trip, to pretend that there was nothing terribly suspicious about it, when in fact there was a lot that was very suspicious about it." Of course, he emphasizes, this doesn't mean there was a conspiracy.

Zaid, Mark

Background: Washington lawyer who represents whistleblowers in their cases against the federal government. Frequently litigates against the CIA. Has been very active in the JFK-assassination-documents area for decades.

What he thinks today: Zaid doesn't think that the document releases change the overall dynamic of the case, but they are nevertheless important because they have helped historians and researchers connect a few more dots. "What it's doing is filling in gaps, particularly for historians, that means very valuable information so that we know more about what our intelligence agencies and foreign policy was during the Cold War, especially during the early '60s into the 1970s."

But Zaid, in a December 2021 interview on Priess's "Lawfare" podcast, said that "some documents we may never get, particularly because there are statutes that prevent them from being released...IRS documents, court records that are sealed."

Zaid is no fan of the CIA. He calls its office that handles Freedom of Information Act requests "the most obstructionist and unfriendly of those I have dealt with during the last two decades." Why the lack of transparency? He offers a possible reason: "Those people, those staff who worked in the embassy [the Soviet and Cuban Embassies in Mexico City] were in their mid-twenties. They're in their early-to-mid-eighties. Now, some of these people are likely still alive. And you can imagine what the Cuban government or maybe the Russian government now might do to them or their families were it found out that they revealed information to the CIA as traitors to their country sixty years ago."

CHAPTER THREE

A More Innocent Era

"Innocence always calls mutely for protection when we would be so much wiser to guard ourselves against it."

—GRAHAM GREENE

Overview

The assassination of President Kennedy has often been described in "before" and "after" terms, a demarcation line between a placid, post-war America that was confident, wealthy, and on the move, and one that became mired in division, uncertainty, cynicism, and scandal.

How much the assassination played in the opening of this pandora's box of ills is debatable. Yet it is undeniable that Kennedy's brutal murder was quickly followed by Vietnam, social unrest, a series of riots, a surge in crime, other political assassinations, Watergate, and all the rest. This was all accompanied by political instability: In the three decades between 1933 and 1961, we had three presidents. In the next sixteen years, we had five. Kennedy was murdered; his successor was hounded out of office after one term. The president who replaced him resigned in disgrace, and the election bid of his caretaker successor was rejected. His replacement lasted just one rocky term.

Of course, America was hardly innocent before Kennedy's motorcade turned onto Elm Street. Yet relative to all which followed, it can certainly seem like it was. There was also a certain degree of innocence about our presidents and the protection we once gave them. Compared with the multiple layers of protection that envelop presidents today, it seems lax, often shockingly so. But it was a different era, a more complacent one, and it's a misnomer to think, as conspiracy buffs often do, that the security around President Kennedy on November 22, 1963, was suspiciously, perhaps deliberately loose. No, it was the product of a bygone time, one in which Kennedy and his predecessors going back decades eagerly participated. Let's take a look.

* * *

Hours before his assassination on April 14, 1865, Abraham Lincoln signed legislation creating the United States Secret Service. But it wouldn't have saved the president that night, nor would it have saved James Garfield in 1881 or William McKinley in 1901 when they, too, fell victim to assassins' bullets. That's because the original mission of the Secret Service had nothing to do with protecting presidents; it was tasked with thwarting currency counterfeiting. All three murders were easily preventable, and it was only after McKinley's death that Congress requested that the Secret Service take on the grave responsibility of keeping the president of the United States safe.[1]

It's a wonder, in fact, that additional presidents escaped harm. Even after Garfield was shot—at a train station that is now the site of the National Gallery of Art's West Building—the White House remained wide open until the mid-1890s, allowing members of the public to just stroll in.

This came to an end after President Grover Cleveland and First Lady Frances Cleveland began to worry about the safety of their daughter Ruth. Their nanny routinely took little Ruthie out on the South Lawn, where she was barraged with public fawning. Mrs. Cleveland ordered the gates to be locked. She also learned of a plot to kidnap her children during a family vacation in Massachusetts and asked for additional security. The president also arranged for some twenty-seven Washington police officers to protect the perimeter of the eighteen-acre White House grounds.

But Cleveland's successor, McKinley, wasn't as security conscious. When he moved into the White House in 1897, he ordered guard boxes on the front lawn removed. He went on early-morning walks alone, apparently untroubled by the murder of two of his predecessors in the prior three decades. "I have never done any man a wrong, and believe no man will ever do me one," he said naïvely. The president's friends, not convinced, urged McKinley to at least allow one plainclothes Secret Service officer to shadow him on his morning strolls.[2]

Other measures—the simple locking of windows, and a halt to large public receptions, for example—were also taken. Still, McKinley scoffed. He even did so after an August 27, 1901, report in the *Washington Post*, which warned of an assassination plot. "Mr. McKinley laughed at the report," the *Post* story said, "characterizing it as a canard, and again expressing the belief that he was enough of the people to trust the people."[3]

Ten days later, touring the Pan-American Exposition in Buffalo, he was shot twice by a Polish anarchist named Leon Czolgosz. The president died eight days later, the third chief executive to be murdered in thirty-six years.

The McKinley assassination prompted changes. Secret Service agents would protect the president full time, yet just two agents were assigned to this crucial task.* Two agents to cover Theodore Roosevelt, the youngest and probably the most energetic of presidents, a man who was always on the go, frequently in public.

Like John F. Kennedy six decades later, TR often chafed at his (thin) protective screen. "The secret service men are a very small but very necessary thorn in the flesh," Roosevelt wrote in 1906. And despite Congress's request that the Secret Service formally guard the president

* The Secret Service began informal protection of President Grover Cleveland in 1894, but only on a part-time basis. William McKinley also had official, part-time protection—but not on the day he was shot.

full time, it didn't get around to providing the funds to do so until it passed the Sundry Civil Expenses Act for 1907.

September 3, 1902—Pittsfield, Massachusetts

In a little-known incident nearly a year to the day after President McKinley's shooting, Roosevelt is thrown from his carriage after it is smashed into by a speeding trolley car. It is an accident, and luck is with the president: he is only bruised. But William Craig, a six-foot-four former member of the British military who serves as TR's personal bodyguard, is killed.

Shortly before he was killed, Craig told a Massachusetts newspaper, the *Worcester Telegram*, of the constant danger to the president. "The danger lies in some fanatic getting up to the president and shooting or stabbing so quietly that it cannot be prevented," he said. "If no outsiders are allowed within ten feet of the president—and twenty-five feet is still better—the danger is greatly lessened."

Craig added that whenever he was near Roosevelt, he kept his hand in his coat, holding his revolver, ready to fire at any moment.

The scare did little, if anything, to alter presidential security. Roosevelt continued to get about in an open, horse-drawn carriage, with some but often minimal security around him. He did not use a motor car at first, but as automobiles gained in popularity, the Secret Service decided to buy one, purchasing a 1907 White Motor Company steam car, which often traveled near Roosevelt's carriage. But the president himself still opted for his carriage, which plodded along the streets of Washington with minimal maneuverability in an emergency.

TR's successor, William Howard Taft, was an early automobile buff. Shortly after he became president in 1909, Congress appropriated $12,000 for the purchase of motor cars for White House use. To accommodate this, Taft had the executive mansion's stables converted into a garage. The government purchased a Model M touring car from the White Motor Company, two Pierce-Arrows, and a Baker

Electric Vehicle. Taft liked cars so much he even attended an auto show in 1910.

And yet the president continued to ride around in his horse and buggy, including escorting his successor, Woodrow Wilson, to the Capitol in one. The outgoing and incoming presidents rode together in the open, for all to see. Photos of Inauguration Day 1913 show minimal security around the two men.

The horse and buggy was finally done away with during Wilson's presidency. He became a car buff, too, and the government shelled out for three more Pierce-Arrow models. For a generation, the Pierce-Arrows would enjoy seventeen years of dominance as the presidential vehicle of choice. They had retractable roofs, but Wilson preferred to have the top down, weather permitting. Fifteen months into his presidency, another world leader was assassinated in an open car, when Archduke Franz Ferdinand, the presumed heir to the Austro-Hungarian Empire, and his wife, Sophie, were gunned down as they were driven through the streets of Sarajevo (the present-day capital of Bosnia and Herzegovina) by a gunman named Gavrilo Princip. The shootings took place minutes after a colleague of Princip's tried to kill the royal couple by throwing a grenade into their car. The assassination of the Archduke sparked the first World War.

Yet the open-car murders in Europe had no discernible impact on presidential security. President Wilson continued to be driven around in the clear, usually with very little close security on either side or to the rear of his vehicle.

Convertibles with minimal security were also the general setup for Wilson's immediate successors, Warren Harding, Calvin Coolidge, and Herbert Hoover. Weather permitting, they, too, were driven around in the open, and while there were Secret Service agents nearby, an examination of photo archives from their respective presidencies shows that each was vulnerable.

February 15, 1933—Miami

This vulnerability came within inches of being disastrous when an unemployed bricklayer named Giuseppe Zangara was able to fire six shots into president-elect Franklin D. Roosevelt's open Buick touring car. Incredibly, Zangara missed FDR. But five people were injured, and one of them, Chicago mayor Anton Cermak, died.

Yet Roosevelt continued to ride around in open cars throughout his presidency. Just three weeks after Zangara's attack, he rode to his inauguration in an open car—a 1933 Lincoln—with outgoing President Hoover, proceeding slowly along Pennsylvania Avenue to the Capitol.

The most famous vehicle associated with FDR was a 1939 Lincoln, dubbed the "Sunshine Special," most likely for its retractable roof. Like presidents who came before and after him, Roosevelt disliked car roofs that kept him concealed from public view.

The Secret Service did tighten Roosevelt's security during World War II. It modified FDR's cars with armor, bullet-resistant glass, and special rear bumpers. The changes added six feet to the Sunshine Special's length, and the Lincoln now weighed more than four and a half tons.

After World War II, Harry Truman—who became president when Roosevelt died suddenly in 1945—continued to use the Sunshine Special. But Truman took even bigger security risks than driving around in an open car. The president insisted on taking walks each morning throughout downtown Washington.

Walking at the quick 120-steps-per-minute pace he learned in the Army, the president emerged from the White House practically every morning at roughly the same time. Truman cherished his walks, saying it kept him fit while also clearing his mind before facing the tough decisions that awaited him in the Oval Office. The president usually walked with an agent by his side, and others were nearby, but the dangerous, undeniable fact was that the president of the United States was out in the open each morning, on public streets, and anyone walking down the sidewalk could have gotten unacceptably close to him. Newsreels show him waiting at stoplights to cross and talking with whoever was on the corner; these things made agents so nervous that they began rigging traffic lights on his usual route to turn green so he wouldn't have to stop. When Truman found out, he complained that they were ruining his walks.[4]

Referencing this risky public behavior, David McCullough writes in *Truman*, his magnificent biography of the thirty-third commander in chief, that "Truman gave little thought to his own physical safety while President. When your time was up, it was up, was his feeling and it did not matter much what precautions were taken." Not unlike John F. Kennedy a few years later, McCullough adds, "the unbroken presence of protectors, the feeling of being constantly under guard, grated on him. He never became accustomed to it. He would have preferred less security than more."[5]

As we move closer to November 22, 1963, I thought it would be useful to provide a few typical examples of the way Truman moved about while president; we'll then do the same for Dwight Eisenhower, who became president in 1953. As we'll see, how these presidents chose to ride around—and how the Secret Service chose to guard them—was not materially different than what John F. Kennedy encountered and preferred. All took personal risks in public, preferring to be seen up close by Americans, and to bask in their cheers and warmth. As the title of this chapter says, it was a more innocent era.

June 12, 1948—Berkeley, California

Receiving an honorary degree from the University of California at Berkeley, Truman rides around as usual in a convertible, often standing so bystanders can get a better look at him. Police motorcycles flank the right and left rear of his car, but the nearest Secret Service agents, other than those in the front seat, are relegated to the follow-up car.

June 14—Los Angeles

Sitting up on the edge of the trunk, Truman "is slowly paraded down the street in Los Angeles." He is surrounded by tall buildings with many open windows. There is no security on either his left or right. Agents in the follow-up car appear some ten to fifteen feet away. He speaks at the Ambassador Hotel, future site, nearly twenty years to the date, of the 1968 assassination of Senator Robert Kennedy.

October 18—Miami

In town to speak at an American Legion Convention, Truman is seen standing up as his car is driven slowly down the street. There is no security to the right, no security to the left, and the closest agents, other than the front seat, are in the follow-up car.

There are plenty of examples here, but hopefully you get the point. The president was frequently exposed with security that can only be described as less than what it should have been. Truman wanted to be seen by the American people; he enjoyed sitting on the edge of the trunk, and even standing up, placing himself at even greater risk. The fact that there were numerous tall buildings with scores of open windows seemed to make no difference.

November 1, 1950—Washington

President Truman narrowly escapes assassination when two Puerto Rican nationalists attempt to storm Blair House, a government residence across from the White House. The Trumans are living at Blair House while the executive mansion is undergoing extensive renovations.

It was a record-hot day for the first of November—eighty-five degrees—and the president was taking a nap in his second-floor bedroom, which faced Pennsylvania Avenue. The window was open. The time was 2:19 p.m.

The two gunmen approached the Blair House entrance from different directions, and in the ensuing gun battle, White House policeman Leslie Coffelt was killed, and two others, Officers Joseph Downs and Donald Birdzell, were wounded. One assailant was killed and another wounded.

Truman, hearing the explosions of gunfire just yards below him, rushed to the window. A passerby, seeing the president's face peering down as the battle erupted, shouted "Get back! Get back!" at him. The president did so.

He was lucky. Instead of shooting their way into Blair House, the gunmen could have simply waited twenty minutes to attack Truman when he came out of Blair House to leave for a statue unveiling at Arlington National Cemetery. This was public information after all: the president's schedule had been published, as usual, in the morning newspapers.

After the assassination attempt, security was temporarily tightened, which aggravated Truman. In Missouri four days later, he wrote in his diary of his displeasure about having to ride in a closed car, which would make it harder to be seen.

> Because two crackpots or crazy men tried to shoot me a few days ago my good and efficient guards are nervous. So I'm trying to be as helpful as I can. Would like very much to take a walk this morning but the S[ecret] S[ervice]...and the "Boss" [Bess Truman] and Margie are worried about me—so I won't take my usual walk.
>
> It's hell to be President...[6]

But the closed car wouldn't last. After security fears subsided, Truman would resume some of his earlier habits that were typical of that more innocent era, including traveling in an open car, highly visible—and highly vulnerable.

January 20, 1953—Washington

President Truman and president-elect Dwight Eisenhower ride to Capitol Hill in an open car for Eisenhower's swearing in.

After the inaugural, President Eisenhower rode back to the White House in yet another convertible, a 1953 Cadillac Eldorado. He stood most of the way, as the car slowly passed office buildings on Pennsylvania Avenue. Secret Service agents occasionally walked alongside the car, but not always.

There were also no barriers between the president and crowds—neither metal barriers nor lines of soldiers and police officers.

May 8–9—Fredericksburg, Virginia

Eisenhower rides around in his convertible, so he will always be—as he wished—visible to all. And spectators know where Ike will be because, as is the custom in these days, motorcade routes are published in the newspaper.

What readers didn't know, until the president had safely returned to Washington, was that police learned from an informant about a possible assassination plot involving three men with rifles who planned to ambush Eisenhower. Cops had dealt with the informer before, and "had proved a reliable witness who provided information leading to arrests and convictions."

The Secret Service and police investigated all night long and were unable to find the purported assassins. Security was stepped up, and a twenty-three-minute ceremony involving the president and Mrs. Eisenhower occurred without a hitch. Police Superintendent A. G. Kendall said, "I was under right much tension from the time the president arrived to the time he left."[7]

Convertibles and well-publicized motorcade routes: security had been gravely compromised. Such things wouldn't be done today, of course, but in that more innocent era, no one thought much of it.

January 20, 1957—Washington

After being sworn in for his second term in office, President Eisenhower stands up in his convertible for much of the ride from the Capitol to the White House, waving to the crowd on either side of Pennsylvania Avenue.

At one point an agent next to Eisenhower dropped off and scurried back to the follow-up car, leaving the president, standing up, exposed, and with agents (other than in the first seat) well behind him in the follow-up car.

Once again, a parallel to November 22, 1963, is seen. Conspiracists have made much of the fact that when President Kennedy's motorcade departed Love Field for downtown Dallas, one agent, Don Lawton, was seen beside JFK, only to stop and hold up arms and banter with agents in the follow-up car. To them, sure that something sinister was afoot, this was the proof. But no.[8]

* * *

By now we've seen that presidents routinely took great risks in public. Motorcades routes were known in advance. Convertibles were preferred, and more often than not, Secret Service agents gave presidents more space than seems (at least today) prudent.

But surely when a president traveled overseas, things were different?

They were not. In December 1959, Eisenhower embarked on a grueling eighteen-day, twelve-nation trip through Asia, Europe, and Africa. Secret Service agent Clint Hill, one of Eisenhower's guards, wrote about the journey in his splendid 2017 book, *Five Presidents*.

December 6—Rome, Italy

As he prefers, President Eisenhower drives through the streets of the Italian capital in an open car, to the shrieks of thousands of delighted Romans.[9]

December 6—Ankara, Turkey

Eisenhower rides twenty miles into the Turkish capital in a 1934 Lincoln convertible, frequently standing up and waving. Sidewalks are jammed, often twenty people deep on both sides, "while still more waved from open windows, and up above, balconies and rooftops were packed. . . ."[10]

December 6—Karachi, Pakistan

In this Pakistani seaport city, President Eisenhower rides in an open car, before he and his host Ayub Khan switch to an open, horse-drawn carriage. At times Eisenhower stands up as the carriage makes its way through the mass of spectators. "Even though the crowds were very well-behaved, the exposure of the president at such a slow speed was very precarious."[11]

December 9—Kabul, Afghanistan

Eisenhower and Afghan king Zahir ride in a 1947 Lincoln convertible through the streets of the Afghan capital.

"As we entered the downtown area, the crowds got denser and denser," remembers Hill, "making it difficult for the Afghan police motorcycle riders to keep the path open for the carts following behind. Men and young boys crowded around the slow-moving motorcade, waving small American flags and throwing streamers and confetti, trying to move in closer to see President Eisenhower. It got so bad that Agents Jim Rowley and Dick Floor were perched on the back fender of the car, and at times they had to physically throw overly exuberant young men back into the street as they tried to reach out and touch President Eisenhower."

The president made it safely to the king's residence, but being exposed to massive crowds in a slow-moving, open vehicle accentuated the dangers that the president was placed in.[12]

December 9—New Delhi, India

"*Zindabad Ike!*" Indians cheered. "Long live Ike!" The president rides with Indian prime minister Jawaharlal Nehru in an open-top Cadillac convertible as he makes his way into the Indian capital.

"The streets were lined with people as far as you could see," Hill writes, "and where there was a higher vantage point, be it a roof, a balcony, or a tree limb, those spots too were jammed with people."

So many people had turned out to see the motorcade that at one point, they overwhelmed police and swarmed into the street, bringing the president's convertible to a halt. "There was nowhere for anyone to go," Hill says, who adds that it took well over an hour to travel the ten miles from the airport into town.

"We were lucky the people were friendly. Had there been any animosity, I shudder to think what could have happened...."[13]

December 14—Tehran, Iran

After a warm greeting from the Shah—installed thanks to an Eisenhower-approved coup six years earlier—the president and his host get into another open Cadillac convertible for the ride into the Iranian capital. Thousands of troops, armed with rifles, stand watch on both sides of the road as the exposed president rides by.[14]

December 14—Athens, Greece

Another world capital, another massive and exuberant crowd—and another ride in an open car. Eisenhower joins his host, King Paul, in the back of a gleaming Rolls-Royce convertible. There are no Secret Service agents in the car, which is driven by a Greek military officer, with another Greek aide next to him.

"Darkness was setting in as we made our way through the streets of Athens, making it difficult to see any unusual movement or activity within the throngs of people that lined the motorcade route," Hill writes, adding that "up above people hung out open windows, jamming rooftops and balconies...."[15]

December 21—Madrid, Spain

Riding in his convertible, Eisenhower stands, exposed, for the entire ride from the airport into the Spanish capital. An estimated 1.5 million people line the streets, many "hanging out windows and lined up on rooftops and balconies," as the president rides by.[16]

December 22—Casablanca, Morocco

After arriving in the fabled seaside city, the president joins King Mohammed V in a white Lincoln convertible for the ride into town. Eisenhower stands most of the way, waving and holding his arms out in appreciation. Secret Service agents, in the follow-up car as is usually the case, keep their eyes peeled for trouble. "I was about as tense as I had ever been," Hill writes.

Suddenly, gunfire erupted. Jubilant bystanders were firing rifles into the air in celebration. Notes Hill: "I couldn't help but imagine how quickly the situation could turn to disaster if one man decided to turn his gun on the president. It would be so easy, and there would be nothing we could do to stop it."[17]

What does all this have to do with the Kennedy assassination? Well, it's important to place events of that terrible day in broader context. There are those who think it's somehow fishy that JFK rode through Dallas in an open car. They think it's suspicious that his Secret Service agents were relegated to the follow-up vehicle.

History says otherwise. Each of his predecessors, every one of them, rode around in the open, placing themselves at heightened risk. As we have seen, Secret Service agents were sometimes beside the presidential vehicle, but in many cases they were not. That a motorcade was traveling slowly down a street surrounded by tall, or tallish, buildings, with countless open windows, didn't seem to make much of a difference.

And so it was with John F. Kennedy. Not just in Dallas, but for the bulk of his travels. FDR, Truman, and Eisenhower wanted to be seen. Newspapers told citizens where they would be. In this more innocent and trusting era, it was quite normal. Those presidents were lucky. JFK was too—until November 22, 1963.

* * *

As was the case with these prior presidents, there are far too many examples of Kennedy being driven, as he preferred, in an open car. As we delve into his presidency further into this book, I'll provide a few interesting examples. Here's just one for now:

October 19, 1962—Springfield, Illinois

It is three days after the most dangerous chapter of the Cold War—the Cuban Missile Crisis—began. Yet here is President Kennedy, weighed down with thoughts of nuclear war, motorcading through the streets of Springfield, Illinois. It will be another three days before he speaks to the American people and the world about it. The November midterm election is two weeks away, and the president has made a previous commitment to campaign for Democratic candidates. To maintain the appearance of normality, he decides to keep that commitment.

It was a sparkling fall day, a Friday, and the president rode as he usually did, in his famous 1961 Lincoln Continental. X-100, the Secret Service called it. Because of the splendid weather—"Kennedy weather," his aides called it—the top was off, just like the boss preferred. To the friendly crowds that lined the streets, the president, waving and flashing his trademark smile, appeared as if he hadn't a worry in the world.

But one man, perhaps, wasn't so friendly. As the open car slowly made its way through town, he watched the president—through the scope on his rifle.

He knew Kennedy would be there, because as usual, the president's schedule and motorcade route were published in the local newspaper: in this case, the *Illinois State Journal.* The paper even noted whether a certain vehicle would contain Secret Service agents, some of whom were even mentioned by name.

The first stop for the president was to visit the tomb of the first president to be assassinated, Abraham Lincoln. On the motorcade route, it was only after Kennedy had driven by that two men were spotted with a rifle. But everyone knew—it had been in the paper—that Kennedy was due to return by the same route in about thirty minutes.

The Secret Service would later note that an alert public safety official "saw a rifle barrel with telescopic sight protruding from a second-story window. The local police took into custody and delivered to Special Agents of the Secret Service" two men who were brothers-in-law. Seized at the scene: "a .22 caliber semi-automatic rifle and a full box of .22 long rifle ammunition."

The men admitted "pointing the gun out the window on the parade route. However, they claimed that they had merely been testing the power of the telescopic sight to determine if it would be worthwhile to remove it in order to get a better look at the President when the motorcade returned. As there was no evidence to the contrary, and neither man had any previous record, prosecution was declined." In terms of Kennedy's security, no changes were made.[18]*

Again, that's just one example of what was all too routine in this more innocent era: motorcade routes published in advance, open cars, open windows. Read on for more. But first, let's take a deep dive into the life of Lee Harvey Oswald, and for that, we begin, as stories must, at the beginning.

---

* Devil's advocate: What if this really had been a plot, and the president was killed on that bright autumn day during the Cuban Missile Crisis? How differently might our world be today? Consider that the Soviets had already been caught lying about not having nuclear missiles in Cuba; would subsequent denials about not being involved in the president's assassination be believed—or would it be interpreted as an attempt to decapitate the US government? What would Lyndon Johnson have done? These are questions that but for the grace of God, thankfully would never need to be answered.

CHAPTER FOUR

A Violent and Unstable Childhood: Oswald, October 1939–October 1956

"Lee has [a] vivid fantasy life, turning around the topics of omnipotence and power, through which he tries to compensate for his present shortcomings and frustrations."

—DR. RENATUS HARTOGS, PSYCHIATRIST

The future assassin had a troubled life from the very beginning. His biological father died before he was born, and for most of his childhood, he grew up without a stabilizing father figure. His mother, Marguerite, moved constantly, shuttling Lee between numerous schools in three states and, at one point, an orphanage. The instability made it all but impossible for Lee to form childhood friendships and develop normally. Retreating into a solitary world of comic books and TV shows—including a program that would influence him deeply called I Led 3 Lives*—young Oswald began displaying a violent temper and began to lash out at others.*

October 18, 1939—New Orleans

Lee is born at the old French Hospital on Orleans Street. His father, Robert Edward Lee Oswald Sr., had died two months earlier at age forty-three. His mother, Marguerite Frances Claverie, is thirty-two.

Lee had two older siblings: stepbrother Edward John Pic Jr., seven, and brother Robert, age five.

1941

Marguerite Oswald, widowed and struggling to take care of her three boys, sends her two oldest ones—Robert and John—to an orphanage. But Lee, age two, is too young to be accepted. Marguerite lets a couple move into her home to take care of Lee, only to soon fire them after learning that they had been whipping Lee because he was a "bad, unmanageable child." Marguerite doesn't think a two-year-old baby could be that bad, yet acknowledges that it "was difficult with Lee."[1]

December 26, 1942—New Orleans

The day after Christmas, three-year-old Lee, now old enough to be placed in an orphanage, joins nine-year-old John and eight-year-old Robert at the Bethlehem Children's Home in New Orleans. Lee is only three but has already moved five times.

1944

In January, Lee is suddenly yanked out of the orphanage by Marguerite, who takes him to Dallas, so she can be closer to Texas businessman Edwin Ekdahl.

1945

In May, Marguerite marries Ekdahl. It's her third husband. Lee's just five months shy of his sixth birthday, but his life has been unstable from the beginning. Lee has already lived at seven addresses and had one father and two stepfathers. The constant uprooting takes a toll: It takes Lee two years to finish the first grade, even though his grades are all As and Bs. The moving and instability are endless, but it is just getting started.[2]

Even now, at such a young age, Oswald's behavior began to strike others as unusual. In the fall of 1945, when he and his mother lived in a since-torn-down house on Granbury Road in Fort Worth, a neighbor, Mrs. W. H. Bell, recalled him as a loner who resisted discipline.[3] Another woman, Myrtle Evans, who was close to Marguerite for a while, thought Lee was just plain odd. "The way he kept to himself just wasn't normal," she said in 1964.[4]

1948

Fed up with Marguerite, Ekdahl leaves her and begins divorce proceedings. Marguerite is forced to move into a run-down house. Unable to pay tuition at military school for John and Robert, she moves them in with herself and Lee. Both older boys describe it as "prisonlike," and say that Lee has withdrawn even further, often "brooding for hours." Lee would move three times in 1948 alone, and unsurprisingly, the constant disruption makes it impossible to make friends.[5]

In addition to being fatherless, John, Robert, and Lee also felt neglected by their mother. She skimped on food to the point where the weight of her sons plummeted. Their clothing was so shabby and threadbare that they were mocked by other kids. Among themselves, the brothers got along well and, said John, had a "friendly time" until their mother came home from work. Then, he said, "We all got into that depression again." Said one neighbor: Marguerite was "selfish" and obviously considered her children a "burden."[6]

Imagine the impact all this had on Lee. Instead of having a pair of grounded, loving parents who would guide him through childhood and instill in him the proper values, education, discipline, and social skills to make him a decent citizen and contributing member of society, he had but one parent for most of his childhood, and a highly dysfunctional one at that. Marguerite was selfish, boorish, and unstable, flitting from place to place and job to job, rootless and aimless. John and Robert at least had been exposed to the outside world through military school. But not Lee. His mother's deficiencies would come to define her youngest son as well.

Marguerite's tirades frequently punctured whatever semblance of happiness Lee had as a child. Completely dependent upon her, he learned to "sulk or pout" when she exploded, or retreat to the comfort and fantasy world of television or play with the family dog.

1949

In September, Lee transfers to Ridglea West Elementary School. He's a month shy of his tenth birthday but has lived in thirteen different places and attended six different elementary schools. One of his Ridglea teachers, Mrs. Clyde Livingston, would later describe him as a loner who never had friends and never came out of his shell.[7]

At one school, Clayton Public School in Fort Worth, which Oswald attended from January 1947 to March 1948, schoolmate Philip Vinson recalled that Oswald joined a schoolyard gang and was considered a "tough-guy type." Yet Vinson tagged him as a loner, noting that no one ever played with him after school or went to his home. "I never went to his house, and I never knew anybody who did."[8]

Let's recap: Oswald has no friends and is withdrawn and brooding. He also often slept in the same bed with his mother and did so until he was nearly eleven.

John, Lee's stepbrother, would say after the assassination that if Lee committed the crime, then he was "aided with a little extra push from his mother in the living conditions that she presented to him."

Lee's Aunt, Lillian Murret, would tell the Warren Commission in 1964 that Marguerite was always telling Lee that he was smarter than other kids and let him stay home from school if he didn't want to go. When Lee visited the Murrets, who lived in New Orleans, Lillian thought it strange that Lee just wanted to stay inside all day. When they did take him out, the Murrets noticed right away that "he didn't seem to enjoy himself," and that "he was obviously very unhappy."[9]

It was around this time that others observed something else in Oswald: his explosive violence. "He was quick to anger," recalled Hiram Conway, who lived two doors down from the Oswalds and knew him for nearly four years. After school, Conway said, Oswald liked to throw rocks at other children. "He was vicious almost," Conway said. "He was a bad kid" and "very strange."[10]

Such violence extended further than throwing rocks at children. Another neighbor, Otis Carlton, happened to be visiting the Oswalds one night when Lee chased his stepbrother John through the house with a butcher knife. As a startled Carlton watched, Lee tossed the knife at John, missing him but hitting the wall. Carlton says that Marguerite called this scary incident a "little scuffle" and told Carlton not to worry about it.[11]

1952—New York

In July, Robert Oswald joins the Marines. This makes a big impression on twelve-year-old Lee. He buys a Marine handbook, determined to learn everything about the leathernecks.[12]

John, meantime, was in the Coast Guard and stationed in New York. In August, Marguerite and Lee moved there and moved in with John, his wife of one year (Marge), and their baby, who were in turn living at John's mother-in-law's apartment at 325 East 92d Street in Manhattan.

It quickly turned nasty. One day Marge asked Lee to turn down the TV. Instead, Lee threatened her with a knife. When Marguerite told Lee to put the knife away, he punched her—his own mother—in the face. It was Oswald's second violent eruption involving a knife.

John and Marge told Marguerite and Lee to get out.[13]

Of Lee, John later said that "his feelings toward me became hostile and thereafter [he] remained indifferent to me and never again was I able to communicate with him in any way." Lee and John would not speak with each other for a decade. John added that in subsequent years he noticed that even Marguerite, who had babied Oswald his entire life and lavished him with praise, had lost control of him.[14]

The knife and punching incidents reflect an unstable Oswald's violent and explosive behavior, a pattern that would be displayed time and again over the rest of his life. Yet an examination of conspiracy books shows writers typically glossing over such an inconvenient truth. Notes Gerald Posner in 1993's *Case Closed*: "Best-selling authors like Anthony Summers, Jim Garrison, Mark Lane, Josiah Thompson and Robert J. Groden do not mention the New York City period." Another, Henry Hurt, merely says "Oswald and his domineering, eccentric mother lived in various places, including New York City and Fort Worth." Another, Harold Weisberg, also waters it down: "In August 1952, Oswald and his mother moved to New York City, where an older married son [John] by her first marriage also lived."[15]

It's fair to note here that in addition to the negative influence of his mother, Lee had developmental problems because of a reading disability—dyslexia. Citing this Mayo Clinic diagnosis, which was provided to the Warren Commission in 1964, writer Patricia McMillan surmises that it "must have caused him to feel frustrated from his earliest days in school, as if something impalpable, something he could only sense, was holding him back and keeping him from doing as well as others less intelligent than he." Ominously, she adds that it "left him with a legacy of low self-esteem and disruptive behavior that might have plagued him even if his home life had been a happy one."[16]

Thus, on top of everything else, Oswald, even as a youngster, had a disability that contributed to his lack of social skills and ability to assimilate into the culture around him; the path of least resistance was the solitude and uncommunicative demeanor for which he would be known by practically everyone who ever interacted with him.

1953—New York

Marguerite and Lee's year and a half as New Yorkers (August 1952–January 1954) will see them move two more times, and Lee attends three different schools. At one school—P.S. 117 in the Bronx—he skips forty-eight of sixty-four school days and not surprisingly is flunking nearly all his classes.

After moving yet again, Lee refused to attend his next school—P.S. 44, which was also in the Bronx—at all. A judge declared him a truant, and Lee, all of thirteen years old, was ordered to undergo a psychiatric evaluation.

There's a common thread here. The violence that Lee displayed at home—threatening family members with knives, punching Marguerite—was on full display at school as well. Writes Posner: "Comments from his teachers noted that he was 'quick-tempered,' 'constantly losing control,' and 'getting into battles with others.'" And as was the case in Texas, it's observed that Lee makes no effort to mix with other children.[17]

April 16—New York

Lee undergoes a three-week psychiatric evaluation at a facility called Youth House. Even though he has been doted on by Marguerite for his entire short life, he tells social worker Evelyn Strickman that his mother "never gave a damn about him." In her report, Strickman writes that Lee "feels almost as if there's a veil between him and other people through which they cannot reach him, but he prefers this veil to remain intact."[18]

Strickman added that Lee was "seriously withdrawn, detached and very hard to reach," had "suffered serious psychological damage" and that—ominously—*he had admitted to fantasizing about being powerful and sometimes hurting and killing people* (emphasis mine).[19]

Given what we know about Lee's later behavior as an adult, his inability to make friends, his constant brooding, his preference for long, remote silences, Stickman's observation a decade earlier about Lee's preference to maintain a social barrier with others was, in hindsight, remarkably prescient.

Strickman then handed Lee off to Youth House's staff psychiatrist, Dr. Renatus Hartogs, for yet an additional evaluation.

May 1—New York

Hartogs's evaluation of Oswald begins. He makes quite an impression on the doctor. Eleven years later, Hartogs will be questioned by Warren Commission assistant counsel Wesley J. Liebeler:

> **Mr. LIEBELER:** Do you remember anything else that particularly impressed you about Oswald? The FBI report indicates that you were greatly impressed by the boy, who was only 13½ years old at the time, because he had extremely cold, steely eyes. Do you remember telling that to the agents?
>
> **Dr. HARTOGS:** Yes, yes; that he was not emotional at all; he was in control of his emotions. He showed a cold, detached outer attitude.

Liebler then produced a copy of Harthogs's 1953 evaluation of Oswald. Harthogs confirms that he diagnosed Oswald as having a "personality pattern disturbance with schizoid features and passive aggressive tendencies."

Hartogs didn't say that Oswald had "assaultive or homicidal potential," but he did elaborate on his passive-aggressive tendencies, saying "that we are dealing here with a youngster who was hiding behind a seemingly passive, detached facade aggression hostility."

The testimony continued:

> **Mr. LIEBELER:** Would you describe for us briefly what the passive-aggressive tendencies are, how do they manifest themselves, what do they indicate?
>
> **Dr. HARTOGS:** They indicate a passive retiring surface facade, under which the child hides considerable hostility of various degrees.
>
> **Mr. LIEBELER:** It would indicate to some extent a hiding of hostile tendencies toward others?
>
> **Dr. HARTOGS:** Yes. But usually in a passive-aggressive individual the aggressiveness can be triggered off and provoked in stress situations or if he nourishes his hate and his hostility for a considerable length of time so that the passive surface facade all of a sudden explodes, this can happen. I said here that his fantasy

> life turned around the topics of omnipotence and power. He said also that "I dislike everybody," which is quite interesting, I think, also pertinent.

Why didn't Hartogs explicitly warn of Oswald's potential for violence? In his testimony he said it was implied by the phrase "passive-aggressive," adding that on this basis, he recommended that Lee, then just thirteen, be institutionalized because he was potentially dangerous.

It's worth mentioning again that the conspiracy writers who ignored Lee's violent childhood behavior also ignored the later findings of the only clinical psychiatrist to ever sit down with him. Posner notes that Hartogs "is not even listed in books written by conspiracy writers Mark Lane, Josiah Thompson, Jim Garrison, John Davis, Robert J. Groden and Harrison Livingstone, Robert Blakey, Henry Hurt, David Schema or David Lifton." Among the few who do mention Hartogs downplay his findings. Writes Jim Marrs: "The results were essentially inconclusive. They showed him to be a bright and inquisitive young man who was somewhat tense, withdrawn and hesitant to talk about himself or his feelings." Marrs makes Oswald out to be a stable young man, a good scholar who was modest and shy. Comments from teachers, neighbors, fellow students, and even family members threatened by Lee are seemingly deemed irrelevant.[20]

October 1—New York

A syndicated TV show debuts that, according to Robert Oswald, captivates Lee. *I Led 3 Lives* is about a white-collar worker, his secret life as a communist agent, and a life within that as an FBI operative striving to foil communist plots. Shows about espionage and intrigue enthrall Lee, according to Robert, and are the "training ground for his imagination."

Running from October 1, 1953, to January 1, 1956, it was the only constant in Lee's life. During the twenty-seven months it aired, he lived in five different homes in Manhattan, the Bronx, and New

Orleans and went to three different schools. But no matter where he was, there was always *I Led 3 Lives* to look forward to. Titles from episodes included "Confused Comrade," "Martyr," "Unexpected Trip," "Child Commie," "The Spy" (which aired November 22, 1953)—and "Assassination Plot." It's almost as if these episode titles, and there were many others in a similar vein, defined particular episodes of Oswald's short, delusional, and highly imaginative life.

"Lee was fascinated," Robert Oswald wrote in 1967. "In the early 1950's, Lee watched that show every week without fail. When I left home to join the Marines, he was still watching the reruns."[21]

January 1954—New York and New Orleans

Refusing to allow Lee to be placed in a home for troubled boys, Marguerite flees New York and returns to New Orleans, where Lee was born. They move in with her sister Lillian Murret and husband Charles (Dutz) Murret. It's the seventeenth home Lee has lived in. He soon starts classes at Beauregard Junior High—his tenth school.

Just a few weeks later, they moved again, renting an apartment on St. Mary Street. Lee remained in the same school but, as usual, kept to himself and made no friends.

The apartment was owned by a friend, Myrtle Evans. She hadn't seen Marguerite or Lee in several years and was shocked at the changes in Lee. From her April 7, 1964, interview with Warren Commission Assistant Counsel Albert E. Jenner Jr.:

> **Mrs. EVANS:** Well, he was more spoiled.
>
> **Mr. JENNER:** More than before?
>
> **Mrs. EVANS:** Yes; he had gotten older, and he wanted his way, and he was a teenager then, and like all teenagers, he was very difficult. Of course, I guess all teenagers are that way, because they are not yet grown and they are not a child either. The best of them are very trying, and it is hard to keep them in line. In that respect Lee wasn't any different than any other teenaged boy, I guess.

But Evans didn't know about Lee's explosive temper and tendency to resort to violence. But she soon caught on, deciding that "it seemed to be a situation that was getting worse all the time; so I thought maybe it would be better if I didn't have them around."[22]

Mrs. Evans's husband, Julian, didn't think much of the Oswalds either, particularly Lee. He told a story about the time in 1955, when Lee was fifteen and they went fishing near the home of his (Evans's) sister:

> **Mr. EVANS:** He just seemed to want to be alone, and he just fished by himself, and the odd part of his behavior that we all thought was very strange was the way he would just let the fish die on the bank after he would catch them. Now, the other small boys would catch them and, and if there was enough for eating and everything, they would throw the others back, but not Lee. He would pull them in and just throw them down on the river—I mean on the bank by the pond and just let them lay there, and when he got through he just walked off and left them there. Something like that is hard to understand. He didn't catch them for eating, and he didn't want to throw them back in. He just left them on the bank and walked off after he got tired of fishing. We couldn't understand that at all. It showed how totally inconsiderate he was of everything. It was a good example of how he acted, and his general attitude.[23]

He added that Lee was "arrogant," "real demanding," and "loud" with his mother. He also described him as a jerk:

> **Mr. EVANS:** He was arrogant, and nobody liked him. That was the thing.[24]
>
> **Mr. JENNER:** Did he ever associate with any of the children in the neighborhood?
>
> **Mr. EVANS:** No he didn't. He didn't associate with anybody.

And:

> **Mr. JENNER:** Did you ever feel that you ever got to know Lee Oswald, Mr. Evans?

Mr. EVANS: No; I can't say that I ever did. I don't think anybody did. I don't think anybody even came close to it, because the way he was, nobody could figure him out. It was hard to get to him or to understand him. He didn't want you to get too close to him, for one thing. He never went out of his way to make friends, I mean, from what I knew of him.

Mr. JENNER: He sort of shied away from friends, or people who might have become friends, or who might have tried to be friendly with him?

Mr. EVANS: Yes; that's it. You would try to be nice to him, but he wouldn't appreciate it, and he didn't mind showing you that he didn't appreciate it.[25]

Meanwhile, the psychological problems that had been so accurately diagnosed by social worker Strickman and Dr. Hartogs remained deeply embedded in Oswald. Notes McMillan: "His sense of reality appears to have been so badly impaired that the line between truth and falsehood was wavy, and falsehood was often truer than truth. He lied pointlessly, to no purpose and all the time, even when he had nothing to hide."[26]

Oswald's delusions were soon accompanied by a growing interest in both guns and criminal activity. A Beauregard Junior High classmate, Edward Voebel, testified in 1964 that Oswald, who had a plastic model of a .45 caliber pistol, said he wanted a real gun and decided to steal a Smith & Wesson automatic from a local store.

"He [Oswald] came out with a glass cutter…[and] finally told me his complete plans…." Oswald persuaded Voebel to case out the store, but when they did, Voebel saw that the window was wired for an alarm. Oswald chickened out.[27]

William Wulf was another Beauregard student who found Oswald disturbing. Initially drawn together by a shared interest in astronomy and history, the two began arguing at Wulf's house one day about communism. Wulf was shocked by Oswald's intensity and radicalism. "He impressed me as a boy who could get violent over communism," he said in 1964. He was so alarmed that he told a friend who also happened to know Oswald, Palmer McBride, that "this boy Oswald, if you associated with him, could be construed as a security risk, and especially if you want to get into a job position where the information you know could be of a security nature or of a type that could be of a security risk nature."[28]

Wulf's warning proved to be more than prescient. In early 1956, McBride and Oswald were both employed at Pfisterer Dental Laboratory Company. That connection, and a shared enjoyment of classical music, led McBride to invite Oswald over to listen to records one evening. As they conversed, the topic veered off into politics, and Oswald said something alarming: that he wanted to assassinate President Dwight Eisenhower.[29]

As is the case with Oswald's violent behavior as a youngster, and his later, often vicious beatings of his wife and the April 1963 attempt on General Edwin Walker's life, the Eisenhower incident is rarely mentioned by conspiracy writers—if mentioned at all.

Spring, 1955—New Orleans

The Oswalds soon move again, and that is fine with Myrtle Evans. By now—spring of 1955—Lee Harvey Oswald, fifteen years old, has lived in twenty homes in three states and attended eleven schools. He hasn't had a father figure in his life in years, has burned his bridges with one brother, and rarely sees another.

As he finished the ninth grade at Beauregard Junior High, students were asked to fill out a personal-history form. One question asked students to name their close friends. Oswald answers "none."[30]

July 1956—Fort Worth

Marguerite and Lee move yet again, this time back to a shabby apartment in Fort Worth. From New Orleans to an orphanage, to Dallas, Fort Worth, Covington, Louisiana, back to Fort Worth, to Manhattan, the Bronx, back to New Orleans and back, yet again, to Fort Worth, Lee has now lived in twenty-one different homes, sometimes moving multiple times in one city. There's no father figure in his life. He has done poorly in school after school. He has gotten into trouble in school after school. He has threatened his own relatives with knives. He has punched his own mother. He has admitted disliking everybody. He has admitted having no friends. He has spoken aloud about wanting to kill President Eisenhower. Everyone he has come into contact with—teachers, classmates, neighbors, psychiatrists—considers him angry, bitter, hostile, unfriendly, and cold. He considers himself highly intelligent. He's sixteen years old.

September—Fort Worth

After a few weeks of infrequent attendance at Arlington Heights High School in Fort Worth, Lee drops out. It is the last school he will ever attend.

It was around this time that Oswald bought his first gun, a .22-caliber Marlin bolt-action rifle. He later sold it to his brother Robert.[31]

October 18—Fort Worth

Oswald turns seventeen and decides to join the Marines. But he isn't old enough to enlist on his own, so Robert signs for him as a legal guardian. Lee ships out immediately.

CHAPTER FIVE

Sharpshooter: Oswald in the Marines October 1956—September 1959

"One day he would do something which would make him famous...."

—MACK OSBORNE, FELLOW MARINE

Inspired by his brother, Robert Oswald, and stepbrother, John Pic, Lee enlisted in the Marine Corps in the fall of 1956. After a lost childhood, the Marines offered Oswald two things he never had: stability and authority. It was an opportunity for the young leatherneck to make something of himself. But Oswald—who had always been rebellious and resentful of being told what to do—wasn't cut out for the Marines and its strict discipline. As with most things in his life, disillusionment set in quickly. He got out as soon as he could, but not before mastering one important skill: he learned to shoot a rifle.

October 26—Marine Corps Recruit Depot, San Diego

Oswald reports for boot camp. For a young man who chafed at authority, the Marines might not have been the wisest choice for the seventeen-year old. But he looked up to Robert, who had been a leatherneck, and stepbrother John Pic, who was in the Marine reserves.

On a series of aptitude tests, Oswald scored slightly below average.

Every boot is trained to shoot of course, and Oswald scored 212, high enough for a "sharpshooter" qualification. In Marine Corps terminology, this is better than "marksman," but not as good as "expert," the top ranking. In 1956, the sharpshooter badge that Oswald earned meant that he could hit a ten-inch bull's-eye from at least two hundred yards away eight times out of ten.

Marines typically qualify with the rifle on an annual basis. Before Oswald left the USMC in 1959, he scored 191, this time qualifying as a "marksman." The noncommissioned officer in charge of his training unit, Sgt. James Zahm, called Oswald "a good shot, slightly above average…and as compared to the average male…throughout the United States, he is an excellent shot."[1]

Six months into his hitch, Oswald was given a low-level security clearance to deal with "confidential" material, but not "secret" or "top secret" material." In late summer 1957 he was sent to Japan and stationed at Atsugi Air Base, about twenty miles west of Tokyo. He was assigned to an air control squadron as a radar operator.[2]

Oswald's Atsugi posting is grist for conspiracists, who note that it just happened to be where the U-2—the Central Intelligence Agency's extreme-high-altitude spy plane—was also based. Surely it wasn't coincidental, some think. But six decades later, there's really not much to suggest that Oswald, the high school dropout who unsurprisingly scored low on Marine aptitude tests, was somehow involved in any meaningful way with the super-secret, high-tech aircraft. But we'll discuss it in a moment anyway.

The more salient observation about Oswald at this point in his life was that the personal traits he had harbored as a young man—the temper, the tendency towards violence, the resentment of authority, and the misguided belief that he was intellectually superior to others—carried over into the Marines.

Here he was, a young man—just seventeen—away from home for the first time, and exposed to a rigid, top-to-bottom culture where individuality was weeded out from day one and dissent intolerable. It became apparent rather quickly to both fellow boots (new Marines) and superiors that Oswald was insufficiently lacking in the essential qualities that defined the Marine ethos—warrior skills second to none, absolute faith in the integrity of their unit, and unquestioned character.

One Marine who encountered Oswald remembered him well years later. "Oswald was an argumentative type of person," Allen R. Felde told the FBI in 1964. He "was not popular with the other recruits, and his company was avoided if possible."

Oswald had a dislike "for people of wealth," Felde recalled, but also people in authority, including former president Harry Truman and President Eisenhower. Oswald, the high-school dropout, thought so much of his intellectual abilities that he even criticized Eisenhower's "poor tactics in the utilization of a tank unit at the time of the invasion of Europe," Felde added.[3]

Echoing Felde's views was Daniel Powers, who in 1957 crossed paths with Oswald at Kessler Air Force Base in Mississippi, where they were being trained to operate radar equipment.

Testifying before the Warren Commission on May 1, 1964, Powers remembered Oswald as a "loner" whose "general personality would alienate" others.[4]

It was here that Oswald was dubbed "Ozzie Rabbit" by his fellow Marines, who began to pick on him for being different and not fitting in.

"He was somewhat the frail, little puppy in the litter," Powers said. "He was an odd-ball from the Marine Corps' own definition of what a Marine is supposed to—ideally supposed to be."[5]

Powers and others wondered whether Oswald was gay, something that certainly would have been intolerable in the conservative, ultra-masculine Marine Corps. Author Gerald Posner weighs in as well, noting that while stationed in Japan, Oswald visited a transvestite bar, and while stationed in Southern California, ran into a group of Marines in Tijuana, Mexico, and proceeded to take them to a gay bar, the Flamingo, where he seemed to know the place and people.[6]

But the more germane observations about Oswald remain his negative attitude and resistance to authority. In a 1964 affidavit, another Marine, David Christie Murray Jr. (not "David Christie," as other books have called him) tagged Oswald as a habitual complainer "who was never satisfied with any event or situation," and "had a 'chip on the shoulder' personality which would be likely to involve him in fights."[7]

John E. Donovan, a Marine officer who had the chance to observe Oswald as a radar operator, called him "very competent" and always cool and collected—"I don't recall him being particularly excitable,"* he recalled—but "a little bit nuts on foreign affairs."[8]

Back to Oswald and his posting at Atsugi—home of the U-2, which flew reconnaissance missions over the USSR, China, and North Korea. And the seventeen-year-old Oswald—who had begun to study Russian and show a growing interest in communism and the Soviet Union—was there, too. Surely no coincidence, conspiracists point out.

But Atsugi is a very big base, some 1,249 acres, and like most people stationed there, Oswald unquestionably saw the "Dragon Lady" (the U-2's nickname) take off and/or land, but there is no substantive evidence that he showed any serious interest in the plane, its activities, or general US intelligence efforts in the Far East.[9] It's also worth noting that in contrast to what some conspiracy writers seem to think, Oswald lacked a high-level security clearance. In the 1970s, the House Select Committee on Assassinations determined that all Oswald had was a "confidential" clearance, the lowest-level security clearance available.

So what information did Oswald have access to? More from Donovan's testimony:

> The location of all bases in the west coast area, all radio frequencies for all squadrons, all tactical call signs, and the relative strength

* This is notable given that some conspiracists have said that after President Kennedy's assassination, how could Oswald have been so calm when he appeared ninety seconds later in the Book Depository's break room? Bugliosi also weighs in, noting that "there are those who curiously become very calm in moments of crisis. Oswald gave every indication of being one of those people." (Bugliosi, 840)

> of all squadrons, number and type of aircraft in a squadron, who was the commanding officer, the authentication code of entering and exiting the ADIZ, which stands for Air Defense Identification Zone. He knew the range of our radar. He knew the range of our radio. And he knew the range of the surrounding units' radio and radar.[10]

To the uninitiated, this makes it sound like Oswald was sitting on tons of data that the Soviets would love to have. The location of American bases in Japan were well known to Moscow, and it wasn't exactly difficult to determine radio frequencies, radar capabilities, and more. As for authentication codes, these were changed on a regular basis, and by the time Oswald showed up in Moscow more than two years later, they would have been changed countless times.

The U-2 was (is, for it remains in service today) an extraordinary aircraft. It would vanish from radar screens after climbing to forty-five thousand feet, in itself an extraordinary height. But the plane's pilots would sometimes request information on wind patterns and speeds at altitudes twice as high—ninety thousand feet.

As a radar operator, Oswald certainly knew these basic details. But specific, technical intelligence that Moscow certainly wanted about the U-2 (often called "the black lady of espionage" by the Soviets) concerned things Oswald was not privy to: its high-tech cameras and electronic equipment. U-2 operations were essentially run from a base within a base; aircraft were kept in a special hangar that was watched around the clock by heavily armed guards. "There is no evidence," as Bugliosi notes in *Reclaiming History*, that Oswald's unit "actually dealt with the spy plane's operations, nor is there any evidence that Oswald displayed more than a normal curiosity about the plane."[11]

But we're not finished with Oswald's time in Japan—or the Marines. A month after arriving at Atsugi, Oswald managed to shoot himself in the left arm while playing with a .22 caliber derringer he had bought a few months earlier. "I believe I shot myself," he calmly—again, note his calm—told a fellow Marine, Paul Murphy, who rushed to Oswald's side to investigate.[12]

This led, the next spring, to Oswald's first court-martial. He was found guilty of violating the Uniform Code of Military Justice—laws governing members of the armed forces—and busted from corporal to private (he had been promoted prior to his court-martial), sentenced to twenty days in the brig (suspended if he behaved), and ordered to forfeit twenty-five dollars of his salary for two months. Oswald would later admit that what he considered unfair punishment sparked his first thoughts of defecting to the Soviet Union.

According to Oswald himself, his initial thoughts about defecting were also fueled by encounters with a few members of Japan's communist community. A friend he would make in Dallas, George de Mohrenschildt (more on him later), told the Warren Commission in 1964 that Oswald said he met some Japanese communists who sparked his initial interest in traveling to the USSR. According to de Mohrenschildt's testimony, Oswald—who had clearly been reading Karl Marx—claimed that he saw "the poverty of the Japanese working class, or the proletariat" (we'll hear more about de Mohrenschildt later).[13]

Such testimony, if true, would indicate that Oswald's rationale for defecting to Moscow in the fall of 1959 was ideological. By this time he had been reading about communism since his aborted high school years. He seemed offended, as Mohrenschildt would later claim, that people could work so hard yet have so little. Such resentment of wealth, which in his view came from the exploitation of workers, was one common thread that wove its way through Oswald's life.

It was around this time, some conspiracy writers have alleged, that Oswald began to dabble in espionage. In fact, two writers—Henry Hurt and Anthony Summers—have alleged that Oswald shot himself so he could get away from his unit and engage in spy work. But after all this time, neither has produced any credible, verifiable evidence. Hurt, the author of a book called *Reasonable Doubt*, admits his views are merely "speculative and circumstantial," while Summers has admitted engaging in what he terms "very cautious speculation."[14]

Summers has also dabbled in speculation regarding a second, more serious incident involving Oswald and a gun—and that it was somehow an impetus for him to begin working with the CIA.

Oswald's unit was transferred to Subic Bay, a big US Navy base in the Philippines, in November. On January 5, 1958, another Marine, Private Martin Schrand, was shot to death with his own weapon while on guard duty. An investigation ruled the death accidental. But after President Kennedy's assassination, Summers alleged that another Marine—D. P. Camerata—"heard a rumor" that Oswald may have had something to do with it.

One person writing about how a second person "heard a rumor" from a third person that a fourth person may have been involved in the death of a fifth person is obviously beyond flimsy. It reminds one of those childhood games of "telephone," in which one person whispers something into the ear of the person next to them, and by the time the information reaches the last person in the string, it's distorted beyond reason. After laying all this out, Summers, to his credit, acknowledges that "There is no hard evidence that Lee Oswald was really involved in the death of Marine Schrand."[15]

As we have seen after examining Oswald's unstable childhood and numerous examples of poor attitude, his perceived mistreatment in the Marines shouldn't come as a surprise. He dropped out of schools and had trouble fitting in, making friends, and more. His time in the Marines was no different.

Along with his deteriorating attitude—in fairness often caused by fellow Marines picking on him mercilessly because he didn't fit in—Oswald, instead of fighting back, allowed his anger to build up, until he eventually exploded. He began to belittle others he considered intellectually inferior. He "engaged in several fights," said fellow Marine Peter Francis Connor in a Warren Commission affidavit on May 22, 1964. "He often responded to the orders of his superiors with insolent remarks."[16]

Inherent in this behavior was Oswald's contempt for authority. In his own affidavit on May 19, 1964, former Marine John Rene

Heindel noted that "Oswald was often in trouble for failure to adhere to rules and regulations and gave the impression of disliking any kind of authority." Oswald added, according to Heindel, that he was tired of being "kicked around."[17]

This led to Oswald's second court-martial on June 27, 1958, when he was found guilty of pouring a drink on a Marine he had been having trouble with—Sgt. Miguel Rodriguez—and challenging him to a fight. The confrontation was broken up by military police before it could begin, but Oswald was sentenced to twenty-eight days in the brig and fined fifty-five dollars.[18]

This, then, was Oswald: the boy who was quick to anger. The boy who threw rocks at children. The boy who chased his brother with a knife. The boy who hit his mom. The boy described by a neighbor as "a bad kid…very strange…vicious almost." The boy described by a psychiatrist as having "a fantasy life" about "omnipotence and power," who "hides considerable hostility of various degrees." The boy who said, "I dislike everybody." The teen who expressed an interest in killing President Eisenhower. Then: the Marine oddball who didn't fit. The Marine who lashed out violently at others. The Marine who was court-martialed twice in as many months. The Marine who scored a "sharpshooter" rating on the rifle range.

And yet after his second court-martial, Oswald's hitch wasn't over. He emerged from the brig "cold, withdrawn, and bitter," said fellow Marine Joseph Macedo, and said he blamed the Marine Corps for wounding his pride by tossing him in the brig. He seemed to conflate this bitterness with the United States in general, telling Macedo that he had no desire to return to the US. And there was this: "All the Marine Corps did was to teach you to kill," he told Daniel Powers, according to Powers' testimony.[19] Here, in vivid color, was the "considerable hostility" that his psychiatrist, Dr. Hartogs, had observed in 1953.

This was soon followed by a mental breakdown. In the fall of 1958, Oswald's unit had been sent to Taiwan. While standing guard one night, he suddenly began firing his M-1 rifle at shadows in the woods. He was "shaking and crying" when he was found and kept repeating that he could no longer handle guard duty. He was transferred the next day and placed on general duty.

Oswald's anti-Americanism exploded. He began speaking of "U.S. imperialism" and called other Marines "you Americans."[20]

He didn't want to return to the United States but spent a month's leave in Fort Worth going hunting with Robert and posing with his brother's .22 rifle. He was then sent back to El Toro, California, and began wearing his fondness for all things Russia on his sleeve.

He subscribed to a Russian-language newspaper, struggling to decipher it with a Russian-English dictionary. He played Russian records full blast. He used basic words like "da" (yes) and "nyet" (no) whenever he could. A Marine he roomed with on base, Mack Osborne, said in his May 18, 1964, affidavit to the Warren Commission that Oswald "spent a great deal of his free time reading papers printed in Russian." And Osborne offered this eerie observation:

> I once asked Oswald why he did not go out in the evening like the other men. He replied that he was saving his money, making some statement to the effect that one day he would do something which would make him famous.[21]

Oswald, who as we know had previously spoken of his desire to kill the president of the United States—Dwight Eisenhower—didn't elaborate, but Osborne thinks that Oswald was referring to his percolating desire to defect to the Soviet Union, now less than a year away.

Another Marine, Kerry Wendell Thornley, who met Oswald in 1959, also recalled the future assassin's thirst for fame, telling the Warren Commission that Oswald wanted to be remembered in history books "10,000 years from now." And: "He was concerned with his image in history...."[22]

By this time, Oswald's disgust with the Marines and his desire to defect were more explicit than ever. In El Toro in late 1958, he found comradeship with a fellow Marine, Nelson Delgado, who, much to Oswald's delight, also admired Fidel Castro. Living in the same Quonset hut, they spoke frequently, Delgado remembered:

> He was a complete believer that our way of government was not quite right…he was for, not the Communist way of life, the Castro way of life, the way he was going to lead his people.[23] *

There was a Cuban consulate in Los Angeles, a forty-mile train ride from Irvine, the closest major city to El Toro. Oswald later told Delgado that he had been in contact with diplomats there, apparently in conjunction with an expressed interest in going to Cuba to fight on behalf of Castro.

Delgado recalled Oswald's arrogance, noting how he believed that his Marine superiors "weren't as intelligent as he was in his estimation."[24] Once again, a continuation of the smugness that was so pervasive throughout Oswald's short life.

To this we can add another bit of Kerry Thornley's testimony to the Warren Commission. He said Oswald was "a person who would go out of his way to get into trouble, get some officer or staff sergeant mad at him. He would make wise remarks. He had a general bitter attitude toward the Corps."

A few months of exposure to Oswald was enough for Thornley. Before Oswald was discharged from the Marines in September 1959, Thornley would soon conclude that Oswald was "a nut," that something wasn't quite right with him. The Mr. Jenner in the excerpt below is Albert E. Jenner Jr., the commission's assistant counsel:

> **Mr. THORNLEY:** Later, I did reflect on it, and that, combined with his general habits in relation to his superiors, and to the other men in the outfit, caused me to decide that he had a definite tendency toward irrationality at times, an emotional instability. Once again right away, I didn't know exactly what was the cause of this. A couple of years later I had good reason to think about it some more, at which time I noticed.
>
> **Mr. JENNER:** Now when, please? Before the assassination?
>
> **Mr. THORNLEY:** Yes, while working on my book, *The Idle Warriors*.[25]

---

* Delgado claimed Oswald wasn't very proficient with a rifle, though Oswald's scores on the role range show otherwise.

Written in 1962, but not published until 1991, the book is based on a Marine who defected to the Soviet Union.

August 17—El Toro, California

Oswald requests to be discharged from the Marines, saying his mother needs assistance.[26] The Marines are only too happy to be rid of the twice-court-martialed malcontent, and approve his request on September 4.

But Oswald, lying as he did about so many things, had no intention of going home to his mother. The same day the Marine Corps approved his release, he applied for a passport, saying he wanted to study in Switzerland and Finland. He also indicated that he hoped to travel to Britain, France, Germany, the Dominican Republic, Cuba—and his most desired destination of all: the Soviet Union. It was a routine passport request, and it was issued six days later, on September 10.[27]

Oswald was discharged the next day, September 11. He went straight home, arriving in Fort Worth on the fourteenth. Next stop: Moscow.

CHAPTER SIX

Defector: Oswald in the Soviet Union September 1959–June 1962

"I want to give the people of the United States something to think about."

—LEE HARVEY OSWALD

Contemptuous of America and its capitalist system, whose fruits were distributed unevenly, and a government and military that he considered "repressive," Oswald would flee to the Soviet Union, believing it to be a worker's paradise. He would soon learn otherwise, observing that the USSR was repressive and exploitative in its own way. Realizing that the United States, for all its perceived faults, offered a better life, he swallowed his pride and—with a new wife and newborn daughter in tow—moved back. With Lee Harvey Oswald, the lifelong drifter, dropout, and malcontent, the Eden he was always searching for—the place that would recognize the brilliance that he knew he possessed—was always wherever he was not. As we'll see in a future chapter, it was a pattern that would continue beyond his misguided experiment with Mother Russia.

September 17—Fort Worth

Oswald speaks with a travel agent from New Orleans-based Travel Consultants, Inc. Filling out a "Passenger Immigration Questionnaire," he lies, calling himself a "shipping export agent," and that he plans to be out of the country for two months on a pleasure trip. He pays $220.75 to book passage from New Orleans to Le Havre, France, on a freighter, the SS *Marion Lykes*, scheduled to sail on September 18. Arriving in New Orleans that evening, he checks in at a cheap hotel near the French Quarter.

As his final hours in America dwindled, he wrote to his mother, not mentioning that he was bound for the Soviet Union or that he planned to defect.

The *Marion Lykes* sailed on September 20. Only four passengers were on board, and Oswald seems to have rubbed each of them the wrong way. He shared his cabin with Billy Joe Lord, who had just graduated from high school and was going to France to study. Lord later described Oswald as being "standoffish" and that he was bitter about the way his mother was treated at the Fort Worth drugstore where he worked. The other two passengers were Lt. Col. and Mrs. George B. Church Jr., who also found Oswald unfriendly. The Churches would later testify, as Lord did, about Oswald's "bitterness" about his mother's difficulties. Neither Lord nor the Churches had any idea that Oswald was intent on defecting to the Soviet Union.[1]

October 8—Le Havre, France

Oswald arrives in France. He immediately crosses the English Channel for Britain. Arriving in Southampton the next day, he lies to customs officials, saying that he plans to remain in the United Kingdom for a week before moving on to Switzerland, where he plans to study. In fact, he quickly leaves for Finland.[2]

Let's take a moment here to note one conspiracist claim. Noting that Oswald's passport was stamped at Heathrow Airport on October

10, they claim that there were no direct commercial flights from London to Helsinki that Oswald could have taken to arrive in the Finnish capital on the tenth.

The implication here is that something was afoot. Or, perhaps a reasonable explanation can be found deep within the Warren Commission report, which notes that Oswald probably had a connecting flight: "Oswald could have arrived at 5:05 p.m., flying via Copenhagen, or at 5:35 p.m., via Stockholm. See Official Airline Guide, North American Edition, October 1959, p. C-721."

As this book counts down to November 22, 1963, I'll note a few similar anomalies—there are far too many to mention—which support the view that conspiracy buffs focus too much on small things that can, upon reasonable examination, be explained away. Here, I again bring in Bugliosi, who demolishes the conspiracists as only one of the twentieth century's most accomplished prosecutors could:

> "The Warren Commission critics and conspiracy theorists have succeeded in transforming a case very simple and obvious at its core—Oswald killed Kennedy and acted alone—into its present form of the most complex murder case, BY FAR, in world history.
>
> "Refusing to accept the plain truth, and dedicating their existence for over forty years to convincing the American public of the truth of their own charges, the critics have journeyed to the outer margins of their imaginations. Along the way, they have split hairs and then proceeded to split the split hairs, drawn far-fetched and wholly unreasonable inferences from known facts, and literally invented bogus facts from the grist of rumor and speculation.
>
> "With over 18,000 pages of small print in the 27 Warren Commission volumes alone, and many millions of pages of FBI and CIA documents, any researcher worth his salt can find a sentence here or there to support any ludicrous conspiracy theory he might have. And that, of course, is precisely what the conspiracy community has done."[3]

Now on with our countdown.

October 12—Helsinki, Finland

At the Soviet consulate Oswald applies for a visa. Despite threats he would soon make to American officials in Moscow, he makes no reference to his time stationed at Atsugi Air Base in Japan, where U-2 spy missions were launched.[4]

October 16—Moscow, Soviet Union

"Arrive from Helsinki by train; am met by Intourist representative and taken in car to Hotel Berlin," Oswald writes in what he would ostentatiously call his "historic diary." He registers as a student on a five-day "Deluxe" tourist ticket, is given room 320, and wastes no time getting down to business: "Meet my Intourist guide Rimma Shirakova (I explain to her I wish to apply for Russian citizenship.)"[5]

October 17

Rimma takes Lee on a tour of the Soviet capital—the beating heart of the communist world that Oswald so admires. It culminates in Red Square and the Kremlin. She will recall later that Oswald seems disinterested and never asks any questions.

As the chilly day waned, Oswald finally spoke up. He didn't want to go back to America, he said. He had already made up his mind, he told Rimma, and had his reasons. His mother had remarried—this was one of Oswald's typical lies; Marguerite divorced her third husband in 1948—and no longer had any interest in her younger son. He added one thing, however, that was generally true: nobody in America seemed to have any use for him.

Diary entry:

> "I explain to her (Rimma) that I wish to apply for Soviet citizenship. She is flabbergasted, but agrees to help. She checks with her boss, main office Intourist, then helps me address a letter to Supreme Soviet asking for citizenship."[6]

October 18

Rimma, who knows from Lee's file that it's his twentieth birthday, gives him a gift. It's a book: *The Idiot*, by Dostoyevsky. They return to Red Square to visit the most revered site in all the Soviet Union: the tomb of Lenin, the founder of the Soviet state. Soviet citizens who visit the tomb do so in deeply reverential terms, but Oswald doesn't seem too interested.

Oswald told Rimma that he could share some secrets with the Soviets. But he would soon learn that the Soviets weren't impressed.

October 21

Diary entry (original spelling):

Eve. 6:00

Receive word from police official. I must leave country tonight at 8:00 P.M. as visa expirs. I am shocked! My dreams! I retire to my room. I have $100 left. I have waited for 2 year to be accepted. My fondes dreams are shattered because of a petty official, because of bad planning. I planned too much![7]

Days after telling Rimma that he isn't wanted in America, Oswald learns he's not wanted in the Soviet Union, either. He has nowhere to go. He is a man without a country.

Diary entry (original spelling):

7:00 P.M.

I decide to end it. Soak rist in cold water to numb the pain. Then slash my left wrist. Then plunge wrist into bathtub of hot water. I think, 'when Rimma comes at 8. to find me dead, it will Be a great shock. somewhere, a violin plays, as I watch my life whirl away. I think to myself. 'How easy to die' and 'a sweet death, (to violins).[8]

So melodramatic, so self-pitying. But if Oswald was really trying to kill himself, he didn't try hard enough. Taken to Botkin Hospital, doctors said the cut, about one-and-a-quarter inches long, wasn't very deep. He's patched up with four stitches.

Yuri Nosenko, the KGB officer who defected to the United States in 1964, claimed that after Kennedy's assassination, he had reviewed Oswald's file. "When Oswald regained consciousness (in the hospital), he was asked why he did it," Nosenko told author Gerald Posner. According to Nosenko, Oswald said simply. "I'm not leaving here."

Oswald was given a mental evaluation. "We had two psychiatrists, neither of whom was a KGB doctor, examine him," Nosenko said.

Nosenko told Posner that both doctors "concluded he [Oswald] was mentally unstable. It made us feel one hundred percent that he should be avoided at all costs." A transcript of the examinations, later found in KGB archives, said that one of the doctors concluded that Oswald, as Posner writes, "was capable of more irrational acts."[9]

Norman Mailer, in his own research, mentions only one doctor. Of Oswald, the doctor writes, "Has very definite desire to stay in Soviet Union. No psychosomatic disturbances," and adds "and is not dangerous."[10]

By now, Oswald's visa had expired, yet he remained in the hospital. Not because he was in bad shape, but because officials didn't know what to do with him.

Oswald's Intourist guide, Rimma, visited him on a regular basis. They talked about his first name. "Lee" was difficult to pronounce in Russian, so Rimma suggested the more Slavic-sounding "Alik." Oswald liked it and the name stuck.[11] A seemingly minor thing in 1959, the name "Alik" would loom large in 1963, when Oswald was back in the United States.

October 28

Oswald is released and taken to a new hotel, the Metropole in downtown Moscow. Perched between Red Square and Dzerzhinsky Square, where the butterscotch-colored headquarters of the KGB stands menacingly, and just across from the famed Bolshoi Theater, it's an upgrade for Oswald.

Shortly after his arrival, he got a visit from four Soviet officials.

Diary entry:

> "They ask Do you want to go to your homeland? I say no, I want Soviet citizenship. They say they will see about that...They make notes. 'What papers do you have to show who and what you are?' I give them my discharge papers from the Marine Corps. They say 'Wait for our answer.' I ask, 'How long?' 'Not soon.'"[12]

Helping Oswald's desire to remain in the Soviet Union were international events. Only a month before, Soviet leader Nikita Khrushchev had completed a two-week goodwill tour of the United States. Relations between Washington and Moscow were on the mend. "After years of cold relations between the superpowers," notes Nosenko, "We didn't want to do anything to hurt this new atmosphere or to give a pretext to those who wanted to ruin better relations."

This would drive Moscow's decision on what to do with Oswald. His KGB file notes that Anastas Mikoyan, then a member of the Politburo (the highest policy-making authority in the ruling Communist Party) personally ordered that Oswald's request for asylum be given special consideration.

Oswald had already tried to kill himself once. What if—told he must leave—he tried again? Or succeeded? "Considering the options," Nosenko told Posner, "we decided to let him stay. He seemed harmless enough. We could decide where he worked and lived, and maintain surveillance over him to ensure he did not cause any trouble or was not an American sleeper agent."[13]

Meanwhile, Oswald's penchant for drama and attention would be on full display at the American Embassy.

October 31—American Embassy

Oswald tells receptionist Joan Hallett that he's there to renounce his American citizenship. It isn't every day that an American storms into the embassy to do such a thing, and his arrogant, surly demeanor makes an impression on Hallett and her husband Oliver, a naval attaché.[14]

He was then taken to see consular official Richard Snyder.

Oswald's diary entry:

> I say, "I have experienced life in the U.S., American military life, American Imperialism. I am a Marxist and I waited two years for this. I don't want to live in the U.S. or be burdened by American citizenship."[15]

In his testimony before the Warren Commission, Snyder said that Oswald also said that he would tell the Soviets everything he had learned as a radar operator in the Marines—a treasonous matter—though in his diary entry, Oswald made no mention of this.

"His attitude was arrogant and aggressive," Snyder added. "He was a very cocksure young man at that time. He said 'Don't bother wasting my time asking me questions or trying to talk me out of my position.'" Oswald also gave Snyder a written statement that repeated his verbal diatribe.[16]

> I, Lee Harvey Oswald do hereby request that my present citizenship in the United States of america [sic] be revoked. I have entered the Soviet Union for the express purpose of applying for citizenship in the Soviet Union, through the means of naturalization. My request for citizenship is now pending before the Supreme Soviet of the U.S.S.R. I take these steps for political reasons. My request for the revoking of my American citizenship is made only after the longest and most serious consideration. I affirm that my allegiance is to the Union of Soviet Socialist Republics.
>
> Lee H. Oswald[17]

Snyder also testified that Oswald was just like every other "peculiar kind of person" who "occasionally drift into the Soviet Union and state that they want to roll up their sleeves and go to work for socialism for the rest of their lives." But such people, "and I think this is essentially true probably of Oswald," Snyder added, "really knew nothing about Marxism and Leninism, that he professed to be modeling his life after."[18]

"Let's get down to business," Oswald demanded.[19] But October 31 was a Saturday, and Snyder told him that paperwork for such a momentous thing couldn't be processed until Monday. "I turn very mad," Oswald wrote, and left. But on Monday, November 2, Oswald was a no-show.

Back at the Metropol, Oswald got a call from Aline Mosby, a United Press International Reporter. Mosby had been tipped off by Snyder that there was a potential American defector living in the Metropol.

Oswald granted her an interview, and loved the attention.

Diary entry for November 1:

Now I feel slightly axzillarated (exhilarated), not so lonly (lonely).[20]

November 8

Oswald's arrogance comes through in this condescending letter to Robert (in the interest of clarity and legibility, Oswald's poor spelling and grammar have been corrected in certain cases):

> Dear Robert,
>
> Well, what should we talk about? The weather perhaps? Certainly you do not wish me to speak of my decision to remain in the Soviet Union and apply for citizenship here, since I am afraid you would not be able to comprehend my reasons. You really don't know anything about me. Do you know for instance that I have waited to do this for well over a year? Do you know that I

(Example of Russian writing) speak a fair amount of Russian which I have been studying for many months.

I have been told that I will not have to leave the Soviet Union if I did not care to. This then is my decision. I will not leave this country, the Soviet Union, under any conditions. I will never return to the United States, which is a country I hate.

Someday, perhaps soon, and then again perhaps in a few years, I will become a citizen of the Soviet Union, but it is a very legal process, in any event, I will not have to leave the Soviet Union and I will never leave.

I received your telegram and was glad to hear from you. Only one word bothered me. The word "mistake." I assume you mean that I have made a "mistake." It is not for you to tell me this. You cannot understand my reasons for this very serious action.

I will not speak to anyone from the United States over the telephone since it may be taped by the Americans.

If you wish to correspond with me you can write to the below address, but I really don't see what we could talk about. If you want to send me some money, that I can use, but I do not expect to be able to send it back.

Lee[21]

November—Fort Worth

FBI agent John Fain hears that a Fort Worth man by the name of Lee Harvey Oswald is in Moscow trying to defect to the Soviet Union. He opens a file on Oswald.[22]

November 13

Oswald is interviewed again by UPI's Mosby. She would remember him this way:

> "Lee Harvey Oswald struck me as a young boy full of bitterness and hate. Someone not too well educated, certainly not a brilliant

person. I would say he was extremely superficial, very immature, and very misinformed. He told me why he had decided to leave the United States and give up his American citizenship and apply for citizenship in the Soviet Union. He said he had indoctrinated himself for five years through reading books about Marx. But he actually knew very little about communism, and he couldn't apply what he had read to the actual life in Moscow around him. It was as if he were quoting just sentences from *Pravda* and *Izvestia* without really knowing what they meant. When he spoke, he held his chin stiffly and his mouth was tight and thin. When he spoke of the United States, the hostility that he felt for his country was quite evident."

She continued:

"Afterward, I remember thinking what an unbalanced, extremely emotionally immature fellow he was. In fact, when other correspondents in Moscow asked me how the interview had gone, I had described him as being, well, he was just a little weird."[23]

November 16

A Soviet official tells Oswald that he can stay in the USSR until the government can figure out what to do with him. "It is comforting news for me," he writes in his diary.[24]

Apparently feeling more confident about his situation, Oswald gave an interview to another reporter, Priscilla Johnson McMillan, who, like other foreign correspondents, also lived in the Metropol.*

During their conversation, which took place in McMillan's room and lasted several hours, Oswald played the victim, complaining about how he was being treated by the American Embassy.

* McMillan not only came to know Oswald, but incredibly, worked briefly on John F. Kennedy's Senate staff in 1953. They stayed in touch for several years after that. McMillan died in 2021 at the age of ninety-two.

He seemed "bitter," McMillan later wrote, and "did not seem like a fully grown man to me."

Mirroring the observation that Oswald's Intourist guide Shirakova made while showing a disinterested Oswald around Moscow, McMillan noted how she "was astounded by his lack of curiosity and the utter absence of any joy or animal spirit in him."

"I believe what I'm doing is right," Oswald said, then, in a burst of sanctimoniousness, the twenty-year-old turncoat said he wanted to give the American people "something to think about."[25]

November 26

In a 1,298-word diatribe to Robert, Oswald rambles on with a stream of pretentious gobbledygook. He opens by saying "I and my fellow workers and communists would like to see the present capitalist government of the U.S. overthrown," because it represents an unfair, exploitative, repressive system. "I fight for communism," Oswald says, underling the word for emphasis. Scribbling just steps from Red Square and the Kremlin, he adds that "I have always considered this country to be my own." As for America, he writes: "I do not wish to be a part of it, nor do I ever again wish to be used as a tool in its military oppressions."

He mentions the Communist Manifesto, the 1848 pamphlet by German philosophers Karl Marx and Friedrich Engels, which he presumes to understand, before ending with a manifesto of his own:

1. In the event of war, I would kill any American who put a uniform on in defense of the American government—any American.
2. That in my own mind, I have no attachments of any kind in the U.S.
3. That I want to, and I shall, live a normal happy and peaceful life here in the Soviet Union for the rest of my life [original emphasis].
4. That my mother and you are (in spite of what the newspapers said) not objects of affection, but only examples of workers in the U.S.

There's more, but you get the idea.[26]

Let's recap. Here's Oswald, all of twenty years old, the angry, explosive, unstable kid who drifted among a dozen schools as a child, the high school dropout, the kid who plotted to steal a pistol from a gun shop, who pulled a knife on his own family, the twice-court-martialed and demoted Marine, proclaiming after a month isolated in a dingy Moscow hotel room, and several days in a mental ward, that he knew how the world worked. "I am not all bitterness or hate…[but] I would kill <u>any</u> American who put a uniform on in defense of the American government—any American."

No, no bitterness or hatred there at all. America, after all, was a militarily oppressive country, he proclaimed, as he scribbled from the land of the midnight knock on the door, the vast archipelagoes of prison camps, the country that controlled half of Europe by force, and as recently as 1956, had sent tanks into the cobblestoned streets of Budapest to slaughter citizens who wanted greater freedom. But it was American oppression that Oswald was disgusted with.

December

The rest of the year goes by with no news on whether Oswald will be allowed to stay. He keeps to his room, taking all his meals there and trying to learn Russian. And although he's eager to become a Soviet citizen, he continues to show no interest in his surroundings:

> I rarely go outside at all for this month and a half. I see no one, speak to no one, except every now and then Rimma.[27]

January 2, 1960—Washington

Massachusetts Senator John F. Kennedy announces that he is running for president.

January 4

The dam breaks: Oswald learns from Rimma that he will be allowed to stay in the Soviet Union. But not in Moscow. The KGB, which had certainly been reading his rambling letters to Robert (and Robert's to him), deemed him unworthy of living in the Soviet capital. Instead, Oswald was told that he would go to Minsk, the capital of Byelorussia, some 420 miles to the southwest.

Diary entry (original spelling):

> I am called to passport office and finally given a Soviet document, not the soviet citizenship as I so wanted, only a Residence document, not even for foreigners but a paper called, "for those without citizenship." Still I am happy. The official says they are sending me to the city of "Minsk." I ask, "is that in Siberia?" He only laughs. He also tells me that they have arranged for me to receive some money through the Red Cross to pay my hotel bills and expenses. I thank the gentlemen and leave later in the afternoon. I see Rimma. She asks, "are you happy?" "Yes."[28]

Despite threats made at the US Embassy to reveal "secrets" to the Soviets, Oswald doesn't mention, in a questionnaire filled out at the passport office, that he was based in Japan at the Atsugi Air Base.[29]

January 5

Diary entry:

> I go to Red Cross in Moscow for money with Interpreter (a new one). I receive 5000 rubles, a huge sum!! Later in Minsk I am to earn 70 rubles a month at the factory.

Five thousand rubles in 1960 was a fantastic sum, considering that the average salary in 1959 was about 960 rubles a year.[30]

January 7—Byelorussky Train Station, Moscow

Oswald, crying, leaves for Minsk.

> Diary entry:
>
> I wrote my mother and brother letters in which I said "I do not wish to ever contact you again. I am beginning a new life and I don't want *any part* [emphasis original] of the old."[31]

Told that an American defector was headed their way, KGB officials in Minsk established surveillance of Oswald. Upon arrival he was met by Intourist guide Roza Kuznetsova. Within two months, he would be given an apartment all to himself. This was an incredible luxury, given that Soviet families typically lived in one room and shared a kitchen and bathroom. Some conspiracists say this "proves" that Oswald somehow had an in with the authorities. Actually, he was isolated in his apartment because it would be easier for the KGB to monitor this strange young foreigner.

January 13—Minsk, Byelorussian Soviet Socialist Republic

Oswald begins work at the Gorizont Radio Factory. His job—a "'checker' metal worker," as he calls it—is a low-skilled position reflecting his status as nothing more than a cog in a giant factory.[32] Oswald doesn't want to work. The American high-school dropout wants to go to school to study economics, philosophy, and politics. But even if Soviet officials thought him worthy of this, and they do not, there's no question that Oswald's comprehension of the Russian language would have made such advanced studies all but impossible.

January (undated)—Fort Worth

FBI agent Fain interviews both Marguerite and Robert Oswald. Aside from Lee's November 2 letter, there's not much they can add. Marguerite does say that she wired twenty-five dollars to her son.[33]

January 13-16—Minsk

After just a week at Gorizont, Oswald complains in his diary. He dislikes the "picture of Lenin which watches from its place of honour and physical training at 11-11.10 each morning (compulsary) for all (shades of H.G. Wells!!)."

This was one of the main themes that threaded its way through Oswald's life. We've established that he was a malcontent in the many schools he attended. He was a malcontent in the Marine Corps. He was now a malcontent in Minsk, and, as we'll see, would be a malcontent at every future job. Minsk, Dallas, New Orleans, it made no difference: Oswald was never satisfied and always grumbled about the string of dead-end, menial jobs he held. For someone who claimed to be a student of Marxism, with its glorification of the working class, Oswald always thought himself better and smarter than the mere proletariat; the poor attitude that always resulted—there are plenty of examples in the pages ahead—never failed to win contempt from his coworkers, be they Soviet or American.

March—Minsk

Oswald is moved to his own apartment at 4 Kalinin Street (today "vulica Kamunistyčnaja"). In the heart of the city, it has a balcony that offers a sweeping view of the Svislach River. As mentioned previously, his accommodations—though lacking a telephone or TV and "sparsely furnished and dismal"—are much better than that of the typical Soviet citizen. The isolated setup allows for easier surveillance, and teams of KGB agents—about twenty in all—take turns listening in on any conversations he has; there is also a peephole from a neighboring apartment with a magnifying lens into Oswald's bedroom.

Nosenko told Gerald Posner in 1992 that the blanket coverage of Oswald was probably overkill. But not trusting him, and suspecting that he might somehow be an American agent, the Committee for State

Security, as the KGB was formally known, wasn't about to take any chances.*

The typically antisocial Oswald began to form friendships. Some, like Alexander Ziger, an engineer and Polish Jew who had emigrated to the Soviet Union in 1955 and managed a department at Gorizont, may have been innocuous. But many were certainly linked to the KGB. Kuznetsova, the Intourist guide who met Oswald at the train station when he arrived, was one. Oswald took a liking to her, and escorted Kuznetsova to cultural events on a regular basis.

Another female informer who had feigned interest in Oswald, Anna Byeloruskaya, told her KGB handlers, "The general mental development of Oswald is low. His views are limited, and he has a very poor appreciation of music, art and literature." The KGB tried to get Byeloruskaya to lay a trap for Oswald, by telling him that a relative was an important physicist at the Academy of Sciences. Oswald, she would subsequently report, wasn't interested. It would have been the height of naïveté for Oswald not to think that these women were reporting on him, but there is no evidence that he did.[34]

Another informer was Pavel Golovachev, a coworker. Marina Oswald, who we'll soon meet, would say years later that Golovachev was not only Oswald's best friend in the Soviet Union but probably the closest friend he would ever have.[35] Yet Golovachev, the son of a Soviet war hero, was also keeping tabs on Oswald, albeit reluctantly. In a 1993 PBS, interview, Golovachev described how he spied on Oswald:

> "It was like this. Your country asks you—your country demands. 'There is a foreigner here. It's in the country's interests for security, 'and so on.' That was early on, but I told him [Oswald] about it a year later. I had three or four meetings with the KGB people. They gave me little assignments to provoke [Oswald], saying, 'Try this out on him and see what he says.'"[36]

---

* And while the KGB was constantly monitoring Oswald, wondering if he was working with the CIA, US officials in Moscow and Washington, knowing this wasn't the case, wondered whether Oswald—who wanted to shed his American citizenship—was working for Moscow.

But Golovachev told his handlers that Oswald "did not seem to be up to too much that would interest them."

April 27—Fort Worth

FBI agent John Fain talks to Robert Oswald again, "in an effort to locate his mother."[37]

April 28—Fort Worth

Fain talks to Marguerite Oswald again. She tells Fain that she was shocked and upset that Lee had gone to the Soviet Union and, apparently, was trying to become a Soviet citizen.[38]

May 1—Minsk

After months of constant surveillance, the KGB has little on Oswald. Coverage logs reveal a humdrum existence, shuffling back and forth between work and home, with forays, usually alone, to cafes. One typically dull entry covers May 1, which we'll discuss a bit further down:

> PERFORMED FROM 07:00 ON MAY 1, 1960, TILL 01:50 ON MAY 2, 1960
>
> At 10:00 Lee Harvey came out of house N4 on Kalinina Street, came to Pobedy Square where he spent 25 minutes looking at passing parade. After this he went to Kalinina Street and began walking up and down embankment of Svisloch River. Returned home by 11:00.
>
> From 11:00 to 13:00 he came out onto balcony of his apartment more than once. At 13:35 Lee Harvey left his house, got on trolley bus N2 at Pobedy Square, went to Central Square, was last to get off bus, went down Engelsa, Marksa and Lenina Streets to bakery store on Prospekt Stalina.
>
> There he bought 200 gr. of vanilla cookies, then went to café, had cup of coffee with patty at self-service section and hurried

> toward movie theatre Central. Having looked through billboards he bought newspaper, visited bakery for second time, left it immediately, and took trolley bus N1 to Pobedy Square and was home by 14:20.
>
> At 16:50 Lee Harvey left his house and came to house N14 on Krasnaya Street. (Residence of immigrant from Argentina—Ziger.)
>
> At 1:40 Lee Harvey together with other men and women, among whom there were daughters of Ziger, came home. Observation was stopped at this point till morning.[39]

Such banality doesn't prove or disprove anything; but it does reflect ongoing KGB suspicions about Oswald. This was a Soviet agent?

At Ziger's May Day party, Oswald gets some advice from his English-speaking host, which reinforces his growing doubts about living in the Soviet Union.

> Diary entry:
>
> Ziger advises me to go back to U.S.A. Its the first voice of opposition I have heard. I respect Ziger; he has seen the world. He says many things and relates many things I do not know about the U.S.S.R. I begin to feel uneasy inside, it's true![40]

May 1, 1960, is also important for another reason: It's the day that U-2 pilot Francis Gary Powers was shot down on a spy mission over Sverdlovsk, some 1,400 miles to the east, in western Siberia. Given Oswald's hatred of "American imperialism" and his vow that he would kill any American during wartime, he probably was not displeased at the news, when the Soviet government made the shootdown public a week later. But Oswald makes no mention of it in his diary.

Nor, and more significantly, is there any evidence that Oswald, in his earlier zeal to prove his worth to the Soviets, actually told them anything about the U-2, or anything connected with the spy plane's operations. When KGB archives became available following the 1991 collapse of the Soviet Union, "there is no suggestion," as Bugliosi, among others, noted, "that Oswald ever gave the Soviets intelligence information or that they were interested in him as a source."[41]

There are two points to be made. As mentioned before, Oswald really didn't know that much about the U-2—and certainly nothing that the Soviets didn't already know. Yes, he had been at Atsugi, but U-2 operations were conducted from a different and specially guarded part of the base. But Oswald never told the Soviets he had even been stationed there, and even if he had, "Our intelligence on the U-2 was good and had been for some time," Nosenko told Posner.[42]

Furthermore, there is no hard, reliable evidence that Oswald even had access to the plane or gleaned information about it from anyone who did. Secondly, that the Soviets didn't consider him worth "debriefing" in substance about anything belies the larger conspiracist notion that somehow, Oswald was working with the Kremlin. The KGB blanketed him in Minsk because he wasn't trusted; it wasn't some sort of false flag operation.

Circling back to his May 1 diary entry—in which Oswald reveals dissatisfaction with his life in the Soviet Union—one can surmise that it was beginning to dawn on Oswald that the attention, recognition, and respect he had always craved, and which he believed he would find in the USSR, might not be forthcoming. In Minsk itself, the gray drab repetitiveness of Soviet life began to wear on him. The initial curiosity over his arrival had faded, he was bored with Gorizont, and he hadn't heard a word from the authorities about being allowed to attend university. His disappointment, and the realization that he wasn't considered special, even here, begin to grow.

June—Minsk

Oswald, lonely, meets a coworker, Ella Germann, a "silky, black-hair Jewish beauty," he writes. He later says it was probably love at first sight.[43]

June 18—Minsk

Oswald obtains a hunting license, buys a shotgun, and joins a hunting club that is sponsored by his factory. His first actual hunting trip with his coworkers will be September 10, according to KGB observers who keep tabs on him from a distance. They are concerned that Oswald might somehow use a hunting trip as a cover to observe sensitive military installations that were nearby.

Observe? Golovachev said in 1993, "I would say that he wasn't a spy because when he bought a camera, he couldn't even put film in it. And it was a very basic camera, a Smena-2, which even a Soviet schoolchild could use, and he couldn't." Golovachev also told author Guy Russo that Oswald couldn't even fix the simplest defect in a radio while working at the factory.[44]

And the hunting? Golovachev claimed that when Oswald attended training sessions that the hunting club held, he wasn't very proficient with his shotgun.[45] Whether this is true or not certainly cannot be confirmed, but this hasn't stopped conspiracy buffs from claiming that it "proves" that Oswald couldn't possibly have shot President Kennedy. How could he have hit a moving target like a man in a car that was moving away from him at a speed of eleven miles per hour, they ask? Perhaps Oswald had difficulty with a shotgun. But with a very different weapon—a high-powered rifle—the former Marine, as we've mentioned, had already qualified, according to Sgt. James Zahm, the noncommissioned officer in charge of the Marine marksmanship training unit, as an "excellent shot."

There's another tale of Oswald's bumbling incompetence. Another Gorizont coworker claimed Oswald was "possibly" working on some sort of "secret radio transmitter." Golovachev says this was rubbish, noting that Oswald couldn't even use the cheap Soviet radio he had bought. "He complained that he couldn't receive certain broadcasts. So, with a kitchen knife, I adjusted the capacitor and it worked fine." He also said that one time, while trying to insert batteries into another portable radio, he wound up ripping out two wires.[46]

"I have no doubt he was not a CIA agent," said Golovachev. "His knowledge was too primitive." He told Russia's ITAR-Tass news agency in 1992 that Oswald was "a weak man, not very bright or intellectual."

Lee Oswald, master spy.

For a counter-narrative to the Oswald-was-a-poor-shot narrative (beyond his proven, and repeated, expertise on the Marine rifle range), we bring in one person who knew Oswald better than anybody, possibly save his soon-to-be wife Marina: Robert Oswald.

The Oswald brothers went hunting on numerous occasions; Robert said Lee was more than skilled at hitting even a tiny target like a rabbit. "My experience with him in the field was he usually got his game."[47]

"He usually got his game. . . ."

July 13—Los Angeles

Kennedy wins the Democratic party nomination for president. He selects Lyndon B. Johnson, the shrewd Senate Majority Leader, as his running mate.

Fall 1960—Minsk

For a woman he claims to have fallen in love with at first sight, Oswald barely mentions Germann in his diary. In an entry on October 18th—his twenty-first birthday—he merely calls Ella a woman with whom "I have been going walking with lately." In an undated entry days later, he writes that "a growing loneliness overtakes me in spite of my conquest of Ennatachina, a girl from Riga, studying at the music conservatory in Minsk. After an affair which lasts a few weeks, we part."[48]

Germann probably knew of this, and even though she didn't see Oswald in romantic terms, she was "aggravated that he didn't tell me the truth. I was offended. Right after that, I started not to trust him so much."[49]

Germann didn't know that Oswald had lied about other things as well, notably his claim that his mother back in America was dead.[50]

November 8—Hyannis Port, Massachusetts

Kennedy is elected president.

November 15—Minsk

Oswald scribbles in his diary that he met "four girls rooming at the For. Ian. [Foreign] dormitory in room 212." On December 1, he writes of a "light affair" with one of them, Nell Korobka.

Mailer picks up on the Oswald-as-an-unwanted-person theme here, noting that after visiting the four girls in their dorm room a few times, he "dropped out of sight." Some girls used to gossip that his only reason for coming to the Institute [they attended a Foreign Languages Institute] was because no one else wanted to date him.[51]

December 31—Minsk

Oswald shows up at Germann's apartment with a gift of chocolates. He rings in 1961 with her family.

January 1, 1961—Minsk

A momentous diary entry:

> New Years I spend at home of Ella German. I think I'm in love with her. She has refused my more dishonorable advances. We drink and eat in the presence of her family in a very hospitable atmosphere. Later I go home drunk and happy. Passing the river homeward, I decide to propose to Ella.

Not a word about Ella in his diary between October 18 and January 1, and all of a sudden he wants to propose. The next night he pops the question—and is shocked at the response.

Diary entry from January 2:

> After a pleasant hand-in-hand walk to the local cinema, we come home, standing on the doorstep I propose. She hesitates, then refuses, my love is real but she has none for me.

Besides not loving him, Ella said the fact that Oswald was an American was problematic. She told him: "You understand the world situation. There is too much against you and you don't even know it."

He wrote:

> I am stunned. She snickers at my awkwardness. In turning to go (I am too stunned to think!) I realize she was never serious with me but only exploited my being an American in order to get the envy of the other girls who consider me differed [sic] from the Russian Boys. I am miserable!

You'll recall that Oswald didn't handle rejection well. After not getting his way thirteen months earlier, he slashed his wrists in a suicide bid. Now the woman of his dreams tells him no thanks. What will Oswald do now?

January 4—Minsk

Ella's rejection adds to Oswald's earlier doubts about life in the USSR.

Diary entries:

> Jan 4. One year after I received the residence document I am called in to the passport office and asked if I want citizenship (Russian). I say no—simply extend my residential passport, [they] agree and my document is extended until January 4, 1962.
>
> Jan 4–31 I am stating [starting] to reconsider my desire about staying. The work is drab, the money I get has nowhere to be spent. No nightclubs or bowling alleys, no places of recreation except the trade union dances. I have had enough.

January 20—Washington

Kennedy is sworn in as the thirty-fifth president of the United States.

January 26—The White House

In one of history's most bizarre and bitterest ironies, Marguerite Oswald shows up at the White House and asks to speak with President Kennedy. Mrs. Oswald, fifty-three, is desperate to learn of her son's whereabouts. She knows Lee is in the Soviet Union, of course, but thinks he is a "secret agent" working for the US government. Surely Kennedy could help her, she thinks. Told he is unavailable, she lowers her sights and asks to speak with Secretary of State Dean Rusk. He is busy too.

Finally Marguerite found three lower-level State Department officials to speak with. She asked for money, claiming that because of her son's status, she was entitled to some form of government compensation. The officials dismissed her claim that Oswald was a "secret agent," but said they would try and locate him.[52]

Washington (exact date uncertain)

As Harry Truman did with his morning walks, Kennedy enjoys strolling about from time to time, to the consternation of the Secret Service. Shortly after his inauguration, JFK and his World War II buddy, Paul "Red" Fay—who Kennedy has made undersecretary of the Navy—are walking from the Army-Navy Club back to the White House, half a mile away.

Suddenly a Secret Service agent jumped between Kennedy and a suspicious-looking man. A startled JFK told Fay that he often thought of being assassinated. "I guess there is always the possibility, but that is what the Secret Service is for," the president said. "I guess that is one of the less desirable aspects of the job."[53]

February 1

Diary entry:

> Make my first request to American Embassy, Moscow, for reconsidering my position, I stated, "I would like to go back to U.S."

It's early 1961. Oswald has been in the USSR for all of fifteen months. He knows, has seen with his own eyes, what a terrible place it is—the people are "poor and depressed," and that—as he would say in August 1963—that "It stunk."[54]

To this disillusionment we can add the rejection of a woman he barely knew, a woman he was madly in love with—but who had no deep feelings for him. It was more than enough to convince Oswald that he had made a terrible mistake. But leave? For where? And for what? The hotheaded, arrogant, so-sure-that-I-know-everything Oswald had already told his family that he wasn't coming back to a United States that "I do not wish to be a part of."[55]

Once again, let's review the real Oswald: the young man with the explosive temper. The high school dropout. The twice-court-martialed Marine. The betrayer of his country. Now, he wants out of the land of his dreams. He's unlucky in love. Working in a menial, dead-end job. Won't anyone see his brilliance? Won't anyone give Lee Harvey Oswald the fame and notoriety he desires? Perhaps he was reminded of an episode from his favorite TV show, *I Led 3 Lives*: "Confused Comrade." For this troubled young comrade was certainly that—confused.

Oswald's life, to this point, had resembled a parabola-shaped curve—a U-shape—where things always started out well, with high expectations, only to crash and burn. This was always followed by a decision to try something else, go somewhere else, where, surely, things would be better. His mother had dragged him from Louisiana to Texas to Louisiana to Texas, to New York, to Louisiana for a third time, and then to Texas for a third time. Always, Marguerite would move hoping for some sort of improvement, only for some reason to wind up disappointed, and the cycle would repeat. And repeat again.

As soon as Oswald was responsible for himself, the pattern continued. Surely joining the Marines was the answer. Wrong. What about the Soviet Union? Wrong again. So back to America, then.

His view that the grass was always surely greener elsewhere led to his first known thoughts about Cuba, where Fidel Castro was beginning his third year of building what Oswald considered "true Marxism" on that sunny island, just ninety miles from Florida.

February 28

Diary entry:

> I receive letter from Embassy. Richard E. Snyder stated, "I could come in for an interview any time I wanted."

Remember the arrogance Oswald displayed to the consular officer in 1959? Knowing that moving to the USSR and attempting to dissolve his American citizenship was a grave mistake (though Oswald doesn't say this), you'd think that Oswald would show some humility or contrition. But no. He tells Snyder: "I hope that in recalling the responsibility I have to America that you remember your's [sic] in doing everything you can to help me since I am an American citizen."

All of a sudden, Oswald feels a responsibility to America? And talking down to Snyder, urging him to remember *his* duty?

Insulted yet again by Oswald, Snyder decided that he was in no hurry to help. He told the Warren Commission that while a consular officer "attempts to be as impersonal as he can about these things, in matter of fact it is very difficult to be entirely impersonal," and that "Mr. Oswald had no claim to any unusual attentions of mine, I must say." Evidence, yet again, of this insolent young man rubbing people the wrong way.[56]

Here too, we must take note of another pattern in Oswald's life: *his penchant for sudden, impulsive acts*. He proposed to a girl with little apparent thought. Rejected, he decided to tuck his tail between his legs and return to America. And sometimes Oswald's impulsiveness resulted in violence: pulling a knife on his stepbrother, John; punching his own mother. As we'll soon see, there will be more examples to come.

March 17

A pivotal moment. Still stung by Ella Germann's marriage rejection, Oswald attends a dance at the city's Trade Union Palace. He meets Marina Nikolayevna Prusakova, a nineteen-year-old pharmacology student. As was the case with Ella, he is instantly smitten.

> Diary entry:
>
> Boring, but at the last hour I am introduced to a girl with a French hair-do and red-dress with white slipper. I dance with her, then ask to show her home. I do, along with 5 other admirers. Her name is Marina. We like each other right away. She gives me her phone number and departs home with a not-so-new friend in a taxi. I walk home.
>
> Things moved quickly. Oswald's diary entries for the next six weeks:
>
> March 18–31: We walk. I talk a little about myself, she talks alot about herself. Her name is Marina N. Prusakova.
>
> Apr. 1st–30: We are going steady and I decide I must have her. She puts me off so on April 15, I propose. She accepts.

April 28—Waldorf-Astoria Hotel, New York

Kennedy travels to the thirty-seventh-floor suite of the famed hotel for a meeting with General Douglas MacArthur. Still smarting from the disastrous Bay of Pigs, Kennedy wishes to consult with the eighty-one-year-old five-star general who commanded American forces in the Pacific during World War II and presided over Japan's 1945 surrender and the Allied occupation of it. More controversially, the general—an almost mythical figure in mid-twentieth-century America—commanded United Nations forces in Korea before being fired by President Harry Truman, for what Truman considered insubordination.

Kennedy, who had served under MacArthur as a lowly Lieutenant Junior Grade (JG) commander of a patrol torpedo (PT) boat in the Solomon Islands, deeply admired MacArthur, and seemed almost deferential to him. "The young president [was] obviously proud to appear with the aging legend," the historian Mark Perry would write years later.[57]

William Manchester, who wrote biographies of both men, said MacArthur was "Kennedy's kind of hero: valiant, a patrician, proud of his machismo, and a lover of glory."[58] And so the two men, thirty-eight years apart in age, hit it off. "I could not drag them apart," Kennedy advisor Ken O'Donnell said.[59]

After discussing the Bay of Pigs debacle—MacArthur blamed Eisenhower, whom he had also once commanded, for planning the operation—the conversation turned to Southeast Asia. Kennedy told the general that he was being pressured to send troops to Laos and Vietnam, to fend off growing community insurgencies.

MacArthur advised Kennedy not to get sucked into a ground war. "Anyone wanting to commit ground troops to Asia should have his head examined," he told the president.[60]

April 30

Oswald diary entry:

> April 31 [really the 30th] After a 7 day delay at the marriage bureau because of my unusual passport, they allow us to register as man & wife.[61]

The quickie marriage is another example of Oswald's impulsive, erratic behavior. In January he had begun to "reconsider my desire about staying" in such a "drab" place. "I have had enough," he wrote. Lonely and emotionally needy, his heart had been broken by a woman he barely knew. His answer? A woman he knew even less well. Married forty-four days after meeting in a dingy dance hall.

We've already established, in earlier passages of this book, that Oswald was a habitual liar. Now Marina would be the recipient of his endless falsehoods, starting with the very moment they registered to be married. At ZAGS, the Soviet government office that registered marriages, Oswald wrote on a form that he had been born in 1939.

"You are only twenty-one," she said. "Why did you tell me you were twenty-four?"

"I was afraid you wouldn't take me seriously," he said, acknowledging that he had lied to his wife on a major matter.[62]

It wasn't long before Marina discovered other big lies. Oswald had told her that his mother was dead and that he was an orphan. He told her that he wasn't interested in returning to the United States, which, based on his own diary entries and renewed correspondence with the American Embassy in Moscow, obviously wasn't true. Had Marina read the diary she would also have read this entry from May 1:

> May Day 1961 Found us thinking about our future. In spite of fact I married Marina to hurt Ella, I found myself in love with Marina.[63]

What wife wouldn't enjoy knowing that she was her husband's plan B? That she was being used to hurt another woman? From the get-go, this was nothing near a marriage made in heaven. And it was about to get worse.

It was around this time that Oswald wrote the American Embassy again to discuss "not only for the right to return to the United States, but also for a full guarantee's [sic] that I shall not under any circumstance's [sic] be persecuted for any act pertaining to this case." He added that he now had a Soviet wife. "So with this extra complication," he advised somewhat condescendingly, "I suggest you do some checking up before advising me further." Oswald also made a veiled threat to go over the heads of Embassy officials, if they couldn't help him: "Instead, I shall endeavor to use my relative's [sic] in the United States, to see about getting something done in Washington." Marina knew nothing about any of this.[64]

Lifelong characteristics of Oswald were present throughout his Soviet sojourn. He reminded one of a lone wolf, antisocial, preferring solitude to the company of others. He didn't dislike his Gorizont coworkers; he just wasn't one of them. He ate lunch by himself every day, didn't partake in their drinking binges, and didn't visit their apartments.

And, as most of Oswald's past employers (the Marine Corps) and future employers in America would learn, he was a poor employee.

"Honestly, he was not a good worker," said Leonid Botvinik, a Gorizont coworker, in a 1993 interview. "He would bring all kinds of magazines to read at work, and he was always dissatisfied.... At first, we were curious why an American would suddenly appear in our midst, and some of us felt sorry for him. But after a while, most people came to regard him with a kind of antipathy."[65]

Another coworker, Leonid Tsagoikov, remembered Oswald decades later as "a lazybones who always put his feet up on his worktable," which Tsagoikov considered a brazen disrespect of workplace etiquette.[66]

His factory bosses didn't think much of Oswald either, sending a critical letter to city officials: Oswald's job performance, it said, was "unsatisfactory," and that he "reacts in an over-sensitive manner to remarks from the foreman and is careless in his work. Citizen L.H. Oswald takes no part in the social life of the shop and keeps very much to himself."[67]

May 16—Ottawa, Canada

Planting a ceremonial tree during a state visit to Canada, Kennedy re-injures his back. He has suffered from back pain most of his life, and a series of dangerous spinal operations, which nearly killed him, haven't really helped.

Kennedy's health problems were extensive and a closely guarded secret during his presidency. As a young man, he was so sick that his thoughts turned often to death. "Took a peak [sic] at my chart yesterday and could see that they were mentally measuring me for a coffin," he wrote a friend in January 1936.[68] As we'll see later on, Kennedy's fascination with his own mortality never went away.

Kennedy's back was probably first injured in 1937 during a football game at Harvard. For the rest of his life, he regularly wore a back brace. It was helpful in that it enabled him to move about more easily, but there was a downside: he could not bend forward easily.

June (undated)—The White House

The Secret Service takes possession of a new car for the president: A modified 1961 Lincoln Continental. Custom built by the Ford Motor Company and Cincinnati-based engineering firm Hess & Eisenhardt, its numerous features include:

- a hydraulic rear seat that could be raised 10½ inches, so the president could be better seen
- four retractable steps for Secret Service agents
- two steps on rear bumper for additional agents
- auxiliary ("jump") seats for extra passengers

The jump seats hugged the transmission hump, meaning that whoever sat in them would not be directly in front of the president.[69]

X-100 also had three roofs, which could be used depending on the weather and the president's wishes. One was made of standard cloth, another of lightweight metal, and a third of transparent plastic.

The overall objective in this more innocent era was to maximize the president's visibility, not his safety. X-100 wasn't armored, and yet it was so heavy—7,800 pounds without any passengers—that its 350-horsepower engine, "though adequate for normal use, did not facilitate quick acceleration."[70]

June—Minsk and Fort Worth

Oswald and his mother resume correspondence. Marguerite, frantic to hear from her son, is delighted, and over the next year will receive seventeen letters from him.

At first, Oswald made innocuous requests: books and copies of *Time* magazine for him, fashion magazines for Marina. But now that he wanted to return home, he asked for more. Some things were over the top, like asking Marguerite to get her own employer to write an affidavit of support on Marina's behalf, which could expedite her entry into the United States. He also asked her to plead with relief agencies like the Red Cross for money.

Notes McMillan: "He manipulated Marguerite, always with twin purposes of exploiting her, yet at the same time keeping her at a distance." What a son he was.[71]

Oswald's lie that his mother was dead and that he was an orphan was exposed when Marguerite's letters began arriving. In one, she enclosed a recent photo.

"That's my mother. She's gained some weight," Oswald said, perhaps forgetting that he had told Marina that his mother was no longer alive.

"You told me your mother was dead."

"Well, I don't want to talk about my mother," Oswald shot back.

Stupid me! Marina thought to herself, realizing she'd been conned.[72]

Other disappointments soon followed. Marina realized her husband was also cheap. She wanted to fix up their apartment, and he would always say "No, we have everything we need." He began to show a domineering side. If she was even ten minutes late coming home from work, he would grill her: "Where were you? How come you're late?" She began to feel "a little distaste for him," and sometimes "felt distant from him."[73]

Then there was the time they discussed a small metered device—a *schyotchik*—on the wall of their apartment. It had no apparent purpose, so they assumed—this was a police state, after all—that it must be a listening device. This led to speculation about whether any of their friends were informers. Marina asked about Pavel Golovachev. Oswald's response: "I'd trust him a lot sooner than I'd trust you."[74]

As 1961 wore on, Oswald's ambivalence towards Marina and his dissatisfaction with his menial job grew. And there were new complaints and perceived slights. Just five days after getting married, he got a rejection letter from Moscow's prestigious Lumumba University. He also signed up for a factory-organized weekend in Riga, the capital of Latvia, one of the Soviet republics, and Leningrad. He planned to take Marina. But he was given his money back and told the trip had been canceled. But Oswald soon learned that it hadn't been canceled; he was dropped from the trip because as a foreigner, he had been denied permission to make the trip. "It's so underhanded," he fumed. Oswald, the deceiver, was furious about being deceived.[75]

The marriage soon acquired a new twist when Marina learned that she was pregnant.

Late June—Minsk

Oswald comes clean, telling Marina of his desire to return to America. It took three days of begging for her to agree to go with him, if they could even leave. He had had enough. "One more winter in Russia and I'm going to die," he told her.[76]

July 8—Moscow

Oswald impulsively flies to Moscow and proceeds to the American Embassy. It is Saturday, he has no appointment, and no one knows he is coming. Richard Snyder, the same consular officer he dealt with in the fall of 1959, is upstairs in his apartment and comes down to meet him.

Their 1959 encounter had left a sour taste in Snyder's mouth, and he certainly remembered the arrogant young man. But Oswald, increasingly bitter that his Soviet experiment hadn't worked out, seemed subdued now. Snyder cabled the State Department:

> Twenty months of the realities of life in the Soviet Union have clearly had a maturing effect on Oswald. He stated frankly that he had learned a hard lesson the hard way and that he had been completely relieved of his illusions about the Soviet Union at the

> same time that he acquired a new understanding and appreciation of the United States and the meaning of freedom. Much of the arrogance and bravado which characterized him in his first visit to the Embassy appears to have left him.[77]

But Oswald's rare humility was accompanied by something not so rare: more lies. He told Snyder that at no time since his arrival in the Soviet Union had he ever asked for Soviet citizenship. Actually, he had on October 16, 1959—the very first day he set foot on Soviet soil (he never formally applied, however). He also told Snyder that he had never been quizzed by Soviet officials about his background, which certainly wasn't true. He also claimed that in a Radio Moscow interview, he had said nothing that would hurt the United States. Yet Oswald himself wrote later that in giving the interview, he had "sold himself" and betrayed American interests.[78]

July 10—Moscow

Marina Oswald, at her husband's request, joins him in the Soviet capital. The next day she meets with another consular officer, John McVickar, who advises and assists her with an immigrant visa application.[79]

July 14—Minsk

Back in Minsk, Oswald writes to his brother Robert, saying he and his new wife "are doing everything we can to get out." And, nearly two years after arriving in what he thought would be the land of his dreams, he trashes his adopted country:

> "The Russians can be crule [sic] and very crude at times. They gave a cross examination to my wife on the first day we came back from Moscow, they knew everything because they spy, and read the mails. But we shall continue to try and get out. We shall not retreat. As for your package we never received it, I suppose they swiped that too, the bastards.[80]

The flighty, unstable Oswald, who only so recently had no use for his brother, ends by saying he hopes to see him and to "write often."

Marina, meanwhile, got the cold shoulder at both the pharmacy where she worked and, more disturbingly, from her own family. She had flown off to Moscow and visited the American Embassy in secret without telling anyone; she considered this a lie of omission and confronted her husband.

"I can't live like that," she said. "I can't open my mouth without giving you away as a liar. You lied about your mother and your age. You lied when you said you couldn't return to America. Now you're making me lie." And: "When will there be an end to it?"[81]

It would never end. Unlike discoverable lies about his age and mother, Oswald told falsehoods that Marina had no way of unraveling. To give but one example, he told her that a scar on his left elbow was caused by a wound he suffered during combat in Indonesia. In fact, it was caused by his accidental discharge of his pistol. A chess player since age thirteen, he told Marina's uncle, who beat him regularly, that it was because he was only just beginning to play.[82] Oswald lied so often and about so many things that Marina came to the conclusion that "He lied not because he needed to but because he liked to—it was his character."[83] And this observation from McMillan: "Marina soon realized that her husband's secretiveness was of another kind entirely. He told lies without purpose or point, lies that were bound to be found out. He liked having secrets for their own sake. He simply enjoyed concealment. For him it was not a matter of life and death but a matter of choice."[84] Often, conspiracists blinded by Oswald's "I'm just a patsy" line on the evening of the assassination are unfamiliar with, or unable to reconcile, an inconvenient truth: that their "patsy" was an incontrovertible, lifelong liar.

July 19—Minsk

A KGB surveillance reveals the rickety state of the Oswald marriage.

Wife: All you know how to do is torture....

(LHO goes out, yells something from the kitchen)

Wife: Go find yourself a girl who knows how to cook...I work, I don't have time to prepare cutlets for you. You don't want soup, you don't want kasha, just tasty tidbits, please!

LHO: I can go eat at a restaurant.

Wife: Go to hell! When are you ever going to leave me alone?

LHO: But you don't know how to do anything.

Wife: Leave me alone!

And condensed snippets from August 3:

Wife: (yells) I'm tired of everything!

LHO: You haven't done anything.

Wife: Well, what have you done for me?

LHO: Silence!

Wife: I'm not going to live with you.

LHO: Thank God!

Wife: You're always finding fault; nothing's enough, everything's bad.

LHO: You're ridiculous, Lazy and crude.

Wife: Get out! I'm not your housekeeper.

And:

Wife: Alka [Marina's nickname for Oswald], do you hate me when you yell at me?

LHO: Yes.

Wife: Why are you afraid of people? What scared you?

LHO: (yells angrily) Shut up, shut up...You stand there and blab.

Wife: You're afraid of everybody!

LHO: Shut up!

Wife: Are you afraid that they'll steal everything from you, a pot of gold you have (laughing). At times like this you could kill me...

Here we see, from the KGB transcripts, further confirmation of what we've already established: that Lee Harvey Oswald was insecure, resentful, unstable, hateful—even towards his wife, as he admits—and possessed an explosive temper.[85]

August 8—Glenview, Illinois

The Marine Corps Reserve, hearing of Oswald's defection to the Soviet Union, recommends that he be "separated from the Marine Corps Reserve as undesirable."[86]

August 18—The State Department

Cable to US Embassy/Moscow: "We concur in the conclusion of the Embassy that Mr. Oswald has expatriated himself under the pertinent laws of the United States" and therefore the renewal of his passport to return to the US "is authorized."[87]

October 14—Minsk

With Marina visiting an aunt in Kharkov, Oswald goes alone to his favorite opera, Pyotr Tchaikovsky's *The Queen of Spades*. He's also seen a movie version numerous times and has bought the record album too.

McMillan says Oswald was so enthralled by one particular aria that—according to Marina—he played it constantly—as many as twenty times a night. It contained some rather ominous lyrics:

> I love you. I love you beyond measure.
> I cannot conceive of life without you.
> I would perform a heroic deed of unheard-of-prowess for your sake…[88]

October 17—The White House

Dr. Hans Kraus, a prominent New York orthopedic surgeon, examines Kennedy and is alarmed at his condition. Asked to touch his toes, JFK can't reach beyond his knees, he can't do a single sit-up, and his leg muscles are "as taut as piano wires." Kraus tells him to start exercising. "You will be a cripple if you don't," the surgeon warns. "Five days a week. And you need to start now."

Kraus began flying to Washington three days a week to oversee an exercise regimen, and after a month noticed "a definite increase of strength and flexibility in his patient." He wrote in his patient's file that Kennedy might be able to ditch his back brace "in the not too distant future."[89]

Fall (undated)—Minsk

With Oswald stripped of any illusions about life under Soviet communism, his interest in Cuba and its young new leader, Fidel Castro, grows. He takes Marina to a movie about him. He starts calling Castro "a hero" and "a man of talent."[90]

Fall (undated)—Minsk and Fort Worth

By now, Marguerite Oswald has been sending packages to Lee and Marina on a regular basis. Lee devours *Time* magazine, and Marina likes seeing pictures of President Kennedy and his glamorous wife Jacqueline. It is probably in the pages of *Time* that Lee first reads of Edwin A. Walker, a former general who resigned his commission under pressure for allegedly trying to influence the votes of soldiers under his command. We'll hear more about Walker shortly.

December 25—Minsk

On Christmas Day (not officially celebrated in the Soviet Union), Marina is summoned to the Soviet Passport Office and told that she and Oswald's exit visas have been approved—they are free to leave the Soviet Union. Oswald scribbles in his diary: "Its [sic] great (I think!)."[91]

January 2, 1962—Minsk

Oswald writes to his mother and asks her to contact the Red Cross and through it, the International Rescue Committee, to give him $800 so he can return to the United States. On the twenty-sixth, he writes the IRC himself twice and ups his gift request to $1,000.[92] The man who hates capitalism is looking for another handout.

January 11—Capitol Hill

For a president derided by some as soft on national security, Kennedy lays out some statistics during his State of the Union address:

> In the past twelve months our military posture has steadily improved. We increased the previous defense budget by 15 percent—not in the expectation of war but for the preservation of peace. We more than doubled our acquisition rate of Polaris submarines—we doubled the production capacity for Minuteman missiles—and increased by 50 percent the number of manned bombers standing ready on a fifteen-minute alert. This year the combined force levels planned under our new Defense budget—including nearly three hundred additional Polaris and Minuteman missiles—have been precisely calculated to insure the continuing strength of our nuclear deterrent.[93]

January—Minsk

Rumors sweep Minsk that an assassination attempt has been made—near Minsk itself—on the life of Nikita Khrushchev.

According to Pricilla Johnson McMillan, the Soviet leader, accompanied by Polish leader Władysław Gomułka, was staying at a nearby hunting preserve. She writes that the incident was shrouded in secrecy, but that the "least fanciful" scenario involved one of Khrushchev's bodyguards trying to shoot him. "The Oswalds heard about the incident in frightened colorful undertones" from Marina's aunt, who happened to work in Khrushchev's dacha. "The account may have been imprinted even more indelibly on Alik's (Oswald's) mind," because the aunt's account was whispered and because she was so obviously terrified."[94]

January 18—The White House

Kennedy gives final approval to "Operation Hades" (later changed to "Ranch Hand")—a massive chemical-weapons program to defoliate the forests of Vietnam, Cambodia, and Laos with an herbicide that came to be known as Agent Orange. Over the next nine years, some eighteen to twenty million gallons will be dropped.

Conspiracists who say Kennedy was "eliminated" by the "military-industrial complex" for being soft on communism rarely mention Operation Hades/Ranch Hand and the role his administration had in launching it.[95]

January 30—Minsk

In a letter from his mother, Oswald learns of his undesirable discharge from the Marines. He thinks this is a "dishonorable" discharge and writes to John Connally asking for help. Oswald mistakenly believes that Connally is secretary of the Navy, but Connally resigned in December to run for governor of Texas.

As usual, Oswald lied, telling Connally that he had received an honorable discharge from the Marines in 1959. He hadn't. He had received a hardship/dependency discharge. Oswald also blamed the press for news coverage of his defection to Russia, complaining that it had been "blown up into another 'turncoat sensation,'" which was the reason for his "dishonorable discharge." Again, we see Oswald refusing to take personal responsibility for his actions.[96]

February 15—Minsk

Marina gives birth to the Oswalds' first daughter. They name her June.

February 23—Austin, Texas

Connally writes to Oswald, saying he has passed his letter along to the new Navy secretary, Fred Korth. Oswald's discharge status will never be changed.[97]

March (undated)—Washington

The U.S. Immigration and Naturalization Service (INS) objects to allowing Oswald back into the United States, on the grounds that his loyalty to the United States is in question. The State Department disagrees, saying "We're better off with the subject in the U.S. than in Russia." State's position is based on a policy that said it was "potentially less embarrassing for the United States to have its unpredictables and malcontents" at home rather than sullying America's image abroad. Yet even State considers Oswald an "unstable character, whose actions are entirely unpredictable."[98]

March 15—Minsk

Oswald learns that the INS has approved Marina's application for a visa. Five days later, she quits her job at the pharmacy.[99]

March 23—Berkeley, California

Visiting the Lawrence Radiation Laboratory in California, Kennedy travels the way he prefers to—and, as we've seen the way his predecessors often preferred to—in his open 1961 Lincoln Continental, with no Secret Service agents on the back of the car. Sitting with the president in the back seat of X100 is California governor Edmund G. "Pat" Brown.

Late March—Minsk

Marina, hurt by her relatives' anger about the possibility of her leaving, tells Oswald she will not accompany him to the United States after all. Oswald, upset that his wife and child would abandon him, will later break down in tears and cry, "What have I to live for? What am I to do now?" His emotional distress eventually convinces Marina to change her mind.[100]

May 10—Moscow

The American Embassy informs Oswald that it is "now in a position to take final action on your wife's visa application." It suggests that both Oswalds come to Moscow to sign one final batch of documents.[101]

As usual, Oswald, with his knack for rubbing just about everyone the wrong way, irritated embassy officials who had the unpleasant misfortune of interacting with him. Consular officers disliked him intensely, growing particularly weary of Oswald's claim that as a veteran, he should be flown home at government expense on a government aircraft. "He expected the embassy, like an indulgent mother, to forgive, forget and to go to extraordinary lengths to bring him back." Oswald, who, of course, was simultaneously fighting other American officials to reverse his undesirable discharge, would ultimately be loaned just enough money to travel on a steamship.[102]

May 16—Minsk

Oswald quits his dead-end job at the Gorizont factory, a rare instance of him leaving a job voluntarily. "I ask to be released from work as of May 18, 1962. I expect to be leaving," he tells the plant director in a letter.[103] Gorizont's management, which has long considered Oswald a lazy, unproductive employee and social outcast, will shed no tears at his hasty departure.

By now, Oswald's Soviet relatives were fed up with him as well. Marina's uncle Ilya pleaded with her to reconsider, saying Oswald was unstable. "He flits from side to side," he said, "and is unhappy everywhere. Maybe he'll go back and not like it there, and then he'll want to come back here. But he'll never be allowed to come back. People are tired of nursing him over here."

Ilya then delivered the ultimate observation of Lee Harvey Oswald: "He is," he told Marina, "a man who has lost his way."[104]

It was an extraordinarily accurate read on Oswald, except for one thing: Oswald hadn't lost his way. He had never found it to begin with.

May 18—Fort Worth

FBI agent John Fain speaks to Robert Oswald's wife, Vada. She tells him that her brother-in-law and his new wife are about to come to the United States. Fain asks her to let him know when the Oswalds arrive. Vada agrees to do so.[105]

May 23—Minsk

Leaving their Minsk apartment for the final time, the Oswalds board a train for Moscow. Friends and family—despite lingering bitterness—see them off.[106]

June 1—Moscow

In the afternoon, the Oswalds board a train at Byelorussia station and depart for Rotterdam, Holland, where they will sail for New York. Ironically, the train's route takes them back through Minsk; Marina hopes that her family will show up, but no one does. She cries. Oswald tells her: "Don't worry, don't cry. Everything will be alright."[107]

June 2—Brest, Byelorussia

The Oswalds cross the border into Poland. After thirty-two months in the Soviet Union, Lee Harvey Oswald, with a wife and baby in tow, is on his way back to the United States and an uncertain future.

Some conspiracy theorists have pointed to this moment to contend that Oswald by now was somehow working on behalf of the Soviet government. In a 1978 book, author Edward Jay Epstein, whose 1966 work *Inquest* revealed flaws in the Warren Commission's investigation, claimed, based on nothing more than thin circumstantial evidence, that Oswald learned secrets about the CIA's U-2 plane while serving as a Marine radar controller in Japan and that he turned that information over to the Soviets either that year or when he arrived in Moscow two years later. This, Epstein claimed, enabled the Soviets to modify their surface-to-air missiles, like the one used to shoot down Francis Gary Powers on May 1, 1960.

But—to reinforce a prior point—there's no solid evidence that the Soviets regarded Oswald as anything more than a boob. In 1993, no less a figure than Vladimir Semichastny, who had been chairman of the KGB from November 1961 to May 1967, reviewed Oswald's file for the PBS program *Frontline*. "When he came to us [in 1959] and began to ask for asylum here so insistently, the first reaction was to refuse and not to give him permission to stay in the Soviet Union, let alone to give him political asylum," Semichastny said through an interpreter. "Counterintelligence and intelligence, they both looked him over to see what he was capable of. But unfortunately, neither could find any ability at all."[108]

The Soviet government didn't want Oswald to stay in the first place. The KGB considered him a man of low intelligence and emotional instability, who brought no useful skills or knowledge to the table. In fact, the hard-edged men in the Lubyanka—the headquarters of the fearsome intelligence agency—determined that Oswald was a desperate man who would do anything, including use violence, to make a point or get what he wanted. In hindsight, it would prove to be a rather prescient analysis.[109]

Oswald did nothing in Minsk to alter this judgment. He was seen as lazy, bad at his job, and drained resources that were used to keep tabs on him. Bon voyage and good riddance.

What about claims that Oswald was somehow working on behalf of the United States? KGB agents, who for the better part of three years trailed Oswald, eavesdropped on his apartment, intercepted his mail, interviewed his coworkers and neighbors, and dangled sensitive information before him to see if he would take the bait, concluded that he was not.

Semichastny again: "Would the FBI or CIA really use such a pathetic person to work against their archenemy?" He asked rhetorically on *Inside the KGB*, a story which NBC aired on May 25, 1993. "I had always respected the CIA and FBI, and we knew their work and what they were capable of. It was clear that Oswald was not an agent, couldn't be an agent, for the US secret services, either the CIA or FBI."[110]

American officials didn't even know where Oswald was until he resumed contact with the Embassy in February 1961. Meanwhile, as Bugliosi, notes, there is no evidence, based on an analysis of hundreds of pages of documents, letters, diplomatic cables generated by the State Department, the US Embassy in Moscow, the Justice Department, or Immigration and Naturalization Service that Oswald was treated differently or given any sort of special consideration than any other American who had mistakenly gone to the Soviet Union to live and then tried to return.

Oswald had arrived in the Soviet Union in October 1959, a nobody with grandiose visions—his diary, mentioned frequently in preceding pages, was "Historic"—and he was leaving a nobody. His final diary entry, dated March 27, is utterly banal:

> I receive a letter from a Mr. Phillips (a employer of my mother, pledging to support my wife in case of need).

June 4—Rotterdam, Netherlands

The Oswalds board the SS *Maasdam* and sail for New York. Oswald hasn't lost his desire for attention and, in fact, presumes he will get lots of it when he arrives in the United States. He spends much of the Atlantic crossing writing up a series of questions and answers for the hordes of journalists he is sure will engulf him.

June 12—Crossing the Atlantic

As excited as Marina is about traveling to the United States, her husband's dismissive, often nasty treatment gives her a taste of what is to come. Oswald is cheap, surly, and paranoid, and all three behaviors are on display as their ship plods westward across the ocean. When Marina points out that there is a beauty salon on the *Maasdam* and that "the girls come out looking like princesses," Oswald, feigning ignorance, replies "Oh, is there?" He also buys her nothing from any of the shops on board.

On their last night at sea there was a party for passengers. Marina finally made her unhappiness known. Based on her 1964 conversations with Marina, McMillan provides this sad vignette:

Marina: …you don't love me and I feel hurt.

Oswald: If you don't care for me the way I am, go away.

Marina: Where am I to go? There's only one way to go. And that's the ocean.

Oswald: Okay, Go.

Marina fled in tears. She walked around the deck—it was cold and rainy, but she had nowhere else to go—before returning to their cabin, deciding that "Junie needs me even if Alka doesn't."

When Oswald returned later, his loutish behavior continued: "You're here, are you?"

"Only because of the baby."[111]

Oswald's treatment of his wife would soon get worse.

June 13—Hoboken, New Jersey

The Oswalds arrive in the United States and clear immigration and customs. No journalists are on hand. Oswald has only sixty-three dollars and doesn't know where he and his family will stay the night or how they will get to Texas. With the help of the Traveler's Aid Society and New York City Welfare Department, the Oswalds are put up at a modest Times Square hotel.[112]

June 14—New York and Dallas

Thanks to $200 wired by Robert, Oswald is able to buy three plane tickets to Dallas. They depart from Idlewild Airport on Delta flight 821 and arrive at Love Field that evening. Oswald, seeing Robert and his family for the first time in years, is immediately disappointed. His first words to his brother:

"No reporters?"[113]

CHAPTER SEVEN

Oswald Returns to America: June 1962–November 1962

"All of them thought he was 'mentally unstable.'"

—KATYA FORD

By the summer of 1962, Oswald—just twenty-two years old—was a high-school dropout, Marine Corps washout, and betrayer to his country, a delusional young man who erred gravely in thinking that defecting to the Soviet Union would solve his problems, only to learn, to his dismay, that it hadn't. Now, with his tail between his legs, he returned to America. But if Oswald couldn't have handled life in the United States before, he had compounded his difficulties now, with a pregnant wife who spoke no English—and wasn't permitted to study it—and a four-month-old daughter. Oswald had no money, no job, no marketable skills—he couldn't even drive a car—and a mother he couldn't stand and wanted little to do with. But this bleak reality did nothing to diminish his belief that he was special, that he was highly intelligent, and that it would only be a matter of time before this became apparent to others.

Meanwhile, as President Eisenhower did before him, Kennedy resists pressure to send combat troops to Vietnam. He meets Douglas MacArthur for a third time, and the old general tells the young president again: avoid a land war in Asia.

The young president also dealt with the most dangerous moment of his short-lived administration—in fact, the most dangerous moment of the entire Cold War: the Cuban Missile Crisis. After the Bay of Pigs, which heightened Kennedy's skepticism about the advice he was getting from his generals, the October 1962 showdown with the Soviet Union revealed a very different John F. Kennedy. The first Cuban crisis made him more distrustful, more disdainful of their counsel. This shift would prove immensely helpful in the second crisis, when Kennedy would stave off their recommendation that Cuba be attacked for as long as possible. JFK's caution, and his eagerness to help Nikita Khrushchev untie, as the Soviet leader put it, the "knot of war," helped to prevent a nuclear holocaust, which historians estimate could have killed a hundred million American and a hundred million Soviet citizens. Kennedy's skepticism about the military would later contribute to claims from conspiracists that he was too soft on communism, both in Cuba and in Vietnam.

The president's skepticism about his military advisors was more than warranted. Earlier in the year, the Joint Chiefs planned a series of terror attacks on Americans—Operation Northwoods—which they hoped could be used as a pretext for an American invasion of Cuba. Kennedy read their plan and immediately rejected it. The chiefs often came up with crazy schemes: in 1958, for example, Eisenhower rejected their plan for a nuclear attack on China during the crisis over two disputed islands in the Taiwan Strait: Quemoy and Matsu.

And, as Eisenhower had before him, and Truman and Roosevelt before that, Kennedy continued to travel along routes that were often known to the public, often in convertibles and often with minimal—or no—Secret Service agents on the sides or rear of the presidential car.

June 14—Fort Worth

The Oswalds move in with Robert Oswald and his family at 7313 Davenport Street in Fort Worth. It's a two-bedroom, one-bath ranch house, 1,148 square feet. Robert and his wife, Vada, give their guests one of the bedrooms.

It was tight fit, though for Marina, spending her first night in an American home, it must have seemed palatial. Ownership of private property was forbidden in the Soviet Union, and now she was in a single-family house, with modern appliances and a front and backyard to boot. Seeing American grocery and department stores stuffed to the rafters with every imaginable good, big sleek cars everywhere, fast-food restaurants, neon lights, and people smiling—Russians by nature and culture generally do not smile much—she was surely overwhelmed, and thrilled. Vada, a hairdresser, gave her a makeover, and she loved it.

What she didn't like, however, was what returning to America seemed to have done to her husband. Not knowing English and discouraged by Oswald from learning it, Marina was now isolated and completely dependent upon him. Oswald enjoyed this control. At dinner one night, a minor spat turned into a fight, with Marina fleeing to the bedroom and Oswald following her, shutting the door, and then slapping her (as quietly as possible so Robert and Vada couldn't hear). According to Marina, Oswald then threatened to kill her if she told anyone.[1]

Oswald's assault on his wife would be followed by even more violent and frightening episodes in the months ahead. It's a validation of what others who knew Oswald as a child observed. Let's return to the April 1, 1964, testimony—to give but one example—to the Warren Commission by Hiram Conway, who lived two doors down from a young Oswald in 1948. "He was quick to anger," recalled Conway. And, as he mentioned, Oswald liked to throw rocks at other children. "He was vicious almost," Conway said. "He was a bad kid" and "very strange."

June 15—Fort Worth

Marguerite Oswald arrives at Robert's house and is thrilled to see Lee and meet Marina and June. Despite an absence of nearly three years, Oswald isn't thrilled to see her.[2]

Meanwhile, Oswald continues to be irritated with Marina. He tires of having to translate everything for her and criticizes her for not learning English. "You didn't let me," Marina responds. Oswald says that's no excuse and that she should have studied it anyway.[3]

June 18—Fort Worth

Oswald takes the notes of his time in the Soviet Union to a stenographer he found in the phone book, Pauline Virginia Bates, and asks her to type it up (another skill Oswald lacked). They worked together for three eight-hour days, with Oswald translating it for Bates. Oswald was sure that the broader world would, at some point, be interested in what he had to say. But his wallet wasn't as large as his ego, and after three days he ran out of money. Bates—who said Oswald had "the deadest eyes you ever saw"—was interested in his story and offered to continue working for free, but he declined: "I don't work that way," he said. He took the ten single-typed pages they had completed and left. His manifesto, which he had hoped to convert into a book, would never be completed.[4]*

But what about a job? For a man with little money and a family to feed, that Oswald would make a priority out of whipping his "Historic Diary" and other writings into shape reflects his defective personality: his disregard for others, and his selfish desires, which always seemed to come first.

June 22—Fort Worth

FBI agent Fain learns from the New York office of the FBI and the Holland-America shipping line that Oswald, Marina, and their child arrived in the United States on June 13.[5]

---

* There's no doubt Oswald had hoped to publish a book, because his manuscript includes, in his handwriting, a page titled "furword" (forward), an "About the Author" profile, and a "table of contents" that had forty-five sections or chapters.

June 26—Fort Worth

Fain calls Vada Oswald and asks to speak with Oswald directly. Oswald comes on the line and agrees to meet the FBI agent. Another agent, Tom Carter, sits in on the interview. The FBI men find Oswald to be "tense, kind of drawn up and rigid. A wiry little fellow, kind of raspy."

According to FBI records, Oswald refused to discuss why he had gone to the Soviet Union. He also lied, as usual, about trying to renounce his American citizenship, and Fain, based on prior information about Oswald, knew it.

Like their Soviet counterparts, the Americans were baffled as to why Oswald had gone to the Soviet Union in the first place. The Americans thought Oswald might be a Soviet agent; the Soviets thought Oswald might be an American one. In the end, there's no hard, verifiable evidence that he was, either. But that didn't stop Oswald, the fan of espionage and thriller TV shows and movies, the man who told Marina he would have loved to have a life in the espionage business, from enjoying the speculation.

Like many people who came into contact with Oswald, Fain considered him arrogant and insolent, but later decided that Oswald simply may have been scared of dealing with the FBI.[6]

Meanwhile, the Oswalds were being welcomed into the Dallas-Fort Worth area's Russian community. One of the first people who came to know the future assassin was Max Clark, a local attorney. From his Warren Commission testimony:

> I was extremely interested in, well, life in Russia, and to find out just exactly why he left in the first place and why he came back and he was in a very talkative mood and he talked at great length about his stay there and he seemed to want to make a point with everyone he met that he wanted them to know he was Lee Oswald the defector. He seemed to be quite proud of that distinction. In his opinion he thought that made him stand out and he would always say, "You know who I am?" when he would meet someone for the first time, so he was not trying to keep it a secret and in talking with him I asked him why he went to Russia. He said that

> he was in the Marines and he had read a lot of Karl Marx and he had studied considerably while he was in the Marines and he decided that he would get out of the Marines and he would go to Russia.[7]

"*You know who I am?*" Here, Oswald's thirst for attention, for recognition—not to mention the pride he felt in betraying his country—was on full display. Now for the most extraordinary excerpt from Clark's testimony:

> He told me that he had finally made up his mind that he would never get any place in the Soviet Union and that he was disappointed because it was not like Karl Marx or was not true Communism, in his words, and that he thought it was just as bad as a democracy and he said he wanted to leave there because he just felt there was no hope for him there and he would never be able to get ahead or make his mark so he decided the best bet, for both he and Marina was to leave so he made application to leave.
>
> **Mr. LIEBELER:** (Warren Commission assistant counsel Wesley J. Liebeler) Do you remember him specifically using the words "make his mark" or is that just an expression of yours?
>
> **Mr. CLARK:** That is my expression but my general impression was he wanted to become famous or infamous; that seemed to be his whole life ambition was to become somebody and he just seemed to have the idea that he was made for something else than what he was doing or what particular circumstances he was in.

He wanted to be famous or infamous; that seemed to be his whole life ambition. Towards the end of their interview, which took place two blocks from where President Kennedy's motorcade had passed four months earlier, Liebeler asked Clark for his opinion on whether Oswald might have been some sort of agent for the Soviet Union.

> **Mr. CLARK:** I didn't think he had the intelligence to be an agent.
>
> **Mr. LIEBELER:** You did consider the question prior to the assassination?

Mr. CLARK: I considered it briefly when he first contacted us when he got back here and after talking with him, I felt I didn't think that they were that stupid to use someone that stupid as an agent.[8]

Did the CIA also debrief Oswald after his return from the Soviet Union? The agency typically left the task of interviewing "returning defectors" to the FBI, and in Oswald's case, agents Fain and Carter. As Posner notes, between 1958 and 1963, the CIA interviewed just four out of twenty-two such people and denied for years that it had interviewed Oswald. But subsequent documents discovered at the National Archives indicate that the CIA probably did interview Oswald. Conspiracists are fond of arguing that this cover-up is proof that Oswald was somehow working with Langley. The far more plausible explanation is rooted in the banality of bureaucracy, namely that the CIA, like the FBI, was embarrassed that it had had even innocuous dealings with President Kennedy's killer and sought to protect its reputation.[9]

July (undated)—Fort Worth

The Oswalds move to a new apartment at 1501 West Seventh Street. The two-room apartment was rented by his mother, who wants to live with her son again.

Despite Oswald's disdain for his mother, he had no job, no money, and felt he had imposed on Robert enough. So he, Marina, and June moved in with her. As had been the case during Oswald's unstable childhood, mother and son argued frequently. Marguerite, perhaps upset that she was no longer the only woman in Lee's life, also began to complain about Marina.

Marina's English was rudimentary enough at this point that she was able to decipher one complaint that Marguerite leveled at her one day: "You took my son away from me!"[10]

July 17—Fort Worth

Oswald finds work as a sheet metal worker at the Louv-R-Pak division of Leslie Welding Company. As usual, he considers the job, which pays $1.25 an hour, beneath him, but he needs the money. Also as usual, he lies on his application, claiming he was a sheet metal worker in the Marines, and that he was honorably discharged. No one ever seems to check his background or ask for references.

Nor did Oswald's bosses recall (if they even saw) a story on the front page of the June 8 *Fort Worth Star-Telegram*, headlined "Ex-Resident 'Fed Up' in Russia, May Be Back." In the lead paragraph it said Oswald had renounced his American citizenship. The second noted that he had turned in his American passport in 1959 and vowed to "never return to the United States for any reason," and in the third he was quoted again as saying that leaving the United States in 1959 "was just like getting out of prison." The defector who changed his mind was lucky that neither his new bosses nor his future ones would ever remember any of this.

Louv-R-Pak proved to be an outlier for Oswald: he was actually good at his job. His manager later recalled that Oswald was "one of the best employees he ever had." But the absence of social skills and fitting in remained a liability: "He didn't talk to nobody about nothing, so nobody ever messed with him."[11]

August 10—Fort Worth

The Oswalds move yet again, into a furnished one-bedroom at 2703 Mercedes Street in Fort Worth. He has once again gotten out from under the thumb of the mother he detests. He has now been back in America two months and lived in three places.[12]

Robert Oswald, arriving to help with the move, heard his mother screaming before he even got to the door. Notes Bugliosi: "Marguerite was hysterical, Lee stony, and Marina somewhat bewildered." It was dysfunction personified. When the Oswalds drove off, leaving Marguerite behind, she ran after them. Marina felt sorry for her mother-in-law, a view dismissed by Oswald. "She'll be all right," he said. "It's not the first time."[13]

Oswald's new apartment has been described as a dump, shabby and threadbare, but to Marina, it was spacious, had a small patch of yard, and represented the first time since leaving Minsk that she, Lee, and June would have a place of their own. It also happened to be across the street from a department store, Montgomery Ward, where Marina delighted in the toy and dress departments. Oswald, Marina recalls, usually headed "with the most obvious enjoyment" straight to the gun display.[14]

August 16—Fort Worth

FBI agent Fain and fellow agent Arnold Brown visit Oswald's home. Rather than talk in front of Marina, they speak in their car, with Oswald and Brown in the back seat. Asked again why he went to the Soviet Union, Oswald, who up to that point seemed more comfortable than he was during his June 26 interview, clams up, telling the agents it was a personal matter and none of their business. "I went and I came back. It was just something I did."[15] Oswald also agrees to contact the FBI if the Soviets try to contact him.

Although Fain was dissatisfied with Oswald's evasiveness on why he went to the Soviet Union, he decided that Oswald wasn't a serious security risk. He closed the file on him.

Oswald, not knowing that his FBI file had been closed, told Marina his "persecution" was just beginning and that it would never end. "Because I've been over there they'll never let me live in peace. They think anyone who has been there is a Russian spy." Actually, Fain did agree with something that Oswald said: "I was not that important." Here, for a change, Oswald was being truthful. The Soviets didn't think he was important, a judgment now shared by the Americans.[16]

August (undated)—Fort Worth

After working for a year and a half to get out of the Soviet Union, Oswald writes the Soviet embassy in Washington, requesting "any periodicals or literature which you may put out for the benefit of your citizens living, for a time, in the U.S.A."[17]

"*Living for a time in the U.S.A.*" What an extraordinary letter. Here's Oswald in all his wishy-washy instability, back in America for just two months after arriving with his Russian-born wife and child—and he's already hinting that perhaps his family, or perhaps Marina, might one day return to the Soviet Union.

This upset Marina when she learned of it. She was slowly acclimating to America and had no desire to go back. "Do anything, Alka, but don't ever make me go back," she pleaded. Notes McMillan: "The conflicts that had sent him to Russia in the first place had been resolved neither by his defection nor by his decision to come home. Emotionally, he was in the same place he had always been."

Just with a lot more baggage.[18]

August 16—The White House

Kennedy meets with MacArthur a third time. It is unplanned. The general is in Washington for a congressional event, and learning of his visit, the president invites him for a chat.

Much had changed since their two previous talks. A mini-crisis in Laos had been resolved, with the US and Soviet Union agreeing to the seating of a coalition government there. But the situation in South Vietnam had worsened, with pressure mounting on the Diem government from a well-armed insurgency; this led to new pressure on Kennedy to send more US troops.

In this particular regard, Kennedy appreciated his friendship with the wise old general. MacArthur's repeated warnings about getting drawn into a land war in Asia would prove useful. Whenever the current crop of generals urged him to step up the fight in Vietnam, JFK would play the MacArthur card. "Well now," the president would say, "you go back and convince General MacArthur, then I'll be convinced."[19]

Mid-August—Fort Worth

By now, Marina Oswald is a hit with Dallas-Fort Worth's small but close-knit Russian community. She is a graceful, charming beauty, and quickly becomes the recipient of assistance from benefactors who take pity on the shabby conditions that she is forced to live in.

But her husband soon wore out his welcome with most, thanks to his glaring lack of social skills, which included a marked lack of appreciation for the help that had been extended to his family. Instead of showing gratitude and humility, Oswald was resentful. It also became quickly apparent to others that the Oswald marriage was a physically abusive one.

Oswald's conversational skills, never robust, were generally limited to the only topic that ever seemed to interest him: politics. A local college student, twenty-one-year-old Paul Gregory, had been taking Russian lessons from Marina. It turns out that Gregory had graduated from the same high school that Oswald had briefly attended, and Lee, as usual, felt compelled to lie, telling Gregory that he too had graduated.*

In 2013, Gregory, writing in the *New York Times*, said that he had "become as close—or, as Robert Oswald would later say, almost the only—friend of Lee and Marina Oswald's from virtually the moment they arrived in Fort Worth, in June 1962, until the end of that November." He continued: "My friendship with him was perhaps the longest he'd ever had." This is surely remarkable, given Oswald's cold and narcissistic personality, which generally turned off just about everyone else.[20]

---

* Paul Gregory was the son of a local petroleum engineer, Peter Paul Gregory. After Oswald arrived in Fort Worth in June, he called the Texas Employment Office asking about job opportunities and wanted to know if anybody spoke Russian. He was given the name of the senior Gregory, who had fled Russia in 1919. It turned out that Paul, the son, was interested in learning Russian.

One night, the two young men were discussing world events, and Oswald, displaying his growing interest in Cuba, expressed enthusiasm for Fidel Castro. He also said that Nikita Khrushchev was "simply brilliant." The conversation then turned to President Kennedy. Oswald said he liked Kennedy, calling him "a good leader." Gregory later told the Warren Commission that Oswald was "hot tempered, not very smart, and slightly mixed up," a man who had "an inability to grasp things" and was "always ready to flare up."[21]

August 25—Fort Worth

Gregory and his father Paul throw a dinner party for the Oswalds, as a way of introducing them to additional members of the local émigré community. Among them is a widower named George Bouhe. He is eager to meet the Oswalds but wonders about Lee. Why did he go to Russia? Is it possible that he is a Soviet spy?

Bouhe asked Max Clark whether it was prudent to meet Oswald. Clark and his wife, Gali, had their own reasons to wonder about Oswald. When Oswald had called the employment office in June looking for both work and local Russian speakers, he was given, in addition to Paul David Gregory's name, that of Gali, a descendant of Russian nobility. Unlike Oswald's bosses at Louv-R-Pak, Gali had remembered the June 8 newspaper article about Oswald and, based solely on what she had read, considered him a traitor to the United States. When Oswald had called Gali, she considered his demeanor to be abrasive.

Yet Max Clark told Bouhe that there was probably no harm to be done in meeting Oswald. Plus, they were eager to meet Marina.

Priscilla Johnson McMillan, writing extensively of that evening, says that as guests were saying their goodbyes, it was commonly understood that Marina was a "sensation," but that Oswald was "mild mannered but cold." In Minsk, after all, Oswald had been, albeit briefly, an object of curiosity—a foreigner, and an American at that—whom everyone wanted to meet. But deep in the heart of Texas, the opposite was true. It was Marina who was the star attraction, while

Oswald played second fiddle. After all, "the émigrés were better educated, more widely traveled and more experienced than he was…he did not have much to tell them—that they wanted to hear, anyway. They sized him up as a half-educated American boy" and considered his views naïve. They would help him "as much and as long, as he would allow—and as they could stand."[22]

As much as they could stand. They couldn't stand Oswald much now, and even that sliver of toleration would soon dwindle to nothing. Oswald wore out his welcome with the émigré community within weeks, and were it not for their concern for Marina and June, it would have been a lot faster than that.

Notes Bugliosi: "Oswald's Russian speaking acquaintances had any number of reasons to dislike him," which one of those acquaintances, Alexander Kleinlerer, rattled off: "His political philosophy, his criticism of the United States, his apparent lack of interest in anyone but himself and his treatment of Marina." All of them, said yet another one, Katya Ford, were sure that Oswald was "mentally unstable." Yet another, Jeanne de Mohrenschildt, said Oswald was always "very, very disagreeable."[23]

Oswald's mean-spiritedness and lack of social skills were such that he never bothered to express gratitude to anyone for the help—groceries, items for June, clothes—that was always being extended to his wife and child. In fact, he seemed threatened by, and resentful, of it. Once he told Marina that the Russian community was spoiling her.

"Since you can't spoil me," she responded, "why shouldn't they?"

Oswald instantly flew into a rage. He slapped her hard across her face. "Don't ever say that again," he hissed. "I'll be the one to spoil you—when I can." But he never could and never did.[24]

Meanwhile, the émigrés also "sensed Oswald's contempt for them, his feelings that they were people of petty, material interests, whereas *he* cared for higher things." They also believed that Oswald "hated anyone who was in a position of authority, simply because he wanted to be there himself…he wanted to be a 'big wheel,' and as one émigré, Anna

Meller, said, he hated everything. He was "all anti- the Soviet Union, anti- the United States, anti-society in general and anti-us."[25]

August 30—Fort Worth

A Fain report on Oswald states that he "agreed to contact the FBI if at any time any individual made any contact of any nature under suspicious circumstances with him."

September—Fort Worth

Marguerite Oswald begins showing up at Oswald's apartment bearing gifts. She does so when Oswald is at work, and when he finds out that his mother has visited he orders Marina not to let her in. When Marina protests, saying Oswald had no right to treat his mother that way, Lee explodes, slapping her four or five times.[26]

The slapping turned into outright beatings as Oswald's violence escalated. Visiting one day against her son's wishes, Marguerite noticed that Marina had a black eye. She confronted her son. "Lee, who do you mean by striking Marina?" Oswald told his mother to butt out. The beatings would increase in frequency—once or twice a week. The sad cycle would go like this: Oswald would beat Marina, who would typically say "Alka, I am not your maid. I am good enough not to have you hit me." Oswald would soon ask for forgiveness and buy her a trinket, or something for June. A few days later, it would happen again. When she spoke with McMillan in 1964 about the beatings, Marina recalled, as she was being thrashed by her husband, the cold, remote look in his eyes.[27] Bugliosi notes, "Underlying it all was Lee's need to control Marina, with alternating abuse and tantalizing offers of affection." That seems partially correct. Perhaps what was underlying it all was what Katya Ford and others deduced: that Oswald was mentally unstable. That, combined with his insecurity and his lifelong penchant for violence.

September 6—Washington

Like Eisenhower's behind-the-scenes meddling in places like Iran and Guatemala, and his initial planning for "Operation Zapata"—the Bay of Pigs operation—the use of covert, unorthodox, non–US military means is the Kennedy administration's preferred way of bringing about regime change in another country. Its approval of "Operation Hades" (later changed to "Ranch Hand")—the massive chemical weapons program to defoliate forests of Vietnam, Cambodia, and Laos—is one example of this.

Eight months later, a similar idea was proposed for Cuba. According to documents released in 2021, a group of White House, Pentagon, and CIA officials—the so-called "Operation Mongoose" group—met to discuss "sabotage operations" in Cuba. One idea involved "agricultural sabotage," which involved the introduction of "biological agents which would appear to be of natural origin" to destroy crops.

Given that Attorney General Robert Kennedy and National Security Advisor McGeorge Bundy attended the meeting, it's impossible to think that President Kennedy himself was unaware of such thinking. In a memo written after the meeting, it was noted that Bundy "had no worries about any such sabotage which could clearly be made to appear as the result of local Cuban disaffection or of a natural disaster, but that we must avoid external activities such as release of chemicals, etc. unless they could be completely covered up."[28]

Chemical and biological warfare? In both Vietnam and Cuba? And yet the conspiracists would have us believe that Kennedy was murdered by government elements who believed he was too meek of a commander in chief.

October 7—Fort Worth

Some of the émigré community, visiting Marina and doing their best to tolerate Oswald, learn from him that he has lost his job at Leslie

Welding. To this group, whose contempt he could not hide from, Oswald says he is behind on the rent, is moving to Dallas, and needs a job fast.

There's no evidence Oswald explicitly asked for any help. He merely announced that he was in a pickle and then sat back, presuming that Marina's friends would come to the rescue.

They would, but little did they know that Oswald was telling another one of his lies. He hadn't been let go. He was sick of his job and was planning to just walk away. After his guests said that they would help—largely out of concern for Marina—Oswald, reassured, went to work on Monday, October 8, and simply left at the end of the day without telling anyone. His bosses had no idea what had happened until they got a letter a few days later asking that his last two paychecks be sent to a post office box in Dallas.[29] He had been on the job just eighty-three days, typical for his instability and flightiness.

Why lie? Because Oswald, while condescending towards the émigré community and their focus (as he saw it) on comfort and the good life, needed their help and thought that cooking up a sympathetic story would make him more likely to get it. And he did. One woman at the party, Elena Hall, invited Marina and June to live with her in Fort Worth while Lee looked for a job, this time in Dallas, where employment opportunities were more abundant. Hall's ex-husband, John, offered to make a job call on Oswald's behalf.

It was Oswald at his cynical, hypocritical best. Contemptuous of others who were doing better than him—obviously a sign that they were "materialistic"—while milking each one for something. Money, groceries, and clothes. Shelter for Marina from one, a call about a job from another. Never the giver, always the taker.

October 8–14—Dallas

It's not known where Oswald spent his first week in Dallas. Conspiracy theorists see something fishy here. Where was he? No one knows. Obviously suspicious, right? Bugliosi snickers: "Before the assassination, no one had any reason to have Oswald under surveillance, watching his every move. The conspiracy theorists, however, do not accept this obvious fact and expect every day and minute of his time to be accounted for." Whenever it isn't, he was clearly off meeting with people who wanted to kill President Kennedy. That certainly must be the explanation, right?[30]

Sarcasm aside, the truth as to his real whereabouts that week are almost certainly far more banal. Oswald was starting a new job and had very little money—not even enough to send for his wife and child. As he did so often, including the final weeks of his life, he stayed at the YMCA and the cheapest rooming houses he could find. As we'll soon see, Oswald also spent a week in one such house in October 1963, only to get kicked out for being a poor tenant. Perhaps a similar situation occurred in October 1962.

October 9—Dallas

Oswald, now on his own in Dallas, rents a post office box, listing his address as 3519 Fairmont Street in that city. He has never lived at this address, which is the home of Alexandra and Gary Taylor, the daughter and son-in-law of a George de Mohrenschildt.

Born in Russia six years before the Bolshevik revolution of 1917, George de Mohrenschildt was a critical figure in this stage of Oswald's life. Introduced to the Oswalds through their mutual friend George Bouhe, de Mohrenschildt was a globe-trotting, swashbuckling, thrice-married petroleum geologist and professor who traveled easily among Dallas's conservative elite, including Big D luminaries like oil barons Clint Murchison, H. L. Hunt, John W. Mecom Sr., and Sid Richardson.

Among de Mohrenschildt's other acquaintances were the attorney Max Clark and J. Walton Moore, who de Mohrenschildt correctly surmised was some sort of US government operative.* Like George

* According to a CIA classified document obtained by the House Select Committee on Assassinations, Moore was an agent of the CIA's Domestic Contacts Division in Dallas.

Bouhe, de Mohrenschildt wanted to make sure that it was okay to meet the Oswalds and asked around. Testifying in 1964 to the Warren Commission, de Mohrenschildt said he was told—but didn't remember by who—that Oswald "seems to be OK," and that "he is a harmless lunatic."

Oswald had moved to Dallas, in fact, at de Mohrenschildt's urging, and since he had decided that Oswald was "OK," tried to help him find work. He arranged for an interview for Oswald with a friend (sometime between October 9 and 11) at an electric log company. The executive, Samuel Ballen, spent two hours with Oswald, later telling the Warren Commission that he ultimately decided that after initially "feeling very sorry" for Oswald, soon came around to the view that "he was too much of a hard-headed individual and that I would probably regret hiring him." Ballen also suspected that Oswald "probably would not fit in" with his coworkers. Given all that we know about Oswald's work record and demeanor, it's fair to say that Ballen's instincts were razor sharp.[31]

Oswald also turned again to the Texas Employment Commission, whose offices he had visited in Fort Worth over the summer. After taking a series of tests, he was judged to have "outstanding verbal-clerical potential," a far cry from the kind of jobs he believed were his due.[32]

He was sent to a local graphic arts firm, Jaggars-Chiles-Stovall, which had a need for a trainee. The head of its photo department, John Graef, hired him, and Oswald started the next day (October 12). His starting wage was $1.35 an hour (about $12.25 in 2021 terms).[33] Out of work less than a week, Oswald had again taken advantage of the generosity extended to him by others.

Having secured new employment—again thanks to help from members of the émigré community—Oswald proceeded to show his thanks by treating them with contempt. "He felt free to be as directly insulting to them as he liked," notes Bugliosi, "despite the fact that they were continuing to help Marina." The very day he started at Jaggars, he called Bouhe, who had done so much for him and Marina, and without any small talk, without expressing any appreciation for the assistance he had been given he simply offered a curt "I am doing fine. Bye." He then pulled the same stunt over the next few days. Bouhe, feeling used and insulted, pulled the plug on Oswald, and other émigrés resolved to do the same.[34]

For reasons that will soon become apparent, the Jaggars job, with its graphics, printing, and photo departments, would play a critical role in Oswald's future actions.

October 14—Niagara Falls, New York

Speaking at the local airport, Kennedy is introduced to the family of Secret Service agent Winston Lawson's family.

Kennedy smiled, shook hands and said, "Well, he must be doing a good job. Nobody's shot me yet."[35]

October 15—Dallas

On his new job just three days, Oswald doesn't have the money for even the kind of crummy apartment that he had Marina were living in in Fort Worth.[36] He checks into the YMCA, paying $2.25 a night, lying that his place of residence is "Toro, California," an obvious reference to the Marine Corps base (El Toro) he had been stationed at.

He had no reason to lie—"He was muddying a background that no one was following," Bugliosi points out.

October 16—The White House

Kennedy is informed that the Soviet Union is placing nuclear missiles in Cuba that are capable of destroying most of the United States. It is the beginning of the Cuban Missile Crisis—a thirteen-day standoff—that nearly leads to nuclear war between the US and Soviet Union.

October 17—The White House

Kennedy orders John McCone, his Central Intelligence Agency director, to brief former president Eisenhower on the Cuban situation. Eisenhower tells McCone that he is supportive of the president's initial steps on the crisis.

October 18—The White House

Kennedy holds a previously scheduled meeting in the Oval Office with Soviet foreign minister Andrei Gromyko and Soviet ambassador Anatoly Dobrynin. The two Soviet diplomats lie to the president, telling him that there are no nuclear facilities in Cuba. Kennedy, who has photographic evidence of such facilities, plays coy and does not let on about what he knows.

As the crisis unfolded, national security advisor Bundy encouraged the president to consider all possible courses of action and sometimes played devil's advocate or changed his mind. For example, Bundy made the case for doing nothing about the Soviet missiles in Cuba. On October 18 he argued that "we would be better off to merely take note of the existence of these missiles, and to wait until the crunch comes in Berlin." The next day he changed his mind and favored decisive action—a surprise air strike, as the blockade would not be enough to remove the missiles from Cuba.

October 19 to November 3—Dallas and Fort Worth

Oswald checks out of the Y, and for a few days stays with Marina and June at Elena Hall's home in Fort Worth. But no one knows where he has been the rest of time. By now he is working at Jaggars; the comments surrounding the period of October 8 to 14 apply once more.

The new job was beneficial to Oswald. He learned how to operate complex camera equipment, work in a darkroom, and make clean photographic prints.[37]

As had been the case throughout his adult life—from the Marines to Gorizont to Louv-R-Pak—Oswald soon proved himself to be a social misfit at his latest job. One Jaggars worker tasked with training him, Dennis Ofstein, later told the Warren Commission that Oswald "didn't get along with people and that several people had words with him at times about the way he barged around the plant, and one of the fellows back in the photosetter department almost got in a fight with him one day, and I believe it was Mr. Graef that stepped in and broke it up before it got started."

Oswald, always the outcast, ate his lunch alone, never inviting anyone to eat with him, and never accepting the few invitations he got to eat with anyone else.[38]

October 22—The White House

In a dramatic Oval Office address, Kennedy goes public with his knowledge of Soviet nuclear missiles in Cuba. The president demands their removal, announces a naval "quarantine" of Cuba and warns bluntly that any Soviet missiles fired anywhere in the Western hemisphere will be regarded as an attack on the US, "requiring a full retaliatory response."

November 3—Dallas

Oswald rents an apartment for his family, at 604 Elsbeth Street in Oak Cliff. The Taylors drive them and their belongings over the next day.

Marina was shocked at the apartment, which Oswald leased for sixty-eight dollars a month. Based on her first glimpse of the run-down building—weeds and garbage were everywhere—she braced herself to enter the unit.

It was "filthy dirty—a pigsty," she recalled, an opinion shared by Alexandra Taylor. "It was terrible," she said. "Very dirty, very badly kept, really quite a slum." The floor was slanted and bumpy.

At first Marina didn't even want to move in but resigned herself to the ordeal and stayed up until five o'clock the next morning trying to scrub away the grime. Lee, she said, did little to help.

New surroundings did nothing to change the Oswald's deteriorating marriage. Their fighting resumed and was so loud at times that other tenants complained to the landlords, Mr. and Mrs. Mahlon Tobias, who lived in the building themselves. It was noted that a window in a back door was broken, apparently the result of one of Lee's frequent outbursts. In the past, their squabbles and Lee's vicious attacks might have been followed by sex, but now even that had vanished. "He sleeps with me just once a month, and I never get any satisfaction out of it," Marina told the only émigré friends the Oswalds had left—the de Mohrenschildts.[39] And risking further abuse, she even shared this embarrassing, intimate detail right in front of Lee.

Arguably the force behind the tensions between the Oswalds stemmed from Lee's insistence on controlling Marina, and Marina's desire to better assimilate into her new surroundings. She wanted to learn English, a more than reasonable pursuit, but Lee refused to allow it. In 2013, Paul Gregory wrote:

> He argued that it would jeopardize his fluency in Russian, but more important, it was a way he leveraged control over her. During one visit to a Rexall drugstore that August, Lee became visibly angry when a pharmacist offered to hire Marina, who had worked at a hospital pharmacy in Minsk, once her language skills improved. The job, after all, could have made her the family breadwinner.[40]

Oswald was both domineering and insecure at the same time. In a booming Texas economy in 1962, he could barely provide for her and June, but flew into a rage at the idea of Marina—a newly arrived immigrant—potentially earning more than he did.

His insecurity was such that he once exploded because members of the émigré community tried to help her out financially. He called his wife a "whore" for accepting money and possessions that he was

Library of Congress

Surveys show that a significant number of Americans believe conspiracy theories about many things, including the moon landings, aliens in Roswell, the 9/11 attacks, Princess Diana's death, and more. Here: practicing for the moon landing at a Grumman Aviation facility on Long Island, 1969.

Library of Congress

It took the 882-foot-long *Titanic* two-and-a-half hours to sink on a clear night. But survivors, shown before their rescue on April 15, 1912, disagreed over whether it broke in two. Yet many JFK conspiracy buffs look at film of a six-second event, or blurry trees, and are convinced they know exactly what happened.

FDR Library

Despite nearly being shot three weeks earlier in Miami—an attack that killed the mayor of Chicago—President-elect Roosevelt and President Hoover rode in an open car, on a route that was known to all, to FDR's inaugural address. March 4, 1933.

Truman Presidential Library

A slow-moving convertible with agents relegated to a follow up car? That's how presidents before Dallas often preferred it. Here: President Truman beneath tall buildings and open windows in Portland, Oregon, June 1945.

National Archives

August 15, 1946: With one Secret Service agent beside him, Truman departs the White House for his morning walk. It was a well-known ritual, and the president sometimes stopped to speak with well-wishers as cars drove by.

Eisenhower Presidential Library

President Eisenhower in Taipei, Taiwan, June 18, 1960.

Library of Congress

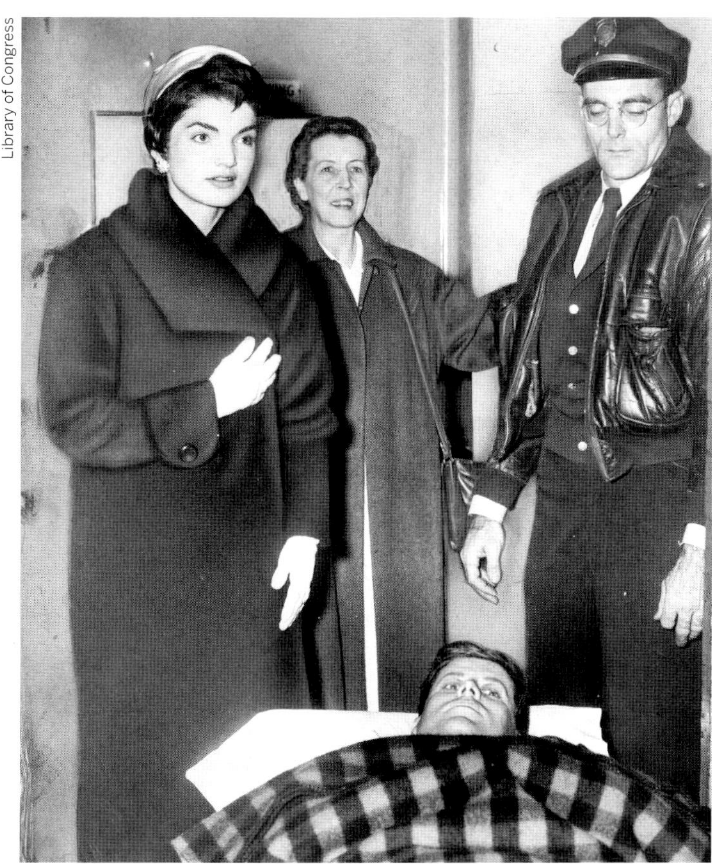

Kennedy with his wife Jacqueline on December 21, 1954, following dangerous spinal surgery. His brushes with death left him with a cavalier attitude towards danger and security. He once said he wouldn't live beyond age forty-five. He was off by just eighteen months.

Kennedy Library

Like his predecessors, Kennedy preferred motorcades that allowed him maximum visibility. Here, with guards on the follow-up car, he stands. Pueblo, Colorado, August 17, 1962.

Library of Congress

March 27, 1963: Kennedy and Morocco's King Hassan II stand as they proceed through downtown Washington.

Kennedy Library

Nashville, May 18, 1963.

"Anyone wanting to commit ground troops to Asia should have his head examined," General Douglas MacArthur told President Kennedy. JFK used the legendary general's advice against his own generals, who wanted to send hundreds of thousands of troops to Vietnam.

Karen Apricot, Creative Commons, via Wikipedia Commons

Oswald's childhood was highly unstable. Born in October 1939, he would live in twenty-one different homes (including an orphanage) before dropping out of high school to join the Marines seventeen years later. Here: his first address, 2109 Alvar Street in New Orleans, shown in 2007.

Retreating into a solitary world of comic books and TV shows, Oswald was enthralled with a TV show called "I Led Three Lives" about an FBI operative striving to foil communist plots. Episode titles included "Confused Comrade," "Martyr," "Unexpected Trip," "Child Commie," and "The Spy" (which aired November 22, 1953). "Lee watched that show every week without fail," his brother Robert said. "When I left home to join the Marines, he was still watching the re-runs."

FD-302 (Rev. 1-25-60) FEDERAL BUREAU OF INVESTIGATION

Date 12/2/63

Dr. RENATUS HARTOGS advised that he is the Chief Psychiatrist for the Youth House of New York City, and, in this capacity, conducts psychiatric interviews of many children and youths referred to him by the Youth House.

Dr. HARTOGS related that upon reading a story in a New York newspaper concerning a psychiatric interview of LEE HARVEY OSWALD, he realized that from the terminology used in the psychiatric report that he himself had conducted the interview of OSWALD. He stated that the specific phrases used in the psychiatric report of "potentially dangerous" and "incipient schizophrenia" are phrases that are peculiar to his type analysis, and he knows of no other psychiatrist who uses them.

Dr. HARTOGS stated that when he reflected on the interview, he recalled the fact that he was greatly impressed with OSWALD in that the boy, who was 13½ years old at the time of the examination, had extremely cold, steely eyes. Dr. HARTOGS stated that OSWALD was referred to him by the Youth House as the result of OSWALD's chronic truancy from public school, and, despite the fact that OSWALD had no record of violence, he recommended institutionalizing him as a result of his psychiatric examination, which indicated OSWALD's potential dangerousness. Dr. HARTOGS further added that he was so impressed with the OSWALD case that he made it the subject of a seminar that he gave at the Youth House to parole officers and students of psychiatry.

Dr. HARTOGS again emphasized that despite the lack of violence in OSWALD's past, he felt that he was potentially disturbed and dangerous, and that he should have institutional care.

When questioned as to whether he had retained a copy of the psychiatric report that he submitted following his interview of OSWALD, Dr. HARTOGS stated that some years after his interview of OSWALD, he moved his office and destroyed all his old files, which included the OSWALD file. He advised that he was unable to recall any further information at this time concerning OSWALD.

On 12/2/63 at 7 East 86th Street, New York City File # 89-75

by SAS FRANK R. GERRITY and NORMAN A. MURRAY, JR./rm Date dictated 12/2/63

This document contains neither recommendations nor conclusions of the FBI. It is the property of the FBI and is loaned to your agency; it and its contents are not to be distributed outside your agency.

At age two, Oswald was observed as an "ill-behaved child who threw his toys." At age seven, he threw a knife at his step-brother. In 1953, Oswald was examined by a New York psychiatrist, who remembered—a decade later—his thirteen-year-old subject's cold, steely eyes, and the possibility that he was disturbed and potentially dangerous.

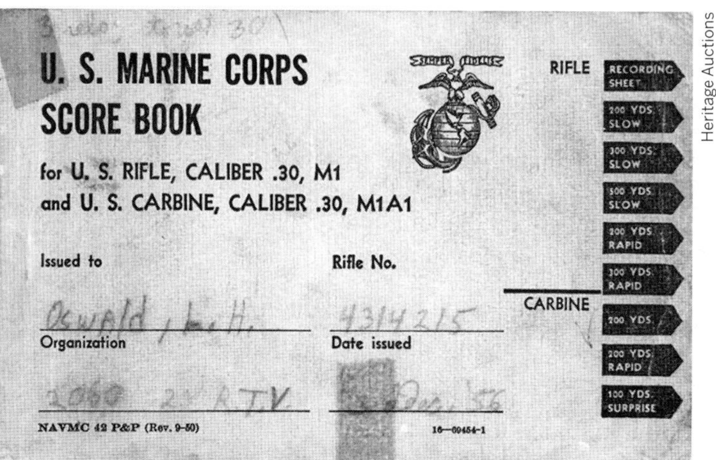

U. S. MARINE CORPS
SCORE BOOK

for U. S. RIFLE, CALIBER .30, M1
and U. S. CARBINE, CALIBER .30, M1A1

SEMPER FIDELIS

Issued to: Oswald, L. H.
Rifle No.: 4314215
Organization: 2060 2d RTV
Date issued: [illegible] Dec. 56

RIFLE: RECORDING SHEET; 200 YDS. SLOW; 300 YDS. SLOW; 500 YDS. SLOW; 200 YDS. RAPID; 300 YDS. RAPID
CARBINE: 200 YDS.; 200 YDS. RAPID; 100 YDS. SURPRISE

NAVMC 42 P&P (Rev. 9-50)
16—69454-1

Heritage Auctions

In December 1956, Marine recruit Oswald qualified as a "sharpshooter," meaning he could hit a ten-inch target eight out of ten times from two hundred yards away. As he peered through the scope mounted atop his rifle in Dallas on November 22, 1963, his target—President Kennedy—was about eighty-eight yards away. It sold at auction in 2008 for $20,315.

National Archives

Oswald, a complainer and a malcontent throughout his short life, didn't adjust well to Marine Corps discipline. He was court-martialed twice during his three years in uniform. He also expressed interest in assassinating President Eisenhower.

NrDEX-M

AIR

(Security Classification)

FOREIGN SERVICE DESPATCH

DO NOT TYPE IN THIS SPACE

PPT

FROM: Amembassy MOSCOW — DESP. NO. 234

TO: THE DEPARTMENT OF STATE, WASHINGTON. — November 2, 1959 (DATE)

REF: Ourtel 1304, October 31, 1959

For Dept. Use Only	ACTION	DEPT.
	F-2	INR 5, SCA 3, SCS-2, SY-2, ... , S/S-2, ...
	REC'D	OTHER
		CIA-15

SUBJECT: CITIZENSHIP: Lee Harvey OSWALD

Mr. Lee Harvey OSWALD, an American citizen, appeared at this Embassy October 31, 1959 and stated to Second Secretary Richard E. Snyder that he wishes to renounce his American citizenship and that he had applied to become a citizen of the Soviet Union. He presented to the interviewing officer his passport and the following signed, undated, handwritten statement, the original of which is retained by the Embassy (misspellings are as in original):

"I Lee Harvey (cq) Oswald do hereby request that my present citizenship in the United States of america, be revoked.

"I have entered the Soviet Union for the express purpose of appling for citizenship in the Soviet Union, through the means of naturalization.

"My request for citizenship is now pending before the Surprem Soviet of the U.S.S.R.

"I take these steps for political reasons. My request for the revoking of my American citizenship is made only after the longest and most serious considerations.

"I affirm that my allegiance is to the Union of Soviet Socialist Republics."

s/ Lee H. Oswald

Oswald is the bearer of Passport No. 1733242, issued September 10, 1959 (retained at the Embassy). The passport shows that he was born in New Orleans, Louisiana, on October 18, 1939, and gives his occupation as "shipping export agent". Oswald gave his last address in the United States as that of his mother at 1936 Collinwood Street, Fort Worth, Texas. A telegram subsequently received at the Embassy for him indicates that a brother, Robert L. Oswald, resides at 7313 Davenport, Fort Worth, Texas. He stated that he was discharged from the U. S. Marine Corps on September 11, 1959. Highest grade achieved was corporal. Oswald evidently applied for his passport to the Agency at San Francisco while still in service. He stated that he had contemplated the action which he took for about two years before his discharge. He departed from the United States through New Orleans with the intent of traveling to the Soviet Union through Northern Europe. He states that he first applied for a Soviet tourist visa in Helsinki on October 14,

Richard E. Snyder:mc

INFORMATION COPY

October 31, 1959: "I affirm that my allegiance is to the Union of Soviet Socialist Republics," Oswald declared during a meeting at the American Embassy in Moscow. The Soviets at first rejected Oswald, leading to a suicide attempt.

Wikipedia Commons

After being allowed to stay, Oswald was sent to Minsk—far from Moscow, where he thought he deserved to live. He was given a menial factory job, which he quickly grew to resent. Here, in sunglasses, the smug defector relaxes with comrades.

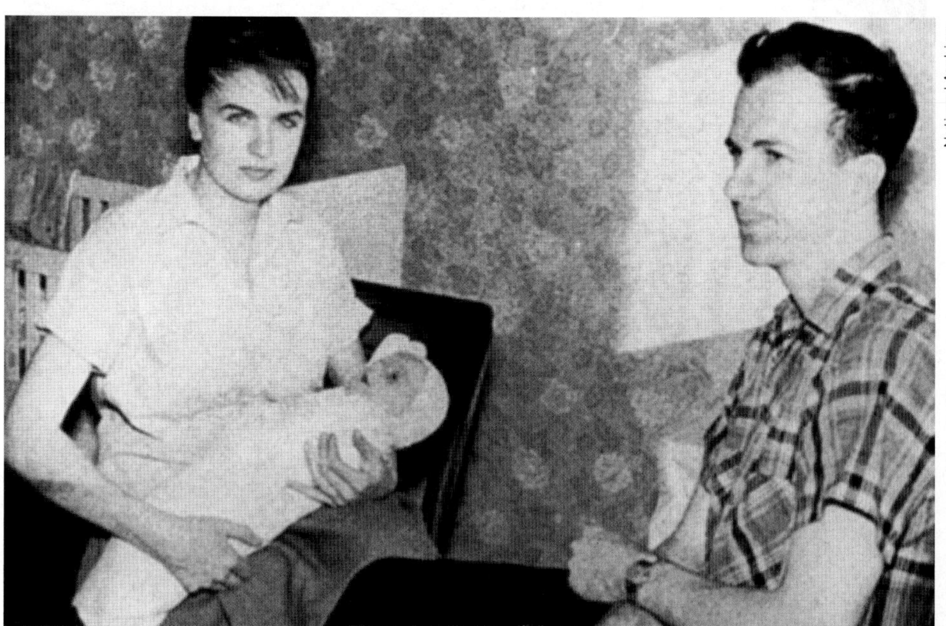

National Archives

Oswald with wife Marina and daughter June in Minsk. In his diary, he wrote that he was still in love with another woman who had rejected his marriage proposal. In America he would beat Marina frequently and prevent her from learning English.

Eisenhower Library

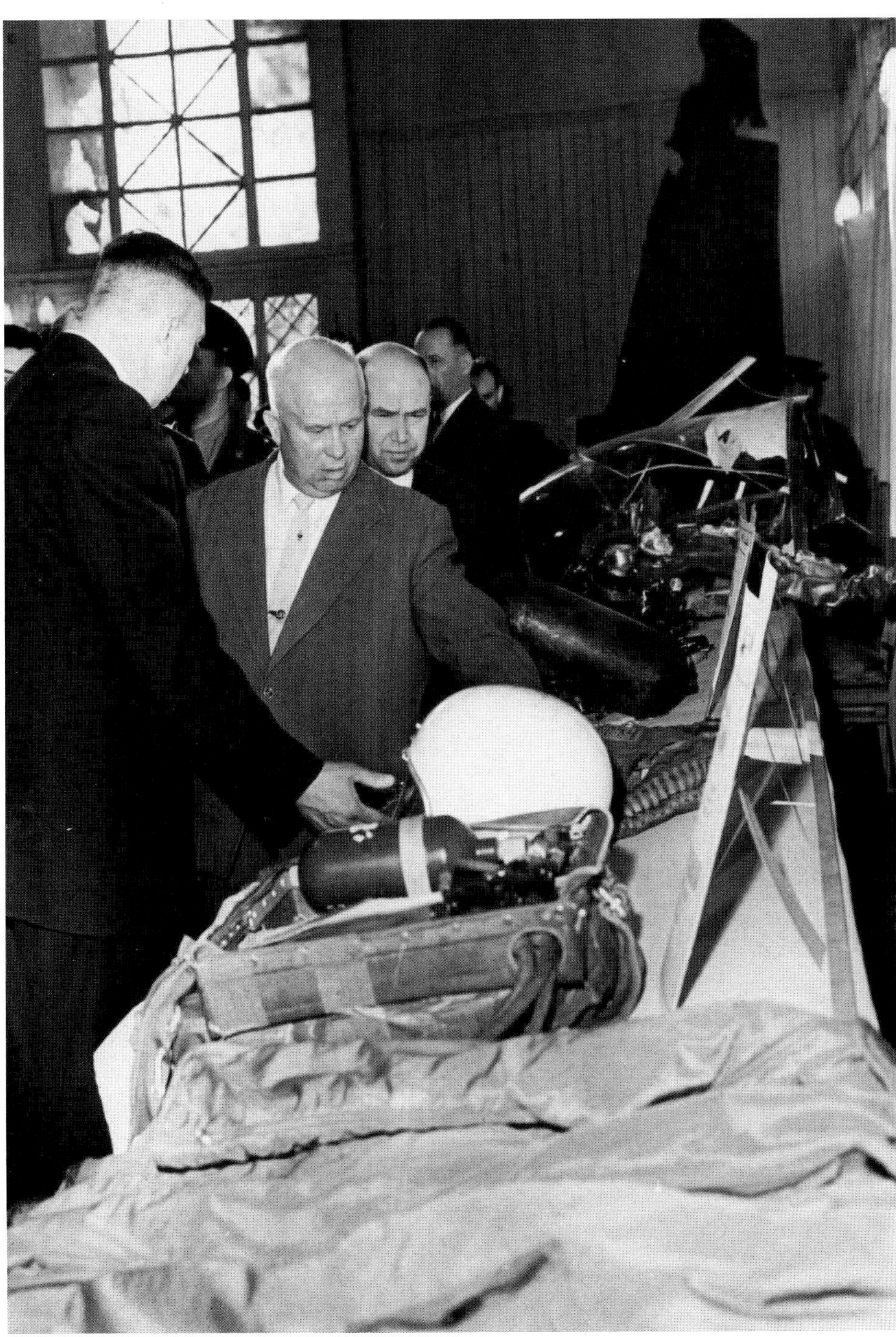

May 1960: Soviet premier Khrushchev examines the wreckage of a downed U-2 spy plane. Some conspiracists think Oswald—a radar operator at an air base prior to his defection—gave the Soviets intelligence on the U-2. Oswald knew how high and fast it could fly, but the Soviets already knew this. The plane's operations were also run from a part of the base that Oswald had no access to.

National Archives

Oswald at around the time of his June 1962 return to the United States. The media-hungry twenty-two-year-old was disappointed that it wasn't covered by the press. "What, no reporters?" he asked his brother.

City of Dallas Municipal Archives

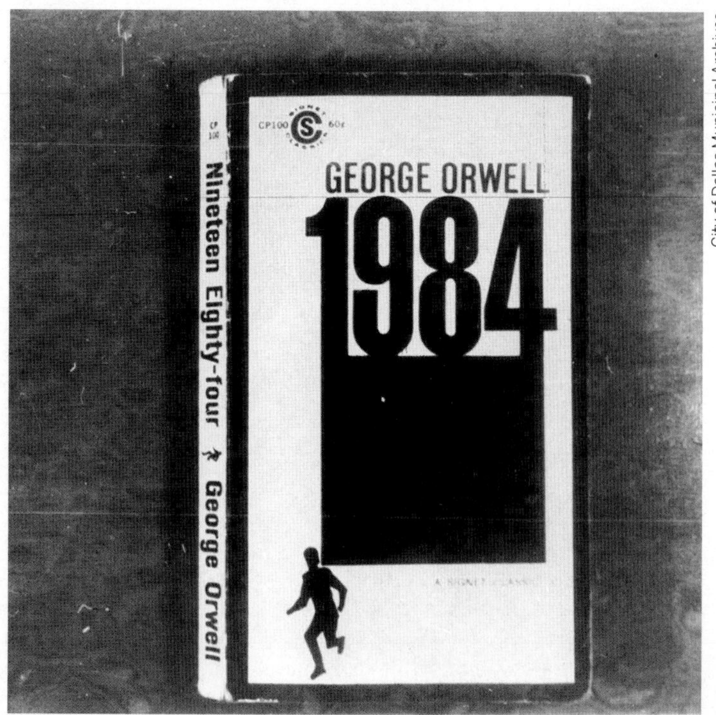

Oswald was a voracious reader. Books he read included Hitler's Mein Kampf, William Shirer's Rise and Fall of the Third Reich, and a biography of Mao Tse-Tung. He also checked out books on American politicians and assassinations. Orwell's 1984 was found among his belongings after the assassination.

City of Dallas Municipal Archives

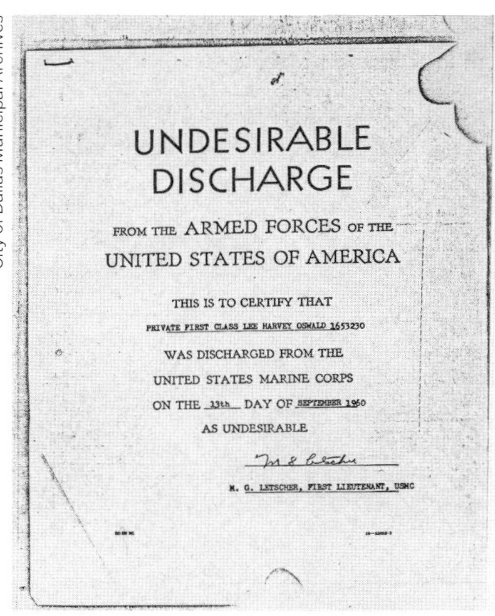

UNDESIRABLE DISCHARGE

FROM THE ARMED FORCES OF THE UNITED STATES OF AMERICA

THIS IS TO CERTIFY THAT

PRIVATE FIRST CLASS LEE HARVEY OSWALD 1653230

WAS DISCHARGED FROM THE UNITED STATES MARINE CORPS

ON THE 13th DAY OF SEPTEMBER 1960

AS UNDESIRABLE

M. G. LETSCHER, FIRST LIEUTENANT, USMC

Oswald was upset that his discharge from the Marines had been changed to "Undesirable" after the Marines learned of his defection to the Soviet Union. He wrote to Navy Secretary John Connally in protest, but Connally had left the job by then to run for governor of Texas.

National Archives

RECEIVED TOO LATE FOR HUNTING SEASON

KLEIN'S LOSS IS YOUR GAIN! SAVE NOW! BUT HURRY!

Cash or Credit NO MONEY DOWN 30 DAY FREE TRIAL

U. S. SPRINGFIELD M1903—30/06 $36.38

U. S. M-1 GARAND RIFLE 30/06 AUTO. $89.95

6.5 ITALIAN CARBINE $12.88 $19.95

SPECIAL PURCHASE! TOP QUALITY! TASCO VARIABLE POWER SCOPE! . . . 3X TO 9X $34.88 $29.88 $19.88

SALE! New Matador 10 Gauge Magnum $129.50

SALE! NEW WINCHESTER FEATHERWEIGHT AUTO SHOTGUN 12 Gauge $98.77

BRAND NEW! U.S. M1 .30 CALIBER CARBINE $78.88

FAMOUS VISCOUNT SHORTWAVE-AM-MARINE PORTABLE RADIO! 3 Bands 8 Transistors COMPARE AT $57.95 ELSEWHERE! $39.95

NEW! FINEST 9 TRANSISTOR WALKIE-TALKIE $49.88

WAR SURPLUS! U.S. MODEL 1917 RIFLE 30/06 CALIBER LAST CALL! HURRY! $29.88

30/06 WITH NEW TASCO HIGH POWER SCOPES INSTALLED READY TO SHOOT

BRAND NEW! FIRST QUALITY! 30-30 or .35 Rem. DELUXE MARLIN 336C! LAST CALL! HURRY! $69.88 $69.88 $94.88 $104.88

SPECIAL WAR SURPLUS PURCHASE! .303 British Caliber ENFIELD SPORTER LAST CALL! HURRY! $19.88 $19.88 $21.88 $46.88

NEW HI-STANDARD .22 DERRINGER $29.95

.38 S & W ENFIELD $12.88

M1917—COLT .45 $29.95

NEW! '63 GUN DIGEST World's Greatest GUN BOOK $3.95

AMMO. SALE! 30 Days Only—Order Today! Swedish Mauser Model 94, metal jacketed, 139 gr. military 6.5 x 55mm ammo. 130 rounds per box. Shipped express, charges collect. E20-T1122X—Box of 130 rounds $7.88

MAIL TODAY! IMMEDIATE DELIVERY! Klein's Sporting Goods KLEIN'S—Dept. 358 227 W. Washington St. Chicago 6, Illinois

100% MONEY BACK GUARANTEE!

March 12, 1963: Using a phony name, Oswald ordered a rifle from this ad in the February 1963 issue of American Rifleman magazine. He chose the Mannlicher-Carcano, shown third from the top in the left row.

March 31, 1963: Conspiracists have long sought to discredit a set of photos taken by Marina Oswald—at her husband's request—of him posing with his newly-purchased rifle and .38. Studies using modern imaging technology have confirmed the authenticity of the photos, which Marina acknowledged taking.

City of Dallas Municipal Archives

Oswald had been plotting to kill Edwin Walker, a retired right-wing general, for weeks—which helps explain his rifle purchase. He took reconnaissance photos of the general's house, which were later found among his belongings. On April 10, 1963, he shot at and barely missed Walker.

4

FD-302 (Rev. 3-3-59)

1

FEDERAL BUREAU OF INVESTIGATION

O-Po 7
Marina 5

Date 11/25/63

Mrs. ELIZABETH GREGORY, 3513 Dorothy Lane South, advised she and her husband first became acquainted with LEE HARVEY OSWALD in the summer of 1962.

She stated that her husband, PETER GREGORY, teaches Russian language at the Fort Worth Public Library and that OSWALD had contacted her husband to determine if OSWALD was capable of translating the Russian language. According to Mrs. GREGORY, her husband gave OSWALD a test and told him that he was capable of translating the Russian language but there was really no demand for it in Fort Worth, Texas.

Mrs. GREGORY stated subsequent to this meeting they invited OSWALD and his wife to a dinner at GREGORY's home and also invited was GEORGE BOUHE of Dallas, Texas. She stated that this was the only contact that she had in her home with OSWALD.

She stated when they learned that OSWALD's wife spoke the Russian language, their son, PAUL GREGORY, took Russian lessons from MARINA OSWALD during the summer of 1962. She stated PAUL visited in the OSWALD home when he lived near Montgomery Ward Company in Fort Worth, Texas, during the summer of 1962 on several occasions while he was taking lessons in Russian.

Mrs. GREGORY stated that PAUL is presently at the University of Oklahoma at Norman, Oklahoma, residing at 1318½ Garfield Street in Norman.

Mrs. GREGORY stated that he has not seen nor talked to OSWALD since PAUL returned to school in September, 1962.

She stated that she had heard of OSWALD through GEORGE BOUHE around Thanksgiving of 1962 and there was some talk of OSWALD having beaten his wife. She stated she could recall no details of what the conversation was regarding OSWALD.

She stated that after OSWALD contacted her husband, she learned that OSWALD had been to Russia and told her husband that he should not have anything to do with OSWALD. She stated after she made this statement, she reconsidered and felt that she may be hypocritical and thereafter/was when her son took lessons from MARINA OSWALD.

CR5

on 11/23/63 at Fort Worth, Texas File # DL 89-43

by Special Agent EARLE HALEY & ARNOLD J. BROWN /rmb Date dictated 11/25/63

294

The Russian émigré community in Texas took a liking to Marina Oswald, but Oswald burned his bridges with his often rude demeanor and lack of gratitude for their assistance. When they learned of his violence—he was a wife beater—it was the final straw.

National Archives

Oswald's "Fair Play for Cuba" committee consisted of one member: himself. He hired two day laborers to help pass out leaflets.

National Archives

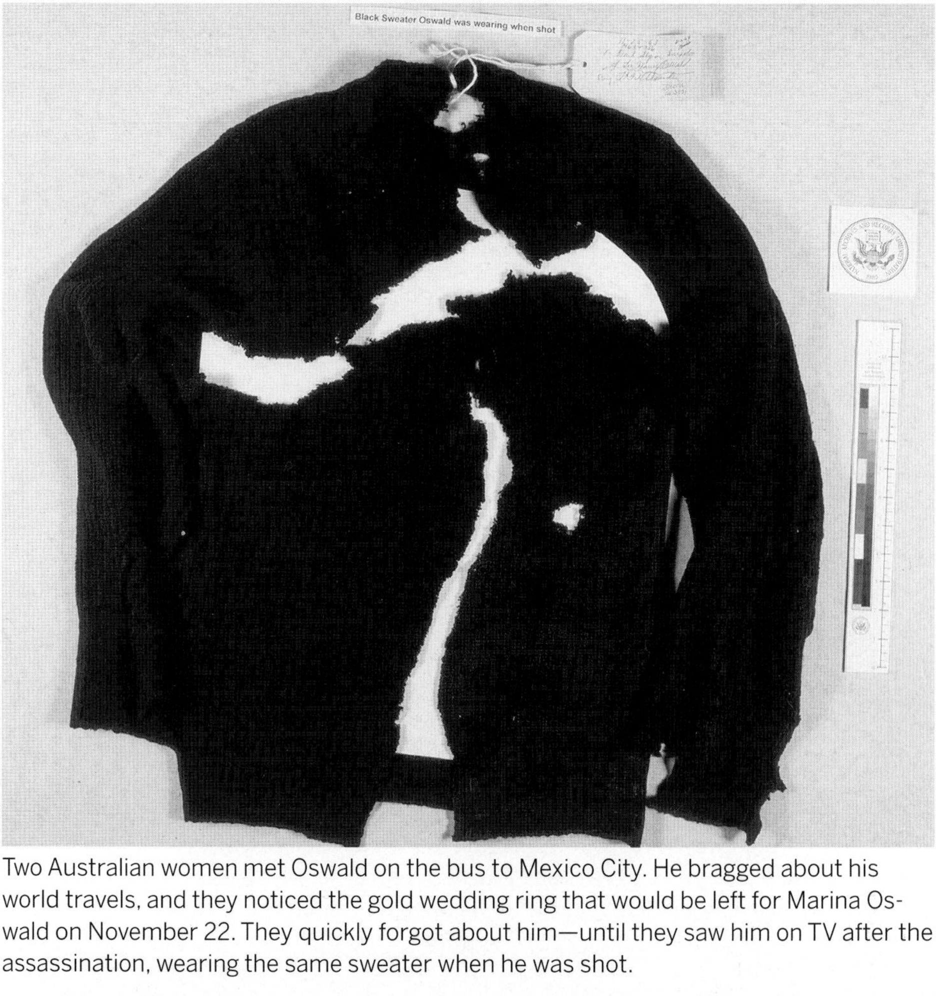

Black Sweater Oswald was wearing when shot

Two Australian women met Oswald on the bus to Mexico City. He bragged about his world travels, and they noticed the gold wedding ring that would be left for Marina Oswald on November 22. They quickly forgot about him—until they saw him on TV after the assassination, wearing the same sweater when he was shot.

one copy)
Date 11/26/63
7010 Bl Justice
Room 7334
Ext 740
☐ Addressograph
☐ Mimeograph

PLEASE FILL OUT APPLICATION BLANK COMPLETELY.............

NAME Oswald LEE H. (LAST NAME FIRST) STREET & NUMBER 2515 W. 5th St. TOWN Irving

PHONE NO BL 31628 SOCIAL SECURITY NO. 433-54-3937 AGE 23 WEIGHT 150 HEIGHT 5'9

PLACE OF BIRTH new Orleans, La HOW LONG LIVED IN DALLAS continuously

FINISHED WHAT GRADE IN SCHOOL 11th NAME SCHOOL Arlington Heights TOWN Ft. worth, Texas

DID YOU ATTEND COLLEGE no HOW LONG — NAME COLLEGE —

RACE C MARRIED (✓) OR SINGLE ( ) HOW MANY DEPENDENTS 2 dependents

WHERE DID YOU LAST WORK U.S.M.C. (three years) NATURE OF WORK air-Wing

REASON FOR LEAVING LAST JOB Honourable discharge

HOW LONG DID YOU WORK ON YOUR LAST JOB three years

WHERE IS YOUR FATHER EMPLOYED Dead NATURE OF WORK —

IS YOUR MOTHER EMPLOYED yes NATURE OF WORK Practical nurse

MEMBER OF ORGANIZATIONS: — CHURCH — LODGE — VETERAN

HAVE YOU ANY PHYSICAL DEFECTS (ANSWER YES OR NO) IF ANSWER IS YES STATE WHAT THEY ARE:

no

DO YOU ROOM AND BOARD no DO YOU LIVE WITH PARENTS no

SHOULD YOU LIKE TO MENTION SOME OF YOUR SPECIAL ABILITIES YOU WOULD LIKE COMPANY TO KNOW IN CONSIDERING YOUR APPLICATION USE THE THREE LINES BELOW.

Clearical (accounting) work in military service, experienced with Ditto, alding and some typing machine and filing system.

DATE OF APPLICATION

Oct. 15, 1963

Lee H Oswald
SIGNATURE OF APPLICANT

K23 D-4364641 PK
FBI LABORATORY

Oswald lied constantly about his background. In his October 15, 1963 application to work at the Texas School Book Depository, he said that he had just gotten out of the Marines and was honorably discharged.

Conspiracists often say that Oswald was "planted" in the Depository when he was hired on October 15, 1963. They overlook two things: 1) the Depository had a second location a quarter-mile away, and Oswald was nearly assigned there until his new boss randomly decided he needed extra help on Elm Street. 2) Kennedy's speaking venue, which dictated the motorcade route, wouldn't be decided—by top JFK aide Kenneth O'Donnell—until mid-November.

Dallas Municipal Archives

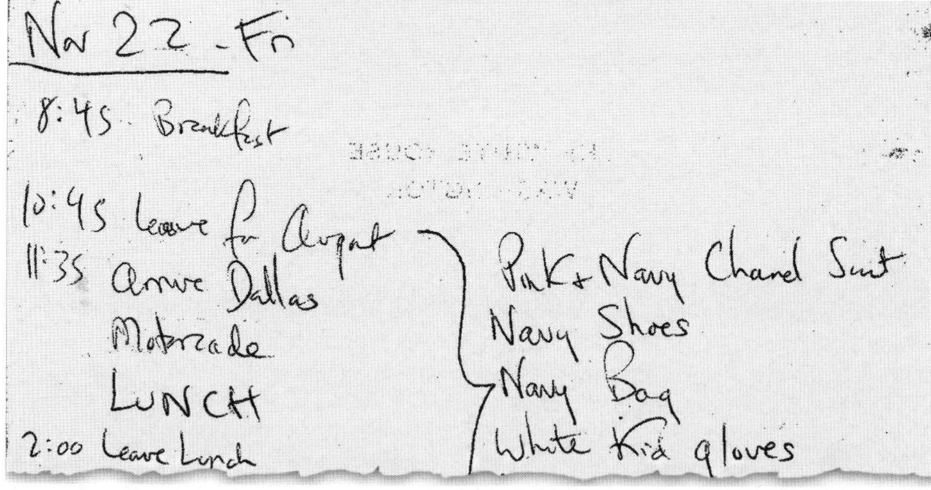

Nov 22 - Fri

8:45 Breakfast

10:45 Leave for Airport
11:35 Arrive Dallas
Motorcade
LUNCH
2:00 Leave Lunch

Pink + Navy Chanel Suit
Navy Shoes
Navy Bag
White Kid gloves

Jacqueline Kennedy chose her attire carefully for Dallas. Her stunning "pink and navy" suit was one of her husband's favorites.

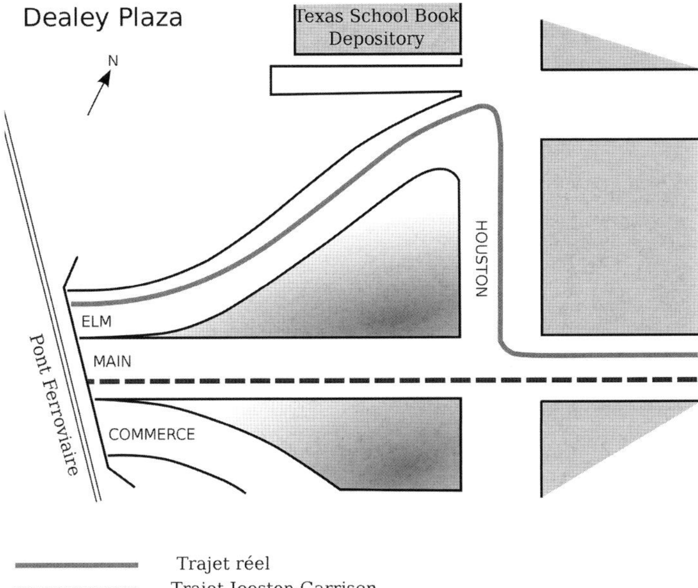

Conspiracists often say that the motorcade route was switched to make Kennedy drive down Elm Street. Actually, the only way to access Stemmons Freeway and the Trade Mart—the site approved by White House aide O'Donnell on November 14—was via Elm Street.

Dallas Municipal Archives

Shown hours after the assassination, the Depository lunchroom is probably where Oswald, just the day before, learned that the presidential motorcade would proceed down Elm Street.

National Archives

November 21: After learning of JFK's motorcade route, Oswald went to the Depository's shipping department and made this bag. He asked Wesley Frazier for a ride to Irving, even though it was Thursday. He said he was going to get curtain rods for his boarding house. Oswald's room already had curtains.

Timcdfw, Wikipedia Commons

November 21: At Ruth Paine's home in Irving, Oswald begged Marina to take him back, saying he would rent an apartment for them in Dallas the next day. She refused. Paine told the author that she noticed the light on in the garage that night and knew that Oswald had been in there.

Commission Exhibit No. 996

WANTED

FOR

TREASON

THIS MAN is wanted for treasonous

THIS MAN is wanted for treasonous

THIS MAN is wanted for treasonous activities against the United States:

1. **Betraying the Constitution (which he swore to uphold):**
   He is turning the sovereignty of the U. S. over to the communist controlled United Nations.
   He is betraying our friends (Cuba, Katanga, Portugal) and befriending our enemies (Russia, Yugoslavia, Poland).
2. **He has been WRONG on innumerable issues affecting the security of the U.S. (United Nations-Berlin wall-Missle removal-Cuba-Wheat deals-Test Ban Treaty, etc.)**
3. **He has been lax in enforcing Communist Registration laws.**
4. **He has given support and encouragement to the Communist inspired racial riots.**
5. **He has illegally invaded a sovereign State with federal troops.**
6. **He has consistantly appointed Anti-Christians to Federal office: Upholds the Supreme Court in its Anti-Christian rulings.**
   Aliens and known Communists abound in Federal offices.
7. **He has been caught in fantastic LIES to the American people (including personal ones like his previous marraige and divorce).**

1514

Leaflets reading "Wanted for Treason," sprouted in Dallas ahead of Kennedy's visit.

National Archives

"OK, OK, I'm going!" Abraham Zapruder told employees of his clothing company, who urged him to go home and get his movie camera on the morning of November 22.

Conspiracists point out, correctly, that a second person was seen on the Depository's sixth floor near Oswald's corner perch. But it wasn't a co-conspirator. It was Depository employee Bonnie Ray Williams eating lunch. He was so close to Oswald, who was hiding behind stacks of boxes, that Oswald, afraid of being discovered, sat perfectly still—like a "statue," said people on the street who saw him. Williams left minutes before the shooting to join his friends on the fifth floor.

Williams and two Depository buddies were on the fifth floor during the assassination. The shots that came from just above them were deafening. They also heard shell casings hitting the floor and debris fell on their heads. Shown seconds after the shooting.

Sixth Floor Museum at Dealey Plaza

incapable of giving her himself. Marina later said that in the ensuing argument, Oswald told her to leave. "If you like them so much, go live with them." Marina, upset, fled. Lee chased her, yelling, "Go. I don't care. I don't need you!"

With the few words of English she knew and some awkward charades with a gas station attendant and waitress at a donut shop, Marina, with June, made her way to the home of Teofil and Anna Meller.

She arrived late at night with her "baby…a couple of diapers and that was all. No coat, no money, nothing," Meller said. Nine time zones from the only world she had ever known, Marina Oswald was now a battered wife fleeing an abusive relationship. She was also slowly starving; Anna took her to a doctor, who said that Marina was "very undernourished."[41]

Word spread quickly and the next day, some of the Texas Russians—who adored Marina but wanted nothing to do with Lee—met to discuss the problem. George Bouhe told Marina to leave Lee, telling her, "I don't think you could have a good life with him." Everyone was eager to help—on one condition: that she never go back to her husband. If she did, they told her, no one would want to help her again.

"I will never go back to that hell," Marina told herself.[42]

November 11—Dallas

After staying with the Mellers for four or five days, Marina wavers, and agrees to meet Oswald at a neutral location: the de Mohrenschildts' apartment.

Both the de Mohrenschildts and Mellers thought Oswald a "megalomaniac," "unbalanced," a "psychopath." They confronted Oswald.

"Do you think it's heroic to beat a woman weaker than you?" George de Mohrenschildt asked him.

"If you cannot live with each other peacefully, without all this awful behavior, you should separate, and see. Maybe you don't really love each other," added Jeanne de Mohrenschildt.

Marina, asserting herself, spoke up, saying she simply couldn't take any more of her husband's beatings.

And yet Oswald, getting it on all sides, refused to take responsibility for his actions.

"I'm not always in the wrong," he said defensively. "Marina has such a long tongue, sometimes I can't hold myself back."[43]

Sometimes I can't hold myself back. This was quite an admission for Oswald, who for the first time admitted that he was a violent man, a man with an explosive temper, a man incapable of controlling his ugly tendency to lash out.

The attempt at reconciliation failed.

After the meeting, George Bouhe—who wanted nothing to do with Oswald—picked up Marina and June at the Mellers' and took them to the home of Declan and Katya Ford. Katya despised Lee; she considered him an "animal."[44]

Now alone, Oswald called Marina each night until she agreed to speak with him. Oswald pleaded with her: he had been invited to Thanksgiving at his brother's house, and it would be an Oswald family reunion. Lee, afraid of the humiliation of going alone, pleaded with her to join him.

After a few days at the Fords' house, Marina found an even better arrangement: she could live indefinitely with another Russian woman, Anna Ray and her American husband. Marina happily accepted.

When Oswald—lonely and fearful that he had lost his wife for good—found out where Marina was, he took the bus to see her. According to Marina, he got on his knees, weeping, and begged her to come back, admitting that he had a "terrible character" but would try and change. Marina, embarrassed but touched by her husband's crying, gave in. She agreed to go home with Oswald.[45]

But Marina's patience was running out. There would soon come a time when she would deal him one final, ultimate rejection.

November 20—The White House

President Kennedy lifts the naval blockade (or "quarantine") he placed around Cuba the month before, after determining that the Soviets have dismantled all missile launch sites and all bombers capable of carrying nuclear weapons.

* * *

We are now up to November 22, 1962. Oswald was back in his familiar lifestyle—moving frequently, job hopping, envying the success of others—while cloaking it in his communist "workers of the world unite" gibberish—and resentful that the world still hadn't recognized his genius. He had been married for a year and a half. He was an abusive husband—violently abusive—and a poor provider to his small family. He was a compulsive liar, a bridge-burning ingrate. Everyone else knew that Oswald had a "terrible character"; now he admitted it himself. For a short period, as he worked to please Marina, he was able to suppress this "Mr. Hyde" that lay within: the dark impulses and explosive violence. But it would not, could not, last. As we will soon see, the unstable man who, years before, had pulled knives on his own family, hit his own mother, and spoken of wanting to assassinate President Dwight Eisenhower, hadn't changed a bit.

CHAPTER EIGHT

The Final Year: November 22, 1962–November 21, 1963

"Oswald's name, such as many others in the Dallas file, was omitted because the FBI saw nothing in Oswald's background to mark him as a potential assassin."

—FBI

By now, we've seen all the variables that, when combined, would spell catastrophe in Dallas. Oswald's lifelong penchant—as a child, in the Marines, towards his own mother and wife—for violence. His lifelong resentment of superiors—teachers, officers in the Marine Corps, factory bosses in Minsk, supervisors at a string of menial jobs. His rampant dishonesty and delusions of grandeur. His jealousies, insecurities, and constant feelings of rejection. His desire for fame and attention. His failures as a husband, father, and provider. His attempt to murder a political opponent of President Kennedy—made possible by a fascination with, and love of, guns.

We've also seen how decades of loose presidential security—open cars, insufficient numbers of agents, and a determination on the part of one chief executive after another to be seen, both at home and abroad—placed themselves at potentially lethal risk. It was truly a different culture and a different era.

Let us now examine that final year—November 22, 1962, to November 21, 1963—and look at all this, plus a series of blunders, oversights, complacency, and sheer historical flukes that would bring Oswald and John F. Kennedy together on Elm Street the next day.

November 22—Fort Worth

It is Thanksgiving Day. Lee and Marina have accepted an invitation from Robert Oswald for dinner. Since Oswald doesn't drive, they take the bus. A home movie is made, and Lee is shown in a short-sleeve dress shirt and sweater vest, perched on a couch with Marina to his left.

It was the last time Lee and Robert Oswald would see each other until a year and a day later—November 23, 1963.

Someone who encountered Oswald that day was Paul Gregory, the young student who had befriended Lee and had taken Russian language lessons from Marina that summer. In 2013, he recalled that day with razor-sharp clarity:

> I arrived at Robert's house as the guests were leaving and then drove Lee, Marina and June back to our house. We said hello to my parents and went into the kitchen to prepare some turkey sandwiches. I tried to keep the conversation casual, but Marina began complaining about Lee even as he sat beside her, largely silent. He treated her Russian friends poorly, she said, and tried to keep her isolated in the house, doing the grocery shopping himself. I listened uncomfortably, sensing his hostility at me for suggesting that he, a self-styled intellectual keeping a "Historic Diary," could not write or punctuate any better than someone just learning English. After an hour or so, I drove them downtown to the bus station for their ride back to Dallas. Marina waved goodbye from the steps. It was Nov. 22, 1962. I never saw them again.[1]

By this point, Oswald had been back in America a mere five months but had already alienated the émigré community that had once been so willing and eager to help. That Oswald had been able to burn so many bridges in such a short period of time was testament to his defective personality—his sullen, uncommunicative, and narcissistic demeanor, his inability to show gratitude for anything, and the physically brutal way in which he treated Marina.

December 7—Los Alamos, New Mexico

President Kennedy sits on the edge of the trunk of his convertible as he is driven to the Los Alamos National Laboratory. As usual, and as he prefers, Secret Service agents are relegated to the follow-up car behind him.

December 21—Havana

Fidel Castro and James Donovan, a former US intelligence officer turned businessman and occasional federal government troubleshooter, sign an agreement to exchange all 1,113 men taken prisoner during the April 1961 Bay of Pigs invasion for $53 million in food and medicine.[2]

January 7, 1963—Dallas

Oswald discovers a letter written by Marina to an old boyfriend. He slaps her twice. "I'll never trust you again," he says.[3] At this point in his life, Oswald, his wife says, is "very unrestrained and very explosive."[4]

January 14—Dallas

Oswald, broke and in need of a job, signs up for a typing course at Crozier Technical School. He begins attending on January 28, with class running from 6:15 to 7:15 p.m. on Mondays, Tuesdays, and Thursdays. But Oswald, who dropped out of numerous schools as a youngster, attends infrequently and stops going altogether in late March.[5]

January 27—Dallas

Using the alias "A. J. Hidell"* for the first time, Oswald orders a .38 caliber Smith & Wesson revolver through the mail from Seaport Traders, Inc., of Los Angeles. He puts $10 down and pays the balance of $19.95 on delivery. A "witness" was needed to purchase the gun. Oswald invents a second fake name: D. F. Drittal. As he did with Marina, he lies about his age, saying he was twenty-eight. Handwriting witnesses—Alwyn Cole of the United States Treasury Department and James C. Cadigan of the FBI—would each later testify that both signatures were in Oswald's handwriting.[6]

Dallas—exact date unknown

Oswald suggests that perhaps Marina should move back to the Soviet Union. Marina, who likes the United States despite the fact that she can't speak English—and Oswald would not permit her to learn it—pleads with him: "Don't ever make me go back!"[7]

February 13—Dallas

The Oswalds attend a dinner party at the home of the de Mohrenschildts. Oswald spends the evening speaking with a German visitor, Volkmar Schmidt.

Schmidt later recalled that Oswald "appeared to be a violent person."[8] And he "felt very angry about the support which the Kennedy administration gave the Bay of Pigs."[9]

---

* Why "A. J. Hidell?" It's possible that Oswald used the name of a marine he knew in Japan—John Heindel, who was often called "Hidell" (rhymes with "Rydell"). But Marina Oswald thinks he used it because it was familiar to "Fidel"—as in Castro. (Bugliosi, 553) As for the A, it was short for "Alik," the name given to Oswald by his coworkers in Minsk. And the J? McMillan says it stood for "James," which she thinks was taken from Ian Fleming's James Bond novels, which Oswald enjoyed (as did President Kennedy). Using phony names recalls his love, a decade before, of his favorite TV show, *I Led 3 Lives*. (McMillan, 406–7)

It was on this night, in fact, that de Mohrenschildt probably, and jokingly, made a remark to Oswald that anyone who killed Edwin Walker —the retired general who was now a leading figure in the far-right John Birch Society—would be doing society a favor.

Marina Oswald would later tell Priscilla McMillan that February 13 may have been a turning point for Oswald, an evening that "influenced Lee's sick fantasy." But, McMillan adds, Oswald was already thinking of killing Walker.[10]

February 15—Dallas

Marina tells Oswald that she is pregnant with their second child.

February 17—Dallas

Oswald begins planning the Walker assassination. He also forces Marina to write a letter to the Soviet embassy in Washington to allow Marina and June to return to the USSR.

Priscilla McMillan notes that the most violent period (to date) of the Oswalds' marriage began at this time. Oswald beat Marina mercilessly, once drawing blood from her nose. He later smashed a window after she locked him out. While this battering went on, there was intermittent begging for forgiveness.

"You know my terrible character," he admitted after one explosion of violence. "When you see I'm in a bad mood, try not to make me mad. You know I can't hold myself in very long now."

You know my terrible character...you know I can't hold myself in very long...

Days later, after a similar incident, she asked him why he was so violent.

"Because I love you. I can't stand it when you make me mad."

Here, Oswald links his violence with his love for Marina...

Marina saw her angry, vengeful husband as a sick person who needed help.[11]

The violence and yelling that burst forth from the Oswalds' shabby apartment frightened their neighbors. One complained to building manager Mahlon Tobias: "I think he's *really* hurt her this time." Said another: "I think that man over there is going to kill that girl."[12]

February 22—Dallas

The Oswalds attend another dinner party, this one at the home of Everett Glover, a chemist for Socony Mobil Oil Co. They meet a pivotal figure: Ruth Paine, a thirty-year old Swarthmore College graduate, committed Quaker, and active member of the American Civil Liberties Union. She was also studying Russian. This is the initial attraction between her and Marina, and the two women hit it off. But the amity between the two women doesn't extend to Lee. There is something about him, from the very beginning, that doesn't sit well with Ruth.

March 2—Dallas

Oswald's steady beating of his wife earns him a warning from the apartment's owners, Mr. and Mrs. William Jurek: stop fighting or move out.

Oswald opted for the latter. Unbeknownst to Marina, he found an apartment at 214 West Neely Street, just a block away. They walked away, with Oswald cheating his landlord out of a few days' rent.[13]

Oswald's reputation as a wifebeater could and should have landed him in jail. Had Marina spoken English, known what options were at her disposal, and had the resources and wherewithal to leave him earlier than she did, the trajectory of Oswald's life as 1963 progressed would likely have been far different.

March 3—Arlington National Cemetery

President Kennedy, visiting Arlington National Cemetery, stands atop its highest point: the Custis-Lee Mansion. Five-year old Caroline visited the week before and has told him about it. JFK is taken in by the sweeping view of the majestic cemetery, Potomac River, and further east, the monuments to presidential heroes.

Kennedy told a friend, Charlie Bartlett: "I could stay here forever."[14]

March 8—The Soviet Embassy

The Soviet embassy in Washington replies to Lee and Marina Oswald's request to return to the Soviet Union. They tell the Oswalds to submit applications and letters from Marina's relatives in the USSR and explain why they want to return. The Soviets tell the Oswalds it will take up to five to six months to process their request.

Had they done so, the Oswalds might have left Dallas prior to November 22.

March 10—Dallas

Oswald takes reconnaissance photos of General Walker's home, at 4011 Turtle Creek Boulevard. The general has been forced into retirement by the Pentagon for spreading right-wing propaganda among those under his command.

Aside from Oswald later admitting to Marina that he tried to kill the general, there is physical evidence. On November 23, the day after President Kennedy's assassination, Dallas police, swarming over the Paine home in Irving, found four photos that Oswald took of the general's home.[15] In the background of one of the photos there was a construction site of another building. Examining the photo months later, a supervisor at the construction site determined that it was taken on the weekend of March 9 and 10.[16] Oswald's time card at Jaggars shows that he worked late on March 9, which was a Saturday, meaning it was almost certain that his recon mission to Walker's home was the next day, the tenth. A voracious newspaper reader, Oswald almost certainly knew that Walker was away on his national anti-communist crusade and knew it was safe to surveil his home.

The photos were also the subject of a confrontation between Oswald and Marina. "What kind of photographs are these?" she demanded to know. Oswald didn't respond.[17]

March 11—Dallas

FBI agent James Hosty visits the Oswald home on Elsbeth Street, only to learn from Mrs. Tobias that they have been tossed out because of their constant fighting. He goes to their new address—214 West Neely—and confirms that they live there.

Hosty was eager to interview Marina, who he considered a possible sleeper agent, but regulations required agents to wait six months to interview new immigrants.[18] *

March 12—Dallas

Two days after conducting reconnaissance of Walker's home, Oswald buys a rifle. Using the same phony name—"A. Hidell"—he used to buy his .38 revolver, he sends a mail order for $21.45 to Klein's Sporting Goods of Chicago, along with a coupon clipped from the February 1963 issue of *American Rifleman* magazine. The fake identification card he used had been fabricated at Jaggars-Chiles-Stovall.[19]

The rifle was a surplus Italian 6.5-millimeter military rifle, a Mannlicher-Carcano manufactured in 1940 at the Terni Arsenal in Italy. The high-powered weapon, serial number C2766, also comes with a four-power (4x) Japanese-made scope. The rifle cost $12.78; the scope an additional $7.17.

Both the mail order (2,202,130,462) and envelope were written in the same handwriting as that used to buy the .38 revolver in January. It was sent to "A. Hidell, P.O. Box 2915 Dallas, Texas." That PO Box—2915—had been rented to "Lee H. Oswald" on September 9, 1962. He would keep it until May 14, 1963.

* This was a bureaucratic stumble by the FBI. By March 1963, Marina Oswald had been in the United States for nine months.

March 20—Los Angeles and Chicago

In quite a coincidence, Seaport Traders in Los Angeles ships its .38 revolver on the same day that Klein's Sporting Goods in Chicago ships its Mannlicher-Carcano rifle. Both are sent to PO Box 2915, Dallas, Texas. The revolver, though, is sent to the offices of REA Express.[20]

March 21—The Pentagon

The joint chiefs of staff ready OPLAN 380-63, a plan for the invasion of Cuba that would take place in 1964. Under the plan, Cuban exiles would infiltrate Cuba in January, American forces would follow on July 15, American air strikes would start on August 3, and "a full-scale invasion, with a goal of the installation of a government friendly to the U.S." would be launched on October 1, 1964.

Conspiracists who think that Kennedy was removed by far-right elements in the Pentagon—so a more amenable President Johnson could take over and move against Cuba—are usually silent when asked if this is so, why Johnson never did. It wasn't as if LBJ was inactive in Latin America, after all: he would order twenty thousand marines to the Dominican Republic in 1965, for instance, to restore order as that country—just to the east of Cuba—descended into civil war.[21]

March 25—Dallas

Oswald picks up his rifle at the post office. He carries it across town to the offices of REA Express and receives his .38 revolver.

Later that week, Marina saw the rifle for the first time. It is partially hidden under a raincoat. She wasn't surprised to see him with a weapon; after all, Oswald owned a shotgun in Minsk, where he went hunting with his workmates. Still, she doesn't like guns in the house and asked why he bought it.

"That for a man to have a rifle—since I am a woman, I don't understand him, and I shouldn't bother him. A fine life," she told the Warren

Commission. McMillan also notes another comment Oswald made to Marina:

"Maybe I'll go hunting sometime."[22]

Late March—Dallas

At the tiny closet that he uses as an "office," Oswald freshens up his political credo. Vincent Bugliosi, in his massive *Reclaiming History*, likens it to "the tradition of Hitler's *Mein Kampf*."

He called communism "that most sublime ideal," just not the Soviet version of it, which left a sour taste in his mouth. Singling out Stalin's mass exterminations, Oswald fumed at the Soviets, which had "committed crimes unsurpassed even by their early day capitalist counterparts."[23]

March 31—Dallas

Oswald asks Marina to take photos of him in the backyard of their apartment building. The neighbors are away, and Oswald wants to pose with his new guns.

In photographs that were soon to become infamous, he stood clad in black—Marina had never seen him dressed this way—with his .38 on his right hip, his rifle in his left hand, and some communist newspapers in the other.

"I asked him why he had dressed himself up like that," Marina said. "I thought he had gone crazy."[24] *

* Conspiracy buffs have long challenged the veracity of the photos. Oswald himself—the habitual liar—claimed they were fake when confronted with them after President Kennedy's assassination. But numerous analyses say otherwise, including a 2015 Dartmouth University study, published in the *Journal of Digital Forensics, Security, and Law,* which used sophisticated 3D imaging technology to analyze key details of the photo, including Oswald's pose, and found that the photo is indeed authentic. It is "highly improbable that anyone could have created such a perfect forgery with the technology available in 1963," said Hany Farid, the study's senior author. "Our detailed analysis of Oswald's pose, the lighting and shadows, and the rifle in his hands refutes the argument of photo tampering." (Jenn Gidman, "Verdict is in on whether Lee Harvey Oswald photo is a fake, thanks to 3D tech," USA Today, Oct. 20. 2015) And Marina herself acknowledged taking them.

March 31—Dallas

After learning from the FBI's New York bureau that Oswald has taken out a subscription to a communist newspaper, the *Daily Worker*, Agent Hosty asks FBI HQ in Washington for permission to reopen the file on Oswald—which was closed in September 1962 by the retiring agent Fain.

April 1—Dallas

Oswald is probably fired on this date, and given one week's notice. One of the founders of the company, Robert Stovall, later says that Oswald was a poor employee.

"He was a constant source of irritation," Stovall said. Asked to elaborate, Stovall told the Warren Commission in 1964 said that Oswald was "inefficient—I wouldn't say he was industrious." Stovall added that Oswald wasn't polite to other employees, either, noting that the simple courtesy of saying "excuse me" for bumping into someone wasn't something he did.[25] *

It was worse than not saying "excuse me" to others. Some employees were so fed up with Oswald's "selfish and aggressive" behavior that they almost got into fistfights with him.[26] That Oswald was also seen reading Russian newspapers in the Jaggars cafeteria was also a source of friction.[27] Added John Graef in his own Commission testimony: "I began hearing—or began noticing—that very few people liked him. He was very difficult to get along with." Graef added that whenever Oswald's name came up, other employees spoke poorly of him; there was a general consensus that he had "an unfriendly way" and "didn't leave a good impression."[28]

Oswald's poor attitude wasn't the only reason for his dismissal. He was also incompetent. Graef said that after four or five months, Oswald was still making mistakes, often the same ones over and over

* As we'll soon see, Stovall would also play an indirect role in Oswald's securing employment in October 1963 at the Texas School Book Depository.

again. "More and more he was being relied upon to produce this exact work and there were too many times—it was his mistakes were above normal—he was making too many mistakes," Graef said. "My impression of his mistakes were somehow that he just couldn't manage to avoid them. It wasn't that he lacked industry or that he didn't try. Whenever he was asked to do a job over he would do it willingly for me, with no—he would be more perturbed at himself that he had made an error, so I think he just couldn't—he somehow couldn't manage to handle work that was exact."

In other words, Oswald knew he wasn't up to the task, knew that he wasn't capable. His errors, Graef said, were "too frequent to allow. There were too many times that these things had to be made over and they added to the final reason for dismissing him."[29]

Graef describes the actual termination of Oswald. "We had a fluctuation in business and I thought 'Well, this is the time to let Lee Harvey Oswald go.'" To spare Oswald any embarrassment, Graef called him into the darkroom, which was illuminated by dim red lights, lowered his voice, and said "Lee, I think this is as good a time to cut it short. Business is pretty slow at this time, but the point is that you haven't been turning the work out like you should." Graef also told him that "There has been friction with other people."

According to Graef's recollection of the moment, Oswald didn't challenge anything Graef said, in fact, and in keeping with his laconic character, said nothing at all. But Grief wasn't finished: "I just don't think that you have the qualities for doing the work that we need."

Finally Oswald, who had been looking at the floor the whole time, spoke: "Well, thank you," he said, and walked away. It was yet another humiliation for the twenty-three-year-old drifter.[30]

Oddly, Graef told Oswald that he would be glad to give him a "good recommendation" to a future employer, "because I think you have tried." But Graef told the Commission that he would have told any future boss of Oswald's difficulties with his coworkers.

I've mentioned before that many conspiracists think the fact that Oswald wound up working in the Texas School Book Depository had to have been fishy. Not at all. Great tragedies often require a string of small random and unconnected events to occur, and Oswald's dismissal from Jaggars and the kind of references that John Graef would provide were among them.

It was probably this same date when Oswald, eager to see the photos Marina had taken of him posing with his guns, developed them in the Jaggars darkroom. He would give one photo to Marina and tell her to keep it for June. On the back it was inscribed: "For Junie from Papa."

An appalled Marina asked why Junie would want a picture with guns.

"To remember Papa by sometime."[31]

April 2—Irving

Ruth and Michael Paine have the Oswalds over for dinner. Michael, an engineer at Bell Helicopter Corp., is appalled at the way Oswald treats Marina; Paine will later call it "medieval torture."[32]

April 3—Dallas

Oswald practices with his rifle for the first time, at the bottom of a nearby levee.[33]

April 4 or 5—Dallas

Jeanne de Mohrenschildt visits Marina Oswald at the Oswalds' Neely Street apartment. Showing her guest around, Marina opens a clothes closet, and there, in the corner, was Lee's rifle. "We are so short of money, and this crazy lunatic buys a rifle," Marina said, according to Jeanne's Warren Commission testimony. This makes de Mohrenschildt probably the only person, besides Marina herself, to see the Carcano among Oswald's possessions.[34]

April 5—Dallas

Oswald practices with his rifle again. Marina sees him with it and is angered. "Don't bother to come home at all," she tells him. "I hope the police catch you."[35]

April 6—Dallas

It's Oswald's last day on the job at Jaggars after getting fired. He still hasn't told Marina.

April 7—Dallas

Once again unemployed and struggling to care for his family, Oswald instead focuses on his plans to kill General Walker. He hides his rifle near Walker's home.

April 10—Dallas

After maintaining his charade about still working at Jaggars, Oswald finally admits to Marina that he lost his job. He lies as usual, claiming it was because "probably the FBI came and asked about me and the boss just didn't want to keep someone the FBI was interested in." He adds for dramatic effect: "When will they leave me alone?"[36]

In the evening, a momentous event: Oswald tries to assassinate Walker—and nearly succeeds.

Firing from what is believed to have been a distance of just one hundred feet, the bullet from his Carcano nicked a wooden window frame, deflecting its path just enough to fly through the general's hair, just missing his head. "I heard a blast and crack right over my head," Walker later said.[37]

Prior to leaving for Walker's home earlier that evening, Oswald left an eleven-point memo for Marina, telling her what to do if he was "alive and taken prisoner" by the police. When he came home around eleven thirty that night, she confronted him, demanding to know what he was doing. "He told me not to ask any questions," but acknowledged that he had tried to kill General Walker.[38] Asked where his rifle was, he said he had buried it.[39]

Conspiracists often point to Oswald's later insistent denials about shooting President Kennedy and owning a rifle. "Denies shooting Pres.," scribbled Capt. J. W. "Will" Fritz, Oswald's primary interrogator while he was in police custody. "Didn't own rifle…says nothing against Pres. does not want to talk further," Fritz also wrote. "Shows photo of gun. Would not discuss photo. Says I made picture super imposed."

Ahh. So in April, Oswald admitted that he had tried to commit murder. Admitted owning a rifle. Admitted burying it after the shooting. But no, conspiracists insist: Oswald was just a patsy. Why? Because he said so.

The attempted assassination of the far-right Walker, and what Marina would later describe as Lee's apparent interest in also killing former Vice President Nixon, erases the claim that the assassination of President Kennedy was somehow politically motivated. Lee Harvey Oswald's actions prior to November 22 tell us that he did not discriminate between left and right. As Jerry Parr, the Secret Service agent who saved President Reagan's life in 1981 told me shortly before his death, Oswald was nothing more than an unbalanced young man looking for attention and fame.

April 11—Dallas

Oswald reviews his bungled attempt to murder General Walker. There is front-page newspaper coverage, which no doubt excites him, but of course there is no mention of him.

According to Marina, he was "very sorry" that he had failed. "It was only an accident that I missed," he told her. According to her Warren Commission testimony, Marina asked Lee to promise that he would not attempt such a harebrained thing again. If he did, she warned him, "I would go to the police." She also asked him what he would do with the reconnaissance photos and notes he had made. Oswald responded that he would "Save it as a keepsake. I'll hide it somewhere."[40]

April 12—Dallas

Jittery and upset about botching the Walker assassination, Oswald suffers anxiety attacks during his sleep. "He shook all over from head to toe four times at intervals of a half hour or so without waking up," Marina said.[41]

Here, I'll contrast Oswald's anxiety about *missing* his intended murder target with the reported deep and comfortable slumber for the two nights he lived after *not missing* President Kennedy. William Manchester notes that on November 23, the morning after:

> It is notable that the one man who enjoyed absolute peace that night—the best, he confided to his brother the next day, that he had ever known—was the assassin. To Robert Oswald and to his interrogators Lee Oswald trumpeted that he was refreshed. Certainly he looked spry.[42]

Why the anxiety attacks about failing to kill, but a good night's rest for succeeding?

That day, Oswald filed for unemployment benefits. The man who was always railing against capitalism and the government was always quick to rely on them when he wasn't competent enough to support himself or his family.

April 13—Dallas

The de Mohrenschildts see Oswald for what will be the final time. It's three days after the attempt on the life of General Walker, and de Mohrenschildt—recalling his recent discussions with Oswald—asks in Russian, "Hey Lee, how come you missed?"

"Shhh," Oswald quickly replies. "Junie's sleeping." There is no denial, no "what on earth are you talking about?" Only "shhh."

Later, Oswald would turn to Marina and ask "Did you telephone them and tell them it was me?"

"Of course not," Marina answered. "I thought you did."

"Maybe he was only kidding," Oswald replied. "But he sure hit the nail on the head."[43]

A year later, de Mohrenschildt said that when he asked Oswald about trying to shoot Walker, that Oswald "smiled at that."[44]

April 14—Dallas

After his failed attempt to kill General Edwin Walker, Oswald recovers his rifle, which he had hidden near some railroad tracks immediately after the attack. Marina, telling her unemployed husband that they needed food, asks him to sell it. He declines. "I'll keep it," he says defiantly.[45]

April 15—The White House

Jacqueline Kennedy is pregnant, says a White House press release, and will deliver her baby by cesarean section in September.[46]

April 17—Dallas

Oswald, unemployed, tells Marina he wants to move to New Orleans to find work.[47]

April 19—Washington

In a speech to newspaper executives, President Kennedy denies that his administration is planning an invasion of Cuba—but predicts that "in five years' time" Castro will not be ruling that country.[48]

April 21—Dallas

It's Sunday and Marina sees that Oswald has put on a suit. His new pistol is at his waist. She asks him where he is going, and why he is getting dressed. "Nixon is coming to town," he answers. "I am going to have a look."

Marina would later say that she had no idea who [Richard] Nixon, the former vice president, was, but that if Lee was going out with his gun to "have a look," she deduced that his life was in danger.

She tricked Oswald into going into the bathroom and then prevented him from coming out by pushing against it as hard as she could, with her feet braced against the wall.

"Let me out!" Oswald yelled. "Open the door!"

Marina refused. "How can you lie to me again after you gave me your word? You promised me you'd never shoot anyone else and here you are starting in all over again." She threatened to call the police.

The standoff continued for several minutes until Oswald calmed down. Marina let him out only after he agreed to hand over his .38 and strip down to his underwear so he couldn't go out.[49]

The exchange may be true, but what wasn't true was Oswald's apparently misguided belief that Nixon was in town. He wasn't. Oswald had seen a story in that morning's *Dallas Morning News* in which Nixon had called on the Kennedy administration to take down the communist Castro government.

Priscilla McMillan, who spent the bulk of July to December 1964 with Marina Oswald, interviewing her, probing, asking questions about Lee—who she had met more than a year before Marina did—speculates that the bizarre "Nixon episode" was a signal from Oswald to his wife that "he might kill somebody else, not just Walker. Lee sent that message," McMillan writes, "but Marina did not understand."

Coming less than two weeks after the attempted murder of Walker, it's more evidence of Lee's rage, his violence, his desire to kill. Marina was aware, McMillan observed, "that Lee would kill abstractly for the sake of his ideas. He had tried to strangle *her* of course." Marina thought her husband was sick.[50]

April 22—Washington

Attorney General Robert Kennedy, in a speech: "We can't just snap our fingers and make Castro go away. But we can fight for this." The comments would be reported in a left-wing publication—the *Militant*—that Oswald subscribed to.[51]

April (undated)—New York

Secret Service agent Jerry Parr describes President Kennedy's nonchalant attitude towards his own safety: "One day I covered the president at the Waldorf, bringing up the rear of the phalanx surrounding him. But he saw a crowd behind a rope line and walked back to greet them, right where I was. For a minute or two I was the only agent close to the president, so I started working the line in front of him, telling the crowd 'Take your hands out of your pockets where I can see them....'"[52]

April 24—Dallas

With a $13.85 bus ticket in hand, Oswald leaves Dallas and moves to New Orleans in search of work.[53] Marina and fifteen-month-old June move in with Ruth Paine at 2515 W. 5th Street in Irving.[54]

April 25—New Orleans

Oswald arrives in New Orleans. He has no money and no job. He moves in temporarily with his aunt and uncle, Lillian and Charles "Dutz" Murret.[55]

April 26—New Orleans

Oswald visits an employment agency. His compulsion to lie is evident once again: he makes up phony previous jobs and lists phony references with phony names and addresses.[56]

May 3—New Orleans

Oswald writes to Marina, saying he's getting fifteen to twenty dollars a week in unemployment. Of course, sponging off his aunt and uncle—with their free room and board—goes a long way. As usual, Oswald doesn't offer to contribute.[57]

May 6—The White House

Kennedy issues "National Security Action Memorandum No. 239," stating his "desirability of a [nuclear] test ban treaty" and his belief in "the value of our proposals on general and complete disarmament." He alludes to the recent Cuban Missile Crisis and "my concern for the consequence of an un-checked continuation of the arms race between ourselves and the Soviet bloc." Kennedy's desire to lower the temperature between Washington and Moscow is received well by the Soviet government.[58]

Hawaii

Defense Secretary McNamara presents the White House's plan for a military withdrawal from South Vietnam. Military officers counter with a time frame that McNamara considers too long. He rejects it, and orders that plans be drawn up to pull one thousand US military personnel from South Vietnam by the end of the year.[59]

May 9—New Orleans

Oswald finds a job. It's another lowly position for the high school dropout: greasing and oiling coffee machines at the Reily Foods Company for $1.50 an hour. Despite his belief that he's an important man, a man of superior intellect and capability, it's the best he can do.

As usual, he lied through his teeth to get the menial job, giving his aunt and uncle's address and claiming he had lived there for twenty-three years. He also claimed his last job was "active duty" in the Marines and that he was a high school graduate and was now in college. About the only thing that was true was his name.[60]

He tells Aunt Lillian, who is pleased that Lee has found work. But she suggests he return to school, and learn a trade, telling him bluntly "you are not really qualified to do anything too much."

Oswald's answer reflected his typical delusion and arrogance:

"No, I don't have to go back to school," he said. "I don't have to learn anything. I know everything."[61]

The last time Oswald had lived in New Orleans was 1955, when he and his mother, Marguerite, had so irritated their landlords, Julian and Myrtle Evans, that they were encouraged to move out. Mr. and Mrs. Evans certainly had no reason to think they'd ever see them again. But now, eight years later, there was a knock on their door. Oswald, newly employed, was looking for an apartment. Mrs. Evans helped him find a rental elsewhere. From Julian Evans's 1964 Warren Commission testimony, we see yet another example of Oswald's shameless ability to lie to everyone about everything (the Mr. Jenner is assistant counsel Albert E. Jenner Jr.):

> **MR. JENNER:** Did your wife question him in your presence about his alleged—attempt to defect to Russia, and whether or not he had renounced his American citizenship?
>
> **MR. EVANS:** Well, yes; she did ask him about that, but he denied it. He said he was only a tourist in Russia, or something like that. He said he just wanted to see the country and how they lived, and that he did not intend to ever give up his American citizenship.

As the interview with Mr. Evans wound down, there was this exchange:

> **MR. JENNER:** What other impressions did you have of this boy?
>
> **MR. EVANS:** Well, I thought he was a psycho. I really did.[62]

Oswald wound up renting a modest one-bedroom apartment at 4907 Magazine Street, a blue-collar neighborhood just blocks from the

Mississippi River. It had a long living room, and a screened-in porch (which we'll discuss shortly) and a small, fenced backyard. The rent was sixty-five dollars a month, and Oswald gave his new landlord, Jessie James Garner, a five-dollar deposit.

The deposit was accompanied, as usual, by another lie. He told Garner that he worked for the Leon Israel Company, which was also on Magazine Street.

After President Kennedy's assassination, Garner gave an interview to Jim Kemp, a reporter with New Orleans TV station WDSU:

Q: What sort of a fellow was he?

A: He was a quiet guy, he didn't pay attention to anybody, he just went on about his business, he never had any friends around, he didn't talk to anybody, he wouldn't even say hello to nobody, he'd just walk straight by with his head up. He walked very straight.

Q: You'd say then he wasn't a very friendly person?

A: Not at all.

Q: What about his wife? Didn't he have a wife and child, I believe?

A: Yes, he had a little Russian wife, she was very cute. She didn't speak English at all, she tried, she'd nod, tell you hello when she'd see you and smile. But that's about all. She'd say she couldn't say anything else.

Q: What about his activities while he lived in the apartment? Was he employed? Did he go to work every day and come home in the evenings?

A: Well, when he first rented the apartment, he was working at some coffee company on Magazine Street (she had discovered his lie about working his place of employment), but the most he worked was about three weeks, then after that he didn't work anymore that I know of because he was at home all the time, going back and forth and he'd do a lot of reading. He'd sit on the porch and read plenty.

Q: Did he ever have any visitors? Any people come to see him?

A: Not that I know of.

May 11—New Orleans

Marina and June Oswald arrive in New Orleans to be reunited with Oswald. They were driven by Ruth Paine. Her station wagon is loaded with the Oswalds' belongings, including, unbeknownst to Ruth, Oswald's rifle.*

Marina had mixed feelings about reuniting with her husband. The last two weeks without him had been "a relief not to have to anticipate Lee's moods every second and try to guess what new and dreadful surprise might be lurking around the corner."[63]

May 14—New Orleans

Left-wing publications Oswald subscribes to make their way to his new apartment. One, called the *Militant*, is highly critical of President Kennedy and Attorney General Robert Kennedy, for hinting that the US government was seeking to oust Castro.

May 18—Nashville

President Kennedy is driven to a speech at Vanderbilt University in X-100. He sits up on the top of his seat so he can be better seen by the crowd along the motorcade route. As is common in these more innocent times, his motorcade route from the airport to the university is published in local newspapers.

May 22—The State Department

At a news conference, Kennedy refuses to promise any troop withdrawals from Vietnam. "There is still a long, hard struggle to go," he says.[64]

---

* Paine told me in 2021—she was then ninety—that had she known of Oswald's attempt to kill Walker, she would have gone to the police. She only learned of it—and the fact that Oswald had secretly stored his rifle in her garage—after the president's assassination.

New Orleans

Oswald, the quiet loner, is a reader. It's known that the books he read included Hitler's *Mein Kampf*, William Shirer's *Rise and Fall of the Third Reich*, and George Orwell's anti-communist classics *Animal Farm* and *1984*.[65] He also read a biography of Leon Trotsky. At Marina's urging he tries *All Quiet on the Western Front* by Erich Marina Remarque, which he apparently doesn't like.

Now settled back in the city of his birth, Oswald went to the New Orleans Public Library, applied for a library card, and took out *Portrait of a Revolutionary: Mao Tse-Tung*, by the biographer Robert Payne. He would soon begin checking out books on American politicians—and assassinations.[66]

May 25—New Orleans

Shortly after Marina's arrival in New Orleans, Oswald tells her he doesn't love her anymore and that she is "in his way." She interprets this to mean his political activities.

She wrote to Ruth Paine back in Texas. "As soon as you left all 'love' stopped. I am very much hurt that Lee's attitude toward me is such that I feel each minute that I am tying him down. He insists that I leave America and I don't want this at all."[67]

Ruth had invited Marina to live with her in October, when the Oswalds' second child was born; Marina may have been hoping to be asked again.[68]

Atoka, Virginia

Rolling up to Army One† in a white station wagon, President and Mrs. Kennedy board the helicopter for the brief flight from their home in the

---

† From 1957 until 1976, helicopter travel for presidents was divided between the Army and Marine Corps. Since 1976, the Marines have had the sole responsibility of transporting the president by helicopter.

Virginia countryside to Washington. A home movie taken mid-flight shows a civilian jetliner crossing directly beneath, and dangerously close to, their flight path.[69]

May 26—New Orleans

Oswald writes to a pro-Castro organization—the New York–based Fair Play for Cuba committee—inquiring about opening a New Orleans chapter.

May 29—New Orleans

Oswald, impatient, asks a local printer to produce leaflets for the Fair Play for Cuba committee. They say:

HANDS OFF CUBA!
Join the Fair Play for Cuba Committee
New Orleans Charter Member Branch
Free Literature, Lectures
Location:
Everyone welcome!

As usual he lied, telling the printer that his name was "Lee Osborne."

Meanwhile, he told Marina that he would "go to Cuba, then China, and you will wait for me in Russia."[70]

Once again we see Oswald's delusion and instability on display: the high school dropout, the vagabond, the greaser of coffee machinery, fancying himself a globe-trotting revolutionary.

Washington

Joined by family and friends, President Kennedy celebrates his forty-sixth birthday.

June 1—Irving

Ruth Paine responds to Marina's lonely letter of May 25. She tells her that she is planning to divorce her husband, Michael.[71]

New Orleans

Oswald checks out a new library book: *The Huey Long Murder Case* by Hermann Bacher Deutsch. It's about the assassination of Huey Long, the governor and senator from Louisiana, who was gunned down in 1935.[72]

June 3—New Orleans

Using his phony name A. J. Hidell again, Oswald rents PO Box 30061. Marina is also listed as someone entitled to receive mail.[73]

June 4—New Orleans

Oswald admits to Marina that the name "A. J. Hidell" (the name he used to order his .38 and his rifle) was made up.

"Do you mean that you have two names?" she asks.

"Yes."[74]

June 5—El Paso

Kennedy decides to make a trip in late November to Texas. The decision is made in Texas itself, where the president meets with Vice President Johnson and Governor Connally at the El Cortez Hotel in El Paso. No specific plans are made at this early stage, but the general idea, the three men agree, is for Kennedy to spend just one day in the Lone Star State, making brief stops in (no particular order) Dallas, Fort Worth, San Antonio, and Houston.[75]

The El Paso trip coincided with a bomb threat against the president. But Kennedy still rode—as he preferred—in an open car into town. Instead of going from his car into the Hotel Cortez, where he was staying, he walked across the street to shake hands with delighted Texans.

June 6—San Diego

Kennedy rides through San Diego in an open car—again, as he prefers—with Secret Service yards behind him in the follow-up car. At times, he stands up so he can be better seen by the crowds who line the streets. The president tours the Marine Corps Recruit Depot, treading on the same ground marine boot Oswald did in 1956.

June 8—New Orleans

You'll recall that days earlier, Oswald admitted to Marina that he invented "A. J. Hidell"—the imaginary witness listed on the Dallas mail order forms he used to buy his rifle and .38. Oswald calls upon his imaginary friend again—only this time he's a New Orleans–based doctor—to stamp a form proving that Oswald has been vaccinated against smallpox. "Dr. A. J. Hidell, P.O. Box 30016, New Orleans," the stamp created by Oswald reads.

Also on that day, a hospital refused to examine Marina—who was five months pregnant—because it was only permitted to examine state residents, and the Oswalds had only been in Louisiana for a few weeks. Oswald was livid. "Everything is money in this country," he raged.

Oswald's anger over money—and his lower-class economic status—manifested itself in resentment over President Kennedy's wealth. "Perhaps he expressed jealously, not only jealously, but envy," Marina said in 1964.[76]

In fact, he did more than that. Marina also said that Oswald, in the wake of his hospital humiliation, complained bitterly about Kennedy's wealth. "His Papa bought him the presidency," Oswald said. "Money paves the way to everything here."[77] *

June 10—American University

Reaching out to the Soviet Union in his quest to ease Cold War tensions, Kennedy says the United States will no longer conduct nuclear tests in the atmosphere. He also proposes a treaty on banning nuclear tests, period: in the atmosphere, underground, underneath the oceans, or in space. JFK also acknowledges the huge sacrifices made by the Russians during World War II—an estimated 26.6 million Soviets, the majority of them civilians, died—and says that both Washington and Moscow should search for common ground:

> Let us not be blind to our differences—but let us also direct attention to our common interests and to the means by which those differences can be resolved. And if we cannot end now our differences, at least we can help make the world safe for diversity. For, in the final analysis, our most basic common link is that we all inhabit this small planet. We all breathe the same air. We all cherish our children's future. And we are all mortal.

What's interesting here is that some conspiracy theorists suspect that the Soviets had something to do with Kennedy's murder five months later. What makes them think that the Kremlin—or Cubans—calculated that they'd be better served with Lyndon Johnson in the Oval Office?

After all, following the previous fall's Cuban Missile Crisis, relations between Washington and Moscow were on the upswing. After coming perilously close to Armageddon—analysts estimate up to one

* There is also evidence that Oswald had praised Kennedy as well. Paul Gregory noted that both Oswald and Marina called JFK a "nice young man," and "I never heard him say anything derogatory about Kennedy. He seemed to admire the man" (WC Testimony, Vol. IX – Page 148). George de Mohrenschildt testified that Oswald had once called Kennedy "an excellent President, full of energy, full of good ideas." (WC Testimony, Vol. IX – Page 255). Though both also made comments that Oswald was unstable.

hundred million Americans and one hundred million Soviets might have been killed in a nuclear exchange—both JFK and Khrushchev recognized that there had to be a better way.

Khrushchev, in fact, was so moved by Kennedy's olive-branch speech that he called it the best address by an American president since Franklin Roosevelt, and Soviet newspapers, state-controlled, were ordered to reprint it in full.

Kennedy later said that he wanted to visit Moscow—no sitting president had ever visited the Soviet capital—a journey he thought could ease tensions further.[78]

June (undated)—New Orleans

Marina finds Oswald's pro-Cuba leaflets. He tells her something she already knows: that he likes Cuba, its system, and its leader, Fidel Castro.

"Do you want them (meaning the Kennedy administration) attacking little Cuba?" he asks.

"No," Marina says, and tells her husband to "sit there and play your childish games." She's unhappy that Oswald is dabbling in politics again, but at least he's not playing with his rifle.

It was also around this time that Marina says she'll go back to the Soviet Union—if he gives her a divorce. He refuses.[79]

June—Dallas—Dealey Plaza

The Texas School Book Depository (TSBD) Company consolidates most of its operations in the former Sexton building (a wholesale grocer) at 411 Elm Street, at the corner of Elm and Houston in the historic West End of Dallas. But the TSBD also has another location at 1917 N. Houston Street, a few blocks north.

After the move, it was noticed that the upper floors of the building were oil-soaked from items which Sexton & Co. had stored. The TSBD's manager, Roy S. Truly, thought the oil would penetrate the depository's cardboard book cartons. He ordered the floors replaced with plywood sheets. This meant work crews would have to move cartons from one side of the vast floor to the other, sometimes stacking them up to allow the floor-laying crew access.

June 19—The White House

Despite his talk of reaching out to Castro, Kennedy approves a CIA program designed to sabotage that island nation's infrastructure.[80]

June 23—Bonn, West Germany

Beginning a tour of Western Europe, Kennedy rides through the West German capital as he prefers—standing exposed in an open car—with Secret Service agents relegated to a follow-up vehicle.

June 24—New Orleans

Hoping to leave the United States for either Cuba or the Soviet Union, Oswald applies for a new passport. Had he been able to leave the US in 1963 as he wished, Oswald would not have been living in Dallas on November 22.

June 25—New Orleans

Oswald receives his new passport.

June 25—Hanau, West Germany

Standing up at times, Kennedy rides in X-100 as he reviews US troops at Fliegerhorst Kaserne, an Army base. An Army officer is with JFK, but Secret Service agents are not on the Lincoln's rear bumper.

June 25—Moscow

Acting on Kennedy's instructions, American negotiator Averell Harriman signals US agreement with Soviet officials on a treaty which would ban testing of nuclear weapons in the atmosphere, in space, or under water.

June 26—West Berlin

Kennedy again rides in the open, standing up next to Mayor Willy Brandt and Chancellor Konrad Adenauer. Unlike the previous day, he is surrounded at times by Secret Service agents who jog alongside his car and/or hug the rear bumper. Excited spectators can be seen reaching out to touch the president's hand; they are pushed back. During some portions of the motorcade, West Berliners hang out of windows and balconies, dropping confetti on the car.

At Checkpoint Charlie, Kennedy climbed the stairs to a wooden platform that allowed him to look over the *mauer*, or wall, into East Berlin itself. Just beyond "no man's land"—the death strip on the communist side—there were numerous buildings and windows. Yet Kennedy stood out in the open, standing still as he took in the view. Armed East German soldiers stared back. It was a nightmare for the Secret Service.

June 26—Dublin, Ireland

Kennedy arrives in his ancestral homeland for a sentimental three-day visit. Before his arrival, Irish authorities received three separate death threats against him.

Two came in the form of anonymous telephone messages to the police, while a third was received by the *Independent* newspaper. One warned that a sniper would be on a rooftop overlooking the route that Kennedy would take from Shannon Airport into Dublin. Another vowed that Kennedy would be done in by a bomb along the way.

Police took no chances, deploying 6,404 officers the evening of Kennedy's arrival—nearly half the country's entire force—with 2,690 lining the motorcade route. Yet newsreels show JFK walking casually on the airport tarmac, and standing, exposed, during an arrival ceremony. After a troop review, he stood still again for nearly three minutes more while delivering remarks.

Despite the threats, Kennedy is shown standing up and waving to crowds; his car was flanked by four police officers on motorcycles and followed by his Secret Service follow-up car.

The crowds were so thick that as Kennedy arrived at the Dublin residence of the American ambassador, his limousine slowed to a crawl, and he was forced to get out and walk. "Crowds don't threaten me," he told the ambassador, Matthew McCloskey. "It's that fellow standing on the roof with a gun that I worry about."[81]

June 27—Dublin

Another day, another risky motorcade as JFK rides through Dublin. A portion of the non-bulletproof bubble top is attached; the president stands up for all to see.

The rest of Kennedy's Irish sojourn—he left on June 29th—also showed him walking and being driven about in public, quite exposed to potential harm.

June 29-30—New Orleans

Acting on Oswald's orders, Marina writes the Soviet Embassy in Washington, asking it to expedite visas for them and daughter June. Such letters, he told her, should contain "more tears and fewer facts." He added a postscript in English, demanding financial assistance from the Soviet government, just as he had from the US government a year earlier.[82]

July 1—New Orleans

Oswald checks out a new book: *Portrait of a President* by William Manchester. It's about John F. Kennedy and the April 1961 to April 1962 period of his presidency. Manchester captured something unique about JFK: That time was short, that every day mattered, and that he was, in political terms, "the biggest target in the land."

As Oswald read, his eyes may have fixated on one particular passage in the book's final pages. It concerned Manchester's observation that JFK had pockets of disapproval around the country, and was not nearly as admired as Abraham Lincoln had been:[83]

> He has a weaker grip on the nation's heartstrings, and the reason isn't that he hasn't been shot.[84] *

What did Oswald think when he read this? The idea to shoot Walker, just weeks earlier, had been given to him by George de Mohrenschildt. Did Manchester inadvertently plant a seed in the mind of the unstable, volatile Oswald?

And for what it's worth, in the days before and after Oswald checked out Manchester's book, he may have seen television coverage of Kennedy's triumphant European tour, which featured JFK riding in one open car after another amid tall buildings with countless open windows. *Lots* of open windows.

After finishing *Portrait of a President*, Oswald then checked out a book by JFK himself, the Pulitzer prize-winning *Profiles in Courage*.[85]

July 1—Rome

From Fiumicino Airport, Kennedy rides into the city in an open car, a distance of some twenty miles. Italian motorcycle policemen flank the vehicle, but Secret Service agents travel well behind.

* Manchester's comment seems odd, given that during the twelve-month period his book covered, Kennedy's Gallup approval hovered steadily in the upper 70s. The final Gallup poll taken before his assassination showed it down some 20 points to 58 percent. Most presidents in our current, hyper-partisan era would be delighted to have 58 percent approval.

July 2—Rome and Naples

Kennedy rides in an open car, often standing so he can be better seen by cheering crowds. As is often the case, bystanders are often just a few yards from the president. The crowds are so thick that his car often slows to a crawl.

July 11—Irving

Ruth Paine writes again to Marina in New Orleans. She invites Marina to move back to Texas and move in with her. "If Lee doesn't wish to live with you any more, and prefers that you go to the Soviet Union, think about the possibility of living with me," she writes. "I would be happy to be an aunt to you and the children."[86]

July 14—New Orleans

Marina responds joyfully to Paine's offer: "Dear, dear Ruth!...Sweet Ruth, I am so grateful for your good and sympathetic heart." Previously, Marina threatened Lee that she would leave him and move in with Ruth and said that "it has been the cause of many of our arguments."[87]

After a hellish thirteen months with her wife-beating husband in America, Marina now had her escape hatch.

July 17—New Orleans

Oswald is so self-absorbed that he doesn't realize it's Marina's birthday until she glumly reminds him. After dinner, he takes her to a drugstore across the street and buys her face powder and a Coca-Cola.[88]

July 19—New Orleans

Oswald is fired—again. Just two months after being hired by the Reily Foods Company as a machinery greaser, he was terminated for being a poor employee. The head of the company's personnel department had weighed firing him for weeks, and his initial supervisor said he would not recommend Oswald to a future employer.[89]

But there was much more than that. Oswald was also insolent and a malcontent. He once asked his supervisor, Charles Le Blanc, "Do you like it here?" Thinking it was a reference to the employer, Le Blanc said yes, that he had been at Reily for eight years.

"Oh, hell, I didn't mean this place," Oswald said. Oswald said he was referring to "this damn country."

But beyond incompetence, laziness, and a poor attitude, Oswald was also considered a kook. Le Blanc told the Warren Commission that Oswald would walk around pointing his forefinger at coworkers and pretend to shoot them.

"He would go, 'Pow!'" Le Blanc said, adding, "Boy, what a crackpot this guy is!"[90]

Oswald's violent nature, his hatred of America, and his desire to shoot someone—anyone, it seems—are on full display here.*

July 22—New Orleans

Oswald, the critic of American capitalism and what he considers its disregard for the little guy, files again for unemployment benefits.

It was also about this time that Oswald had finished Manchester's *Portrait of a President*. In another burst of delusion, he told Marina that in twenty years, he'd be president or prime minister himself.[91]

July 25—New Orleans

Oswald learns that the Marine Corps has rejected his request to review the undesirable discharge he was given in 1959.

---

* Oswald also disappeared frequently from his job to hang out at a garage next door that was run by Adrian Alba. A gun enthusiast, Alba had gun magazines lying around which Oswald would read. He testified that they once had a discussion about what kind of bullets would do the most damage to a human. (Testimony of Adrian Album WC, Vol. X, 233)

He also visits a clothing store run by Carlos Bringuier, who is involved with an anti-Castro group. Oswald, lying, says he wants to fight Castro and his communist government.[92]

August 7—Washington/Hyannis

An event that will later shape events in Dallas: At 11:43 a.m., Kennedy's secretary, Evelyn Lincoln, rushes into the Oval Office to tell the president that Jacqueline Kennedy has gone into labor—five and a half weeks early.

Before rushing to the Cape, JFK learned that Jackie had been rushed to the Otis Air Force Base hospital, where her obstetrician John Walsh was preparing an emergency cesarean procedure. Walsh gave the worried father a mixed message: Jackie would be fine, but a baby born that prematurely had just a 50/50 chance of surviving.[93]

Upon arrival, Kennedy learned that Patrick Bouvier Kennedy—the name he and Jackie had chosen—had been born and weighed four pounds, ten ounces.

But Walsh had bad news: the infant was suffering from "hyaline membrane disease" (today known as respiratory distress syndrome). A film was covering the air sacs on Patrick's lungs, interfering with their ability to supply oxygen to the bloodstream.

It was decided that Patrick should be taken immediately to Boston Children's Hospital, where the facilities were better. This upset Jackie, who didn't want to be separated from her son.

"Nothing must happen to Patrick," JFK told his mother-in-law, Janet Auchincloss, "because I just can't bear to think of the effect it might have on Jackie."[94]

August 9—Boston Children's Hospital

At 4:04 a.m., Patrick Bouvier Kennedy, aged thirty-nine hours, dies. A heartbroken JFK, who was holding his son's tiny fingers when he passed, says quietly, "He put up quite a fight. He was a beautiful baby." He then goes into a nearby boiler room and weeps for ten minutes.

He returned to Otis AFB to see Jackie, and as he described Patrick's final moments, Kennedy broke down again, sinking to his knees and crying.

In their shared grief, Jackie told him: "There's just one thing I couldn't stand," she said in a whisper. "If I ever lose you…"

"I know, I know…," he said quietly.[95]

New Orleans

Oswald is arrested. It happens when Bringuier hears that a pro-Castro demonstrator is handing out "Fair Play for Cuba" leaflets on Canal Street. He and two friends go there—and discover that the pro-Castro demonstrator is Oswald. Bringuier is livid—and we're shown again a prime example of Oswald's deceitful, dishonest behavior.

Passersby turn on Oswald, calling him "Traitor! Communist!" and saying, "Go to Cuba!" Some even said, "Kill him!"

Two cop cars pulled up. Oswald, Bringuier, and his two buddies were tossed in jail. Unable to post bond, Oswald was held overnight; the others paid and were released.

August 10—New Orleans

After spending the night behind bars, Oswald requests to meet with a local FBI agent, and the bureau's local office sends John Quigley. Quigley, a twenty-seven-year FBI veteran, thinks Oswald is lying about the Fair Play for Cuba Committee, because he is evasive and silent when asked numerous questions. Oswald also claims to know who A. J. Hidell is (which is certainly true, given that Oswald had invented him out of thin air).

Quigley described Oswald's overall demeanor as "antagonistic to some extent, not overly so. He certainly was not friendly."

Why did Oswald request an interview with the FBI? In a February 7, 1964, affidavit provided to the Warren Commission, Quigley said "this was a normal situation that has occurred many times of persons in custody of the police wish to talk to an FBI agent. We have them come to our headquarters in New Orleans all the time to talk to us. So I didn't consider this unusual at all."

Quigley later destroyed the notes he took during the interview. Asked by Warren Commission lawyer Sam Stern if it was usual practice to destroy notes after an interview, Quigley said "It is the usual practice to destroy your notes after the completed work has been returned to you for proofing to make certain that the information is accurate, then you do destroy them."[96]

After paying a ten-dollar fine, Oswald was released and went home. Over the next few nights, Marina would heap criticism upon him over his pro-Cuba delusions. "You're nobody special," she would tell him. "One Lee Oswald can't do anything. Do you think you're such a great man that you're the only one who can help?"[97]

Holyhood Cemetery, Chestnut Hill, MA

Making arrangements for Patrick's funeral is too much for Kennedy to bear. A longtime family friend, Frank Morrissey, is asked to help. He chooses a white gown for Patrick and a small white coffin.

Kennedy, distraught, placed a gold Saint Christopher's Medal, one that he had worn since Jackie gave it to him when they were married, inside. It was a small service—Jackie, too upset to attend, remained in the hospital—and after everyone left, Kennedy was left alone with Cardinal Cushing. Kennedy wrapped his arms around the tiny coffin.

"It's awfully lonely here," he said quietly.

"Jack, you had better go along," the Cardinal told him gently. "God is good. Nothing more can be done. Death isn't the end of all, but the beginning."

Prior to the service, Kennedy had ordered the coffin closed, telling Morrissey, "Frank, I want you to make sure they close the coffin when I die."[98]

The death of Patrick Kennedy set off a series of events that would lead to something extraordinary: Jackie's decision to visit Texas three months later with her husband.

August 14—Otis Air Force Base

A rarity: President and Mrs. Kennedy are seen holding hands as they leave the hospital where Jackie has been recuperating since the death of Patrick Kennedy. Displays of public affection between the two—even holding hands—are practically unheard of.

"It was a touching moment," Jackie's Secret Service agent, Clint Hill, told me decades later. Just before they moved into the White House, Jackie herself had said that "I would describe Jack as rather like me in that his life is an iceberg. The public life is above the water—& the private life—is submerged…."[99]

Mid-August

After nearly two years of rehabilitation and exercise under the watchful eye of Dr. Kraus, President Kennedy's condition is vastly improved.

He is able to endure grueling travel, like the recent European trip, golf, and probably most fulfilling of all, toss two-year old John into the air.

Kennedy said that physically, he felt better than at any time in his adult life. Yet, perhaps out of habit, or a nagging worry about regressing, he continued to use his back brace. The back brace that helped him sit up straight.[100]

August 16—Moscow

The Soviet government sends condolences to President and Mrs. Kennedy on the death of Patrick Kennedy.

August 17—New Orleans

Oswald's arrest and pro-Cuban activities win him an invitation to appear on a New Orleans radio program. As usual, he lies numerous times about his background.

August 21—New Orleans

Oswald is invited to appear on the same radio program again—this time with anti-Castro activist Bringuier.

By now host Bill Stuckey had done his homework and learned about Oswald's undesirable discharge from the Marines, his defection to Moscow, and his attempt to renounce his American citizenship—all things that Oswald had previously hidden or lied about. Oswald was distressed at having his lies exposed, and Marina, although not understanding the English, could tell by the tone of her husband's voice on the radio that he lied during the interview. Oswald was devastated.[101]

August 21—New Orleans

Humiliated on the radio, Oswald turns to his best—his only—friend: his rifle.

Marina recalled that on numerous nights, he would sit on the darkened front porch of their shabby apartment, opening and closing the bolt for hours on end, sometimes aiming at imaginary targets. "Fidel needs defenders," he told her. "I'm going to be a revolutionary."[102]

Aug. 24—The State Department

In what would become known as the "Hilsman cable" (or "Cable 243"), presidential advisors Roger Hilsman, Averell Harriman, and Michael Forrestal draft a cable to the new US ambassador in South Vietnam, Henry Cabot Lodge Jr. The cable says that the US should "make detailed plans as to how we might bring about Diem's replacement

[South Vietnam's president Ngô Đình Diem] if this should become necessary."

The cable, which was endorsed by JFK, is later seen as an implied endorsement for the November ouster (and assassination) of Diem and his brother. Kennedy later regretted his support of the cable, which put US support of a coup in South Vietnam on the record.[103]

August—New Orleans (undated)

Craziness: Determined to get to Cuba and help Castro, Oswald decides to hijack a plane and force it to fly to Havana. The scheme reflects everything that Oswald is: a violent man, a delusional man. An unstable crackpot.

He was dead serious. There were no longer direct flights between the United States and Cuba, after all, and he was determined to get to Havana, possibly meet Castro, and fight for his revolutionary cause.

He began working out to prepare. Marina recalls him doing deep-knee bends, arm exercises, leaping about the apartment in his underwear—obviously your typical airplane-hijacking regimen. June Oswald, all of eighteen months old and not realizing her daddy was insane, loved such performances. When he was done prancing about in his skivvies, he rubbed some sort of liniment all over his body and took a cold shower.

June wasn't the only one laughing. "Junie," Marina said, "our papa is out of his mind." She pleaded with her husband. "For God's sake, don't do such a thing."

Oswald's plan was this: he would buy tickets under different names—in 1963, ID wasn't required to buy an airplane ticket—and sit in the front of the cabin with the gun he had purchased in January, while Marina sat in the rear with one. Of course, she didn't have a gun and, thanks to Lee, didn't speak English. At this point, Oswald realized that even by his loony standards, that was a problem. "That script won't do," he admitted. "I'll have to think of something new." He left the room, then bolted back in shouting, "Hands up and don't make any noise!" Oswald told her that if she pulled out a gun, they'd understand. He added that he had been shopping around for a weapon for her to use.

"Only a crazy man would think up something like this," she said.[104]

She was right, of course, but Oswald wasn't dissuaded. According to Marina, he began collecting airline schedules and maps, measuring the distances between places with a ruler and wondering how much fuel it would take to fly to make it to Cuba. He also told Marina that he might need another partner in crime.[105]

It took Oswald about two weeks to realize that even by his untethered-to-reality standards, it was lunacy. Wasn't there an easier way to get to Cuba? Then it hit him: there were direct flights between Mexico City and Havana. He would go to Mexico City, then, and fly from there. All he needed was a visa, and how difficult could that be?*

"I'll go there," he announced to Marina. He considered himself some sort of media figure now—he had been on the radio after all, and in the newspapers—and surely that would impress the Cubans into giving him a visa. "I'll show them my clippings, show them how much I've done for Cuba, and explain how hard it is to help in America. And how above all I want to help Cuba." And, pointing at his Marina's bulging stomach—she was now seven months pregnant—announced he would name his son (it surely would be a boy) "Fidel."[106]

And so Oswald began preparing to travel to Mexico, even though some conspiracists say no, it couldn't possibly have been him.

Saigon

Henry Cabot Lodge Jr., the American Ambassador to South Vietnam, sends a cable reporting—or warning—that "We are launched on a course from which there is no turning back: the overthrow of the [Ngô Đình] Diem government."[107]

---

* On the other hand, if you were loony enough to try and hijack a plane to Cuba, why would an entry visa be a concern?

The White House

Kennedy discusses the Lodge cable with his secretaries of state (Rusk), defense (McNamara), and treasury (Dillon), as well as CIA director McCone. He authorizes a reply to Lodge, which includes the statement that "The USG [United States Government] will support a coup which has good chance of succeeding but plans no direct involvement of U.S. Armed Forces."[108]

At this late stage of the Kennedy presidency, let's take a step back to explore what's happening here. In supporting the overthrow of a foreign government, but declining overt American involvement, the Kennedy administration was, in essence, acting no differently than its predecessor. The presidency of Dwight Eisenhower was bookended by covert operations to topple two governments that were not deemed to be in the American interest. In the early years there were Iran and Guatemala. In the end there was Cuba.

In 1951, Mohammad Mosaddegh was democratically elected as prime minister of Iran. But one of his most significant policies—the nationalization of the Iranian oil industry, which had been built largely by the British in the early twentieth century—didn't sit too well with the British government. In August 1953, the CIA, working with its British equivalent, MI6, engineered Mosaddegh's ouster. The reigning monarch, Mohammad Reza Pahlavi—the Shah—would rule Iran until his own ouster twenty-six years later. His 1979 fall led to the hardline Islamic regime that has been a thorn in America's side ever since. Given the troubles that the United States has had with Iran over the past four-plus decades, historians are justified today in wondering whether American and British meddling seven decades ago was worth it.

The next year, Eisenhower, essentially dusting off a CIA plan that was first formed during the Truman era, ordered the removal of Guatemalan president Jacobo Árbenz. Eisenhower had come into office promising a tough anti-communist line. In this context, Árbenz, a progressive leader, was seen as a problem. But the more salient reason for his ouster was pressure from the powerful banana* conglomerate United Fruit Company (today Chiquita Brands International), which dominated Guatemala.†

Of course, there's much more to these examples of American meddling than oil and bananas—which occurred against the backdrop of the intensifying Cold War competition between the United States and Soviet Union—than can be told here, but the point is that the United States had no qualms about covertly intervening in the internal affairs of others when it saw the need. But not with troops.

Eisenhower's CIA had also formed the basis of the previously discussed Operation Zapata—the Bay of Pigs—that had been such a disaster for Kennedy. Even so, and like his predecessor, JFK—who fancied himself a cold warrior who was determined to face down communism both in southeast Asia and in America's own backyard—was enamored with covert action in both Vietnam and Cuba. But, and also like Eisenhower, Kennedy was cautious. Eisenhower refused significant involvement in Vietnam; in 1961 Kennedy rejected a Pentagon recommendation to send two hundred thousand troops there.[109] Even so, there were now some sixteen thousand American military "advisors" in South Vietnam, up from just eight hundred when he took office. Between this, and the previously discussed order to approve Operation Ranch Hand—the vast use of Agent Orange against communist forces—it can be argued that Kennedy had done far more in Vietnam

---

* Beyond the need to "fight communism," there were personal conflicts galore behind the decision to get rid of Árbenz. Secretary of State John Foster Dulles's New York law firm, Sullivan and Cromwell, represented United Fruit, while his brother Allen—the director of the CIA—had served on its board of trustees and was a major shareholder. Meanwhile, President Eisenhower's personal secretary, Ann Whitman, was married to Ed Whitman, who just happened to be United Fruit's top public relations officer. Ed Whitman even produced a film, "Why the Kremlin Hates Bananas," which portrayed United Fruits on the front lines of the Cold War. (RS#01: Background on the Guatemalan Coup of 1954, educational materials developed through the Baltimore County History Labs Program, a partnership between Baltimore County Public Schools and the UMBC Center for History Education.)

† Guatemala can be considered the source of the term "banana republic," incidentally. It is used to describe a backward or politically unstable country with an economy dependent upon the exportation of a limited-resource product, such as minerals—or bananas.

than his predecessor. And yet assassination conspiracists would have us believe that it was JFK who was soft on communism.

August—New Orleans (undated)

While Oswald is dreaming of being a hijacker and trying to gin up interest in his Fair Play for Cuba Committee (he never does recruit any known members), getting arrested and lying about himself on the radio, another FBI agent in the Crescent City, Warren de Brueys, decides to check him out. He speaks with his former employer, the Reily Foods Co., and his landlady. He concludes that Oswald is just an oddball, a nut. But Oswald isn't considered dangerous—he has made no known threats to anyone.[110]

September 1—New Orleans

Oswald writes to both the Communist Party of the United States and the Socialist Workers Party in New York, asking for contacts in the Washington-Baltimore area—"I and my family are moving to that area in October."

There's no evidence, beyond writing these letters, that Oswald really intended to move to the East Coast.[111]

September 2—Hyannis Port

In an interview with CBS's Walter Cronkite, Kennedy is asked about Vietnam. He chooses his words carefully. "I don't think that unless a greater effort is made by the [South Vietnamese] government to win popular support that the war can be won out there," he says. And knowing that his words would be analyzed in Saigon, he adds for emphasis:

> "In the final analysis, it is their war. They are the ones who have to win it or lose it. We can help them, we can give them equipment, we can send our men out there as advisors, but they have to win it…We are prepared to continue to assist them, but I don't think

the war can be won unless the people support the effort and, in my opinion, in the last two months, the government has gotten out of touch with the people."

The president, under pressure from conservatives to remain in Vietnam, threw them a bone, claiming that "I don't agree with those who say we should withdraw. That would be a great mistake."

And yet Kennedy's real thinking pointed towards shrinking the American footprint in Southeast Asia. Thurston Clarke, in "JFK's Last Hundred Days," points out that "the two statements made no logical sense because his remark about not withdrawing was a smokescreen meant to conceal his real agenda and to avoid being 'damned everywhere as a communist appeaser.'" He had privately told advisors, senior Democrats in Congress and others of that real agenda; the line about staying "was simply not true."[112]

The roots of Kennedy's caution on Vietnam can be traced to a 1951 dinner in Saigon with an American diplomat, Edward Guillen, who told him that fighting a war in Vietnam would be a grave mistake.[113] The shattering French defeat three years later at Dien Bien Phu reinforced this view.

Conspiracists who insist that Kennedy was assassinated for trying to avoid getting sucked into a Vietnam quagmire often forget that JFK's position dovetailed with two of the greatest American military minds of the twentieth century—both deeply conservative Republicans—Eisenhower and MacArthur. One of the first things Eisenhower did as president was to stop the carnage in Korea; he knew better than to get involved in a new, and unwinnable, conflict in Asia. After Dien Bien Phu, White House tapes showed Eisenhower refusing to send US troops to Vietnam. Several hundred advisors were sent later, but overall, Eisenhower did far less than what the military establishment might have expected of a conservative five-star general. "One of Ike's greatest accomplishments," wrote historian Stephen Ambrose in 1981, "was staying out of Vietnam in the face of intense pressure."[114] And, as has been mentioned earlier in this book, MacArthur told JFK to stay out of

Vietnam. His quote to Kennedy is worth repeating: "Anyone wanting to commit ground troops to Asia should have his head examined."[115]

Yet it was Kennedy, many conspiracy theorists insist, who was some sort of outlier who had to be eliminated.

September 5—The White House

Kennedy, who had slipped in his commitment to Dr. Kraus to keep exercising—and hopefully get rid of his back brace—tells secretary Evelyn Lincoln that he was experiencing "discomfort." The back brace, which helps him sit up straight, will continue to be worn.[116]

September 7—Havana

In a joint interview with the Associated Press and United Press International, Castro, according to UPI, calls Kennedy a "cretin." AP's Daniel Harker, however, reports that Castro says something far more controversial, namely that "United States leaders should think that if they are aiding terrorist plans to eliminate Cuban leaders, they themselves will not be safe."[117]

Conspiracists often seize upon this to support their view that Castro may have been involved in the president's murder. But did Castro really say it? The alleged quote ran in the AP's version of the interview. Yet the UPI story, which was picked up by the *New York Times*, didn't mention it at all, an odd omission for something so explosive and newsworthy. It's entirely possible that Castro was misquoted or taken out of context—as politicians and public figures often are.[118]

September 9—The White House

In an interview with NBC's Chet Huntley and David Brinkley, Kennedy is asked whether American aid can be reduced.

"Only if we felt that such a reduction would aid the struggle there. As of today we have not made that judgment."

He was then asked about the domino theory—meaning that if one country in southeast Asia were to fall to Communism, others would quickly topple, like a line of dominoes.*

"I believe it," Kennedy said. For this reason, he said, the United States should remain in Vietnam and that "we should not withdraw." He also knocks down a question from Huntley about whether the CIA makes its own policy in Vietnam.

As he had with Cronkite the week before, Kennedy expressed his view that the United States should remain in Vietnam. The two high-profile comments were almost certainly made for public consumption, and to mollify his hardline critics. The real Kennedy policy was to be found in the private discussions, which revealed his decision to withdraw one thousand advisors by the end of the year.

September 8–9—Hyannis Port

Kennedy thinks of his death again, during a conversation with longtime friend Charles Bartlett. The two old friends, plus their wives—the Bartletts famously introduced JFK and Jackie to each other at a Georgetown dinner party—go out on the Kennedy family yacht, the *Honey Fitz*, even though it is rainy and gloomy. In an interview years later, Bartlett will recall the conversation clearly:

> "It just was interesting that we would discuss it at some length," he said. Kennedy asked him "What Lyndon would be like as President…but of course he had that kind of mind that he was always talking about all the eventualities."
>
> Bartlett told another story:
>
> I do remember one time down in Middleburg [Virginia] we were driving along a back country road, and a car shot by the Secret Service car and us. And he was shaken a little bit by this car going by. And he said, "The secret service should have stopped that car."

* The "domino theory" had first been coined by Eisenhower in 1954.

> And then he disliked the fact that he was showing concern and he said, "Charlie, that man might have shot you." But the thing obviously was on his mind."[119]

Thoughts of death were never far beneath the surface. In her 1968 autobiography, one of Kennedy's doctors, Janet Travell, recalled sitting poolside with him one day in Florida. Suddenly he asked, "What do you think of the rule that for the last hundred years every President of the United States elected in a year divisible by twenty died in office?"[120]

Travell told him not to believe in such coincidences, saying "The odds against it are too great." In Kennedy's mind, they weren't, given that of the thirty-three men who preceded him in the presidency, seven had died in office: one in five.*

That same weekend, Kennedy received a message from Khrushchev, expressing his hope that the nuclear test ban treaty would "lead to a real turning point and the end of the Cold War." Kennedy's reply, via the State Department, called recent US-Soviet communications "encouraging" and stated that the president "hopes it will be possible to proceed with the solution of other problems."[121]

After the narrow avoidance of nuclear war the prior fall, this Kennedy-Khrushchev exchange was the latest in a series of communiques that indicated improving ties between Washington and Moscow. As mentioned, Kennedy's American University speech was the template. But it was hardly different from President Eisenhower's Soviet outreach, which included hosting Khrushchev for a two-week tour of the United States in 1959.

Hardliners were upset with Kennedy because he resisted their entreaties on Vietnam? As mentioned before, Eisenhower's National Security Council and Joint Chiefs actually urged him to drop atomic weapons on at least two occasions: to save the French at Dien Bien Phu in 1954, and during the Taiwan Strait crisis in 1958, when China

---

* William Henry Harrison's death after just a month in office began the streak, followed by Abraham Lincoln, James Garfield, and William McKinley, all of whom were assassinated. Following them were Warren Harding and Franklin D. Roosevelt, both of whom died of natural causes. Kennedy's assassination continued the sad streak, and it nearly continued in 1981, when Ronald Reagan was shot.

shelled the islands of Quemoy and Matsu. Eisenhower, the five-star general turned commander in chief, would have nothing to do with it.

"You guys must be crazy," he told his advisors. "We aren't going to drop an atomic weapon on Asiatic peoples twice in ten years."[122]

It wasn't difficult for Kennedy to reject similarly bad advice. Yet it's JFK who had to be eliminated, conspiracists claim, so the generals could have their war. Kennedy was even like Eisenhower in another way. JFK gave newsmen Cronkite, Huntley, and Brinkley double-talk on Vietnam; Eisenhower delighted in using similar tactics during his day. Asked by his press secretary, James Hagerty, what he would say to reporters about using atomic weapons during the Taiwan crisis, Eisenhower replied, "Jim, don't worry about it. I'll confuse them in the press conference." At the news conference, Ike did just that, giving a long, rambling answer, some three minutes' worth of babbling, and everyone—but the president himself—was confused.[123]

September 12—The White House

Kennedy is shown a report evaluating the prospects of a preemptive nuclear attack on the Soviet Union. The joint chiefs of staff plan says the last three months of 1963 present a good opportunity to take on the Soviets. Kennedy, appalled at the prospect of nuclear conflict, says "preemption is not possible for us." He tries to mollify his defense chiefs: "This is a valuable conclusion growing out of an excellent report. This argues in favor of a conventional force."[124]

Newport, Rhode Island

It's the Kennedys' tenth wedding anniversary. At Hammersmith Farm—Jackie's childhood home and the site of their wedding reception—she gives JFK a warm embrace, a public display of affection that was almost never seen before Patrick's death the month before but was now increasingly common.

She later wrote Charles Bartlett that she and Jack had grown much closer since the baby's death, and that JFK had helped "re-attach" her to life. While JFK would have lived a "worthwhile life" if they hadn't married, she told Bartlett, hers would have been a "wasteland."[125]

September 13—White House

In a press release the White House says President Kennedy will visit Texas later that year. No dates or specific information is given, but newspapers report that Kennedy would have "a breakfast in Dallas, luncheon in Fort Worth, coffee in San Antonio and dinner in Houston."[126]

September 14—Dallas

Buell Wesley Frazier, an Irving, Texas, neighbor of Ruth Paine and Marina Oswald, finds work at the Texas School Book Depository.

The White House

Showing that his comments earlier in the month to NBC and CBS about staying the course in Vietnam didn't reflect his true position, Kennedy lays a trap for President Diem. He tells Defense Secretary Robert McNamara and Joint Chiefs Chairman Maxwell Taylor, who are about to visit Saigon, to tell Diem to make political reforms or the United States will pull out.

Of course, if Diem did make those reforms, it would bolster the case for an American withdrawal, as Taylor later wrote, "in about two years."[127]

September 19—New York

While JFK dines with a friend in Manhattan, two men in a station wagon toss a paint bomb at his parked limo. The car and a Secret Service agent are splattered.[128]

September 20—United Nations

Kennedy tells world leaders of his hope that the Limited Nuclear Test Ban Treaty can serve as a foundation for greater peace efforts in the world. He also reaches out to Moscow in another way, suggesting a joint moon mission between the United States and Soviet Union. In Moscow, the communist party newspaper *Pravda* reports that the Soviet government doesn't reject JFK's offer, but calls it "premature."[129]

Kennedy, through Under Secretary of State Averell Harriman and UN Ambassador Adlai Stevenson, also approved a plan for ABC News journalist Lisa Howard, who knew Fidel Castro, to act as a secret liaison to him.[130]

September 21—Newport

A Presidential Murder Movie: President Kennedy makes a home movie depicting his death.

Robert L. Knudsen, a former White House photographer, said he shot the movie on a weekend in Newport, RI, in September 1963. He told the story in a 1983 book *A Hero for Our Time* by Ralph G. Martin, published by Macmillan.

"The President wrote the script," said Knudsen. "He just called me over one day and said they wanted to have some fun and shoot a movie."

Book excerpt:

> "'The man with the binoculars watched President Kennedy as he got off the Honey Fitz at Newport and walked down the long pier,' the book says.
>
> "Suddenly Kennedy clutched his chest and fell flat on the ground. Walking behind him was the dignified Countess Crespi and her small son. Both simply stepped over the President's body—as if he were not there—and continued walking toward the shore.
>
> "Right behind the countess came Jacqueline Kennedy, and she, too, daintily stepped over her husband's body. Behind her

was Red Fay, Under Secretary of the Navy and Kennedy's PT boat buddy. Fay stumbled and fell directly on the President's body. Just then, a gush of red (probably tomato juice) surged from the President's mouth, covering his sport shirt."

A report by The Associated Press dated Sept. 21, 1963, detailed a movie made in Newport but said it was Fay who lay down on the dock and Kennedy who stumbled over him. It's not known what became of the movie, which is not in the archives of the Kennedy Library in Boston.

September 22—New Orleans

Oswald's landlord, Jessie Garner, sees Lee loading his family's meager belongings into the back of Ruth Paine's station wagon. "I asked him if he was moving, since I was concerned that he owed about fifteen days' rent," Garner said. As he does to everyone, Oswald lies, saying he is staying, but that Marina is returning to Texas to have her baby and will return to New Orleans after that. Neither statement is true.[131]

In contrast to Garner's suspicions, Paine had a different thought as she watched Oswald load the car. She "was impressed" with what she remembered as his willingness to do "virtually all the packing and all the loading of things into the car." It was "gentlemanly," she would recall.

Paine told the Warren Commission in 1964, and this author in 2021, that Oswald was helpful for a very good reason: his rifle was among the belongings he was packing, something he chose to hide from Paine.

September 23—New Orleans

Paine drives Marina and June back to Texas. As they prepare to pull away, Oswald's emotional dependency on his wife is evident.

Said Paine: "He kissed her a very fond goodbye, both at home and then again at the gas station [a couple of blocks away, after Ruth's station wagon got a flat tire]."[132] Marina herself said Oswald was on the verge of tears as they parted. He looked, she said, "as a dog looks at its master."[133]

Oswald, the wifebeater, needed Marina more, as was now evident, than she needed him. As they parted, his eyes were the ones that watered up, not hers. Had Oswald made his way to Cuba, or inexplicably back to the Soviet Union, they might not have ever seen each other again.

Capitol Hill

The Senate ratifies the Nuclear Test Ban Treaty by an overwhelming majority, eighty to nineteen, well beyond the two-thirds majority required by the Constitution.

Presidential speechwriter Ted Sorensen would later say that President Kennedy considered the ratification of the treaty, which would go into effect on October 11, the greatest achievement of his presidency.[134]

New York

Lisa Howard throws a party and invites both William Attwood, a US delegate to the United Nations, and Carlos Lechuga, the Cuban ambassador to the UN, thus enabling Kennedy's liaison and Cuba's ambassador to meet informally.

September 24—Milford, Pennsylvania

Arriving for the dedication of a building for the Forest Service, President Kennedy is driven in a white convertible. A film shows no Secret Service agents on the bumper of the open car.

September 24—New Orleans

Oswald, always short on cash, gets his final unemployment check of thirty-three dollars. He probably cashes it on the twenty-fourth, which fits with Marina's recollection that Oswald always gets his checks on Tuesdays. Indeed, his previous check was cashed the week before—Tuesday the seventeenth.[135]

The date is important, because based on travel and eyewitness records, we know that Oswald was next spotted on Continental Trailways bus 5133, which left Houston for Laredo at 2:35 a.m. on Thursday the twenty-sixth. What isn't clear, after six decades, is his exact whereabouts in between and just how he got to Houston.

He may have left New Orleans on the twenty-fourth and gone not to Houston but Dallas—perhaps driven by two men who took him, that night, to the home of Silvia Odio, the daughter of a prominent anti-Castro activist. One of the men who showed up was reportedly an American named "Leon Oswald." Why would Oswald—whose pro-Castro stance cannot be doubted—meet with a Castro hater (Odio's father had been jailed in Cuba)? Conspiracy theorists say it's proof that Oswald (if it was even him at Odio's door, that is) was being framed for a future Kennedy assassination.* Or perhaps Oswald, who had earlier pretended to be anti-Castro with Carlos Bringuier in New Orleans, was again indulging in one of his professed *I Led 3 Lives* fantasies.

Even after all this time, conspiracy theorists aren't exactly sure. In *JFK and the Unspeakable*, James Douglass can't prove when the meeting occurred, noting vaguely that the Odio incident occurred "in the last week of September 1963,"[136] while John Newman says Oswald "is reported to have visited" Odio's home, but doesn't give a date.[137] Norman Mailer, meantime, agnostic about the assassination, notes that after Marina and Ruth Paine left for Irving, "Lee may or may not have remained in the apartment on Magazine Street for the next couple of days."[138] The University of Virginia's Larry Sabato, a preeminent

* Yet no specific details for Kennedy's Texas trip had been established at this point and wouldn't be until mid-November. Oswald assumed he'd be in Cuba by then—after getting a visa in Mexico City.

assassination scholar, notes that in the 1970s, Odio's testimony before the House Select Committee on Assassinations was "essentially credible," though Odio, when shown a photo of Oswald, said "I am not too sure of the man in that picture." Odio's sister Annie, meanwhile, says she did not hear anyone introduced that night as Leon Oswald.[139]

The most exhaustive individual investigation into this matter, which plays out over several pages of Bugliosi's masterwork, says that "the evidence of time and place compels the conclusion that Oswald could not have visited Odio on September 26 or 27, 1963, and most probably did not do so on September 25." And yet: "There are nevertheless countervailing reasons why we cannot automatically dismiss Odio's allegations—namely her credibility and corroborating evidence." Even so, Bugliosi, arguably the most talented prosecutor to ever set foot in a courtroom, would surely admit that this hardly rises to the "beyond a reasonable doubt" threshold that he had met in 105 of the 106 cases that he won over the course of his spectacular career.

What can be confirmed, however, is that by "the last week of September 1963" Oswald's wife had left him, he had lost yet another job, and he was determined to leave America again—barely a year after returning—to search for the fame and fulfillment that had always eluded him. His life, as Sabato notes, was "once again in shambles."[140]

September 25—Grand Forks, North Dakota

Another day, another open car with no Secret Service agents on the bumper, as Kennedy arrives at the University of North Dakota to give a speech.

Laramie, Wyoming

Arriving in the Cowboy State, Kennedy is driven to the University of Wyoming for another speech in an open car with no Secret Service agents on the bumper.

Billings, Montana

Driving to the Yellowstone County Fairgrounds, Kennedy is seen standing up in his open car, with no Secret Service agents on the bumper.

Houston

Given the certainty that Oswald will leave Houston early on the morning of Thursday, September 26, it's almost certain that he calls the home of Horace and Estelle Twiford and asks to speak to Horace, who is an official with the Socialist Labor Party of Texas. Oswald tells Mrs. Twiford that he is a member of the Fair Play for Cuba Committee and that he wants to discuss a few ideas with Horace before he (another of Oswald's lies) "flies" down to Mexico. Twiford, a merchant seaman, is away; they never speak.

Establishing a timeline for Oswald's whereabouts is critical at this late stage of his life, yet few conspiracy writers mention the Twiford call, which firmly places Oswald in Houston.*

September 26—New Orleans

At 2:35 a.m., Oswald boards Continental Trailways bus No. 5133, en route to Laredo, Texas.

What happened on the bus reveals that had things gone Oswald's way, he never would have been in Dallas on November 22. He intended, and had every reason to believe, that he was on his way to Cuba, according to a conversation he had with a British couple on the bus, John Bryan McFarland and Meryl McFarland.

The McFarlands recalled Oswald saying that he was traveling to Mexico because he could not travel directly to Cuba from the United States as it was against the law.

---

* Twiford's name, address, and two phone numbers were found in Oswald's address book, in his handwriting (CE 18, CE 2335, as described in Posner, 171).

Oswald appeared to embellish his importance, saying he was "the secretary of the New Orleans branch of the Fair Play for Cuba Organization, and that he was on his way to Cuba to see Castro if he could."[141]

Great Falls, Montana

Kennedy is seen standing up in his open car, with no Secret Service agents on the bumper.

Salt Lake City, Utah

As he is driven into Salt Lake City, Kennedy is seen standing up in his open car, with no Secret Service agents on the bumper.

Dallas

Kennedy's Texas trip begins to take shape. The *Dallas Morning News* reports that JFK will tour the Lone Star State November 21–22, including Dallas. The article notes that "specific details have not been worked out."[142]

The White House

A man crashes his pickup truck through the closed iron gates of the White House and drives almost to the North Portico before he is stopped. The driver, thirty-eight-year-old Doyle Allen Hicks of Waynesville, North Carolina, is unarmed and screaming "I want to see the president, the Communists are taking over in North Carolina!"[143]

US-Mexican Border

Between 1:30 and 2:00 p.m., Oswald crosses into Mexico. His tourist card is stamped, and at 2:15, he boards Flecha Roja bus No. 516 for the final leg of his trip to Mexico City.

Two more people remember encountering Oswald: Pamela Mumford and Patricia Winston, both from Australia, young women who were traveling in the United States and Mexico.

"He said that he had heard us speaking English and wondered where we came from," Mumford said.[144] *

To these total strangers, Oswald lied as usual, telling the women of his travels, including his time in the Soviet Union where he claimed that "he was studying there. He had an apartment in Moscow and was studying." Oswald said nothing of Minsk, nothing of being married, Mumford said. "But we noticed he had a gold wedding ring on his left hand."

Oswald also lied about having made "previous trips to Mexico City," Mumford recalled.

September 27—United Nations

At the UN Delegates' Lounge, Attwood meets Lechuga, and tells him a meeting with Castro has been authorized. Lechuga says he will inform Havana.

Mexico City

Before discussing Oswald's time in Mexico City, let's recap. He was clearly identified en route by numerous people who 1) recalled specific details—for example, his passport with the Russian stamps and his gold wedding ring—and 2) identified him on TV after the assassination—wearing the very same clothes they had seen him wearing on the bus.

And in the Mexican capital itself, "the evidence could hardly be more overwhelming," notes Bugliosi, "that Oswald (not an impersonator) did, in fact, go to the Cuban consulate and Soviet embassy for the purpose of securing an in-transit visa to Cuba ostensibly to be used by Oswald on his way to the Soviet Union." Oswald was so eager to get to Havana that he had cooked up a crazy hijacking plot the month before,

* Patricia Winston had gone back to Australia and did not testify.

telling Marina that "Fidel needs defenders," and that he was "going to be a revolutionary."

In fact, this is a good time to discuss what, after the assassination, would become a cottage industry: all the alleged sightings of Oswald in the fall of 1963. Some context is needed. It was weeks, months before the assassination. Oswald was an unremarkable-looking man who rarely spoke to anyone. He never had any money to flash around, and didn't stand out in any way. Yet after November 22, he would magically be remembered, in stories told by people who vividly recalled seeing him everywhere from Hawaii to Florida. Or at bowling alleys, dance parties, and more.[145]

As historian Sabato notes in his magnificent "The Kennedy Half-Century," none of these claims have stood up to rigorous inquiry. "Assassination researchers frequently encounter chronicles that seem promising on the surface," he notes, "but end up leading nowhere or raising a host of unanswerable questions."[146]

Thus: Arriving in Mexico City, Oswald checked into a cheap hotel, the Hotel del Comercio, four blocks from the bus depot. He went to the Cuban embassy and filled out a visa application, which bears the date September 27, 1963. Told by consulate employee Silvia Duran that he needed a photo, Oswald went to a nearby shop for one, which Duran checked to be sure it matched with Oswald.[147]

Oswald laid it on thick, telling Duran he was committed to the Castro cause, whipping out documents showing he worked in the Soviet Union, had a Soviet wife, ran the Fair Play for Cuba Committee (membership: one) and all the rest. It entitled him to a visa, he said.

But Duran said he would have to get a Soviet visa first. Here, the volatile temper that Oswald was known for emerged. Duran called for the assistance of her supervisor, Eusebio Azcue. He told Oswald the same thing, and that it could take up to twenty days.[148] † A shouting

† In 1978, Azcue told the House Select Committee on Assassinations that he wasn't sure if the man he saw at the Embassy and the man in the visa photo was Oswald ("fifteen years [have] gone by," but Duran, who spent much more time with Oswald, never wavered. Another Cuban official, Alfredo Mirabel Diaz, who was in training to replace Azcue, also said it was Oswald (Bugliosi, 1,045).

match erupted, and Oswald was told to leave. He then went to the Soviet Embassy, two blocks away, and demanded a visa. Told it would take at least four months, he erupted in anger. "This won't do for me!" he yelled. He was kicked out.[149]

In addition to the handwriting on the Cuban visa application, which matched the handwriting in Oswald's diary, his demeanor is another tell that it was the real Oswald. He was "highly agitated and angry," Duran said. "We never had any individual that was so insistent or persistent...he was never friendly...he accused us of being bureaucratic and in a very discourteous manner."[150] It was typical Oswald: self-entitled, arrogant, rude, contemptuous of authority. It was astonishing behavior, considering that he was requesting their assistance.

September 28—Las Vegas

Kennedy is driven into Sin City in his open car, with no Secret Service agents on the bumper. To repeat: this was generally (but not always) the preference of Kennedy and his predecessors.

Mexico City

After alienating both Cuban and Soviet officials the day before, Oswald returns for round two. At the Soviet Embassy, he pulls out his .38 and waves it in the air, saying he needs to protect himself from the FBI. A Soviet official manages to grab it and remove its bullets.[151]

"His mood was very bad," said Oleg Nechiporenko, a KGB officer working under diplomatic cover. "Very poor."[152]

Needless to say, he didn't get his way there, nor did he when he went back to the Cuban embassy, where he argued again with Azcue. He left empty-handed, never to return.

Conspiracy theorists doubt that this was even Oswald and point to the fact that there are no verifiable images of him in front of either embassy.

Some have seized upon a snippet of a phone call between FBI Director J. Edgar Hoover and President Lyndon Johnson, the day after the assassination:

> **JOHNSON:** Have you established any more about the [Oswald] visit to the Soviet Embassy in Mexico in September?
>
> **HOOVER:** No, that's one angle that's very confusing for this reason. We have up here the tape and the photograph of the man who was at the Soviet Embassy, using Oswald's name. The picture and the tape do not correspond to this man's voice nor to his appearance. In other words it appears that there is a second person who was at the Soviet Embassy.[153]

Sounds fishy, though it apparently never occurred to either man that typical bureaucratic incompetence might have been to blame. Wrong photo, wrong guy? As Sabato notes, such government incompetence isn't exactly rare, like when "bureaucrats put innocent people on no-fly lists, misplace Social Security records and the like."[154] One internal CIA document noted that its photo system often broke down and only worked about eighty percent of the time. The House Select Committee on Assassinations said in 1978 that it lacked sufficient evidence to "firmly" conclude that there was an Oswald imposter, though conspiracy writers have been quick to seize on the HSCA's next line that "the evidence is of such a nature that the possibility cannot be dismissed."[155]

Since, in the American system of jurisprudence, the burden of proof lies with the accuser, we must say here that statements to the effect "that the possibility cannot be dismissed" fall well short of this standard.

The same argument can be made concerning telephone surveillance of the Soviet embassy. The HSCA determined that the CIA had taped several calls from a man using the name "Lee Oswald." But in the fall of 1963, decades before the digital era, tape recordings were usually recycled and used again after two weeks. "How were we to know that two months later this person, Oswald, would assassinate the president?"

asked David Atlee Phillips, the number-three man at the Mexico City station at the time.[156]

Here, bureaucratic incompetence may come into play. Two researchers, the previously mentioned Jefferson Morley and John Newman (both interviewed, like Sabato, for chapter two of this book), conclude that CIA officials didn't tell the Mexico City station all they knew about Oswald.[157] But if they had, what information—that he had lived in the USSR, had a Soviet wife, was a pro-Castro activist with a minor police record in New Orleans—would indicate that he was a potential presidential assassin? The Walker shooting was unknown. That he owned a cheap mail-order rifle was unknown. But it *was* known that he was trying to leave the United States.

What about the alleged threat made by Oswald during one of his outbursts at the Cuban embassy that he would assassinate President Kennedy? Not even the HSCA in 1978 found this to be credible.[158]

To be sure, there are numerous anomalies concerning Oswald's six-day trip to Mexico City. Documents have been lost. The CIA wouldn't tell the Warren Commission everything it knew—"damning," notes Sabato.[159]

"They lied from the get-go," says Morley.[160] The FBI, in its rush to wrap up the case that Hoover wanted made against Oswald, moved too slowly before the assassination and too quickly after it. And even lone-gunman proponents must admit that the Warren Commission itself, also in a rush to wrap things up in the fall of 1964, neither crossed every *t* nor dotted every *i*.

The inference, after six decades, is that all this surely means, conspiracists argue, that more than one person had a rifle in Dealey Plaza. And yet, when this "Countdown" arrives at November 22, 1963—just a few page turns away—only one man with a rifle was absolutely seen, in fact seen by numerous people, and came within seconds of being photographed. But no one else ever was.

In any case, let's return to sunny Mexico City. Oswald's desperate, angry attempts to go to Cuba or even back to the Soviet Union have gotten him nowhere.

September 30—Mexico City

Oswald calls the Soviet embassy and asks if there is any change in his request for a visa. There isn't.*

October 1—Mexico City

Turned away by the Soviets and the Cubans, Oswald spends the rest of his time in Mexico quietly.

A map found among his belongings after the assassination showed that museums, parks, and a movie theater had been marked off. He also told Marina that he attended a bullfight. There is no verifiable evidence that he was seen with anyone else.[161]

Washington National Airport

Jacqueline Kennedy departs for a two-week vacation in Greece. The trip is a chance for her to rest and recuperate after the death of Patrick Bouvier Kennedy in August.[162]

October 2—Mexico City

Unable to get a visa for either Cuba or the Soviet Union, a dejected Oswald sets off—reluctantly—for the United States, leaving the Mexican capital by bus at 8:30 a.m. Had either Havana or Moscow granted him a visa, he would not have gone back to Texas and would not have been in Dallas on November 22.

---

* A record of this call exists. In a memo dated December 13, 1963, CIA officer John Whitten wrote: "Speaking broken Russian and using his true name, OSWALD was talking to the Embassy guard, OBYEDKOV, who often answers the phone. OSWALD said he had visited the Embassy the previous Saturday (28 September 1963) and spoken to a consul whose name he had forgotten, and who had promised to send a telegram for him to Washington. He wanted to know if there were 'anything new.'" Whitten added that due to the heavy amount of telephone traffic the CIA station vacuumed up in Mexico City, that Oswald's call wasn't transcribed until October 9. By then, Oswald was back in Dallas.

October 3—Dallas

Oswald arrives in Dallas. Embarrassed over yet another failure, he declines to call Marina. He walks from the Greyhound station near Dealey Plaza to the YMCA and checks in, lying that he is a serviceman to dodge paying a fifty-cent membership fee.[163] Two weeks shy of his twenty-fourth birthday, Oswald is unemployed, destitute, possessing few marketable skills, and few friends. His estranged wife is about to give birth to their second child.

Washington

Texas Gov. Connally presides over a meeting of state Democrats to discuss President Kennedy's upcoming trip to the Lone Star State (his rival, Sen. Ralph Yarborough, was not invited). Connally says that JFK wants to visit the state's four biggest cities: San Antonio, Houston, Fort Worth, and Dallas.[164]

Air Force One

Kennedy flies to Arkansas to dedicate a dam. Arkansas senator J. William Fulbright is aboard, and they discuss Kennedy's upcoming trip to Texas. Fulbright issues a stark warning: "Dallas is a very dangerous place...*I* wouldn't go there...don't *you* go." He repeats the warning on the return flight.[165]

October 4—The White House

Gov. Connally meets with Kennedy to discuss the upcoming Texas trip. The broad outlines of JFK's visit are agreed to—Houston, San Antonio, Fort Worth, Dallas, and Austin on Thursday, November 21, and Friday, November 22—but no specific details such as venues, times, motorcades, or the like are worked out. Connally tries to talk Kennedy out of visiting Dallas, saying the city is "too emotional" for a presidential visit. The governor may have another motive: as a conservative, he perhaps wants to play down his association with Kennedy in deeply conservative Big D.[166]

Dallas

For once, Oswald's sordid past catches up with him. Desperate to find work, he spots a help-wanted ad for a typesetter trainee at the Padgett Printing Company and applies. He makes a favorable impression on his would-be-boss Theodore Gangl—until Gangl checks with a reference: Bob Stovall, one of Oswald's former bosses at Jaggars. Stovall told Gangl of Oswald's poor attitude and lazy work habits. He was a troublemaker and may be a communist, Stovall said, adding, "If I was you, I wouldn't hire him."[167]

Oswald wasn't hired. Had he gotten the job, he would have been far from the eventual motorcade route that President Kennedy would take through Dallas seven weeks later.

He swallowed his pride, calling Marina to say he was back in town. He hitchhiked to Ruth Paine's house in Irving and spent the evening railing against both Cuban and Soviet officials for not helping him. Of Cuba, and his now-dashed plans of being a fighter for Castro, a glum Oswald merely told his wife, "No point going *there*."[168]

October 5—The White House

President Kennedy orders further aid to the regime of South Vietnam cut off until President Ngô Đình Diem and his brother, Ngô Đình Nhu, begin to implement political reforms. The withdrawal of American support is a less-than-subtle sign to opposition leaders that American patience with the Diem regime has all but run out.[169]

October 7—The White House

President Kennedy signs the ratified Nuclear Test Ban Treaty.[170]

Dallas

Living apart from Marina, Oswald rents a room in a boarding house at 621 Marsalis Street in the Oak Cliff section of Dallas. He will be evicted a week later after landlady Mary Bledsoe, irritated with his demeanor, kicks him out. Oswald, paranoid, thinks it means the FBI is after him again.

October 9—CIA Headquarters

When Oswald called the Soviet Embassy in Mexico City, his name meant nothing to CIA staffers there. But the name jumps out when the transcripts are reviewed at Langley. Whitten again from his December 13, 1963, memo:

> It was noted that the Lee OSWALD phoning the Soviet Embassy in Mexico City was probably the Lee OSWALD who had defected to the Soviet Union in 1959 and returned to the USA in 1962.[171]

FBI Headquarters

Ahead of President Kennedy's trip to Texas, the FBI gives the Secret Service a list of people it thinks require steady surveillance. Lee Harvey Oswald is not on the list. His name has been removed by Agent Marvin Gheesling, after a determination that Oswald is not a potential assassin.

At this point, federal officials didn't know that Oswald was even in Dallas; he had been in New Orleans, after all, just weeks before. It wasn't known that he owned a rifle, or that he had tried to assassinate Walker in April. It *was* known that he had lived in the Soviet Union and had a Soviet wife. But this, in the FBI's eyes, didn't mean he was a threat to anyone, or deserving of further FBI resources that would be needed to keep constant tabs on him.

October 10—CIA Headquarters

A day after CIA officers realize that the Oswald who was calling and visiting the Soviet Embassy in Mexico City was also the Oswald who had defected in 1959 to the Soviet Union, they pass the information on (claimed CIA Officer Whitten on December 13, 1963) to the FBI, State department (because Oswald is still an American citizen), and the Navy Department (because Oswald is a former Marine). Thus, US officials have knowledge, as of October 9–10, that Oswald was in Mexico City—but not that he has returned to the United States.

October 11—The White House

Kennedy approves National Security Action Memorandum 263. It approves recommendations by Defense Secretary McNamara and Joint Chiefs Chairman Maxwell Taylor that "great progress" is being made in Vietnam, that one thousand military personnel can be withdrawn by the end of 1963, and that a "major part of the U.S. military task can be completed by the end of 1965."[172]

October 14—Irving

Marina Oswald and Ruth Paine attend a morning coffee klatch with neighbors. At one point, the conversation turns to Lee Oswald and the fact that he needs a job. Two possibilities are raised: one at a local bakery and another at a gypsum plant. But each of those jobs requires driving, a skill the inept Oswald lacks. His prospects are few. But another neighbor, Linnie Mae Randall, mentions that her brother, Buell Wesley Frazier, has just gotten a job downtown at a place called the Texas School Book Depository. It is the busy season, Linnie Mae says, and perhaps they can use another man.

Paine called Depository superintendent Roy Truly. Truly told them to have Oswald visit the depository the next day.[173]

Dallas

Oswald rents a small room—five feet by thirteen—in a boarding house at 1026 North Beckley. The cost is eight dollars a week. The room has a single iron-rack bed, a nightstand, a small plastic table, and a wooden dresser. The rooms also have curtains, an important detail that we'll discuss when we get to November 21 and November 22. As usual, he lies about himself, telling landlady Gladys Johnson that his name is "O. H. Lee," an obvious reversal of his real initials.[174]

October 15—Dallas

Desperate for work—he hasn't had a paycheck since being fired from Reily Foods Co. in July—Oswald interviews for a position at the Texas School Book Depository in downtown Dallas. His would-be boss, Roy Truly, likes how Oswald is respectful and calls him "sir." Oswald lies as usual about his past, telling Truly that he just got out of the Marines, and that he got an honorable discharge. Unlike other prospective employers, Truly doesn't bother to check Oswald's references and offers him a position filling book orders for $1.25 an hour. Oswald, as always, thinks the work is beneath him, but needs a paycheck.[175]

The printing company, the bakery, the gypsum plant—had any of those jobs worked out, Oswald would not have been in a position to shoot President Kennedy on November 22.

There's something else many conspiracy theorists overlook: the Texas School Book Depository had a second location in 1963, at 1917 Houston Street, several blocks north of Dealey Plaza. In 1964, Truly told the Warren Commission that he had the option to assign Oswald to either building on his first day at work. "Oswald and another fellow reported for work on the same day [October 15] and I needed one of them for the depository building," he said. "I picked Oswald."[176]

This is another thing that conspiracy theorists often overlook or ignore; Truly's random decision to assign Oswald to one location or another. It's also worth remembering that neither Kennedy's luncheon location or motorcade route for November 22 had been finalized.

October 17—Andrews Air Force Base

Jacqueline Kennedy, refreshed and beaming, returns from her Mediterranean vacation.

October 20—Boston

Kennedy's cavalier attitude towards his own safety is on full display when he walks unannounced into a restaurant he has loved for years. He lingers while enjoying a butterscotch sundae, then strolls down crowded Boylston Street.

Such meanderings meant the Secret Service had, at best, minimal control of the environment and gave the president's agents fits. That evening he was driven to a gala dinner and stood up in his open car—just the way he liked it—so he could be better seen. Everyone knew the route he would take—crowds lined the streets. The president ordered his driver to go slowly.[177]

October 20—Dallas

Marina Oswald gives birth to a daughter: Audrey Marina Rachel Oswald. Lee, who had been hoping for a boy, shows little interest.

October 21—Texas School Book Depository

Oswald, as usual, doesn't make much of an effort to meet his new work colleagues. But one makes an effort to meet him: Buell Wesley Frazier. In his 1964 testimony to the Warren Commission, Frazier will recall that it occurs on a Monday in mid-October, which makes the likely date October 21.

"I went up and introduced and he told me his name was Lee and I said 'We are glad to have you,'" Frazier said.

Oswald learns that Frazier lives in Irving, not far from Marina and Ruth Paine. Frazier later said:

"So I thought he would go home every day like most men do but he told me no, that he wouldn't go home every day and then he asked me could he ride home say like Friday afternoon on weekends and come back on Monday morning and I told him that would be just fine with me."

Frazier doesn't inquire as to the Oswalds' odd living arrangements, figuring it's none of his business.[178]

Washington

Who was the Secret Service watching in the fall of 1963? Thanks to documents released in the fall of 2017, the answer is a lot of people. A 413-page document detailed everyone from Puerto Rican nationals (who had tried to assassinate President Truman thirteen years earlier), Ku Klux Klansmen, and others. All told, said another document, there were more than four hundred people who were considered a potential threat to President Kennedy.[179] *

October 22—The White House

President Kennedy, seeing his wife glowing from her Mediterranean vacation, feels emboldened enough to ask her for a favor: would she accompany him on a campaign swing through Texas in late November? Even with Texan Lyndon Johnson as his running mate, Kennedy barely carried the Lone Star State in 1960—the winning margin was a mere 46,257 votes—and its twenty-five electoral votes will be crucial in 1964. Jackie's presence, JFK judges, will be helpful.

"I'll campaign with you anywhere you want," Jackie said. She opened her red leather appointment book and scribbled "Texas" across November 21, 22, and 23.[180]

* After JFK's murder, one Puerto Rican nationalist on the Secret Service's threat list praised Oswald for thinking big. "Diagnosed schizophrenic paranoid," the Secret Service notes said. "Considered dangerous by doctor."

October 24—Dallas

United Nations Ambassador Adlai Stevenson is attacked by a Dallas mob. Giving an address on UN Day, a group of demonstrators descends upon him. On that night's *CBS Evening News*, Walter Cronkite reports that "one man spat on him and a woman hit him with her placard." One man screams, over and over, that "Kennedy will get his reward in hell. Stevenson is going to die. His heart will stop, stop, stop. And he will burn, burn, burn."[181]

Via his assistant Arthur Schlesinger, Kennedy sent Stevenson a telegram congratulating him on remaining calm during the attack. Stevenson told Schlesinger that he was shocked by the level of hatred in Dallas and questioned whether JFK should visit in late November.[182]

October 25—Dallas

Dallas civic and business leaders send a telegram to Stevenson, apologizing profusely for the previous day's attack. A copy is sent to the White House as well.

It said the city was "outraged and abjectly ashamed of the disgraceful discourtesies you suffered at the hands of a small group of extremists." Mayor Earle Cabell, meantime, blasted the "right wing fanatics" behind the attack, calling them "not conservatives" but "radicals" who were nothing more than "a cancer on the body politic."

Governor Connally called those who attacked Stevenson "a handful of people who let their emotions run away with them," and claimed they were "not representative of the people of Dallas." Meantime, the *Dallas Times Herald* ran a front-page apology, saying "Dallas has been disgraced. There is no other way to view the storm-trooper actions of last night's frightening attack on Adlai Stevenson."[183]

October 28—Dallas

Dallas resident Nellie Doyle, alarmed at the hostile right-wing atmosphere in her city, writes a letter to White House press secretary Pierre Salinger, urging him to tell Kennedy not to visit:

> Although I do not consider myself an 'alarmist', I do fervently hope that President Kennedy can be dissuaded from appearing in the city of Dallas, Texas, as much as I would appreciate and enjoy hearing and seeing him.
>
> This "hoodlum mob" here in Dallas is frenzied and infuriated because their attack upon Ambassador Adlai Stevenson on the 24th, backfired on them. I have heard that some of them have said that they "have just started".
>
> No number of policemen, plainclothes men nor militia can control the "air", Mr. Salinger—it is a dreadful thought, but all remember the fate of President McKinley.
>
> These people are crazy, or crazed, and I am sure that we must realize that their actions in the future are unpredictable.

Dallas

Even though key details of President Kennedy's visit to Dallas have yet to be settled, a variety of prominent locals worry about it. Examples include:

- Two brothers of Texas Senator Ralph Yarborough—both lawyers—send their brother nearly identical accounts of the dangerous, anti-Kennedy hatred in Dallas.
- US District Judge Sarah T. Hughes dreads an incident in Dallas (she would famously administer the oath of office to Lyndon Johnson on November 22).
- Austin newspaper editor Ronnie Dugger, on Kennedy's upcoming trip to Dallas: "He will not get through this without something happening to him."

- US attorney H. Barefoot Sanders, the senior Department of Justice official in that part of Texas, and a friend of Vice President Johnson's, tells LBJ advisor Cliff Carter that visiting Dallas is "inadvisable."
- "I think we ought to see whether or not we can persuade President Kennedy to change his mind about visiting Dallas," Stanley Marcus, president of luxury retailer Neiman Marcus, tells his top executives. "Frankly, I don't think this city is safe for it."[184]

October 29—Austin

Democratic National Committee advance man Jerry Bruno lunches with Governor Connally. The next day he begins a tour of Kennedy's upcoming trip. In Dallas on October 30 and November 1, he considers several sites for JFK's November 22 speech—which will then determine the motorcade route. Bruno's preference is the ballroom at the Sheraton-Dallas Hotel. But it has been booked by a women's group, and the hotel management says it will not ask them to move. It's a mile from Dealey Plaza, where Oswald now works.

Dallas's Memorial Auditorium, about half a mile from Dealey Plaza, was next. It was available, but Democratic officials told Bruno that its very size—it had a seating capacity of seven thousand—could mean that cranks or protestors might get in and embarrass the president.

This left Bruno with three venues. There was the Women's Building, near the Cotton Bowl, on the opposite side of town from Dealey Plaza. And there were Market Hall and the Trade Mart, across from each other and just off Stemmons Freeway (I-35), which skirts Dallas's West End—site of Dealey Plaza and the Texas School Book Depository.

But Market Hall was also booked for a Pepsi-Cola convention taken by the bottlers' association. Bruno saw no need to bother them.*

* Which explains why Richard Nixon was in Dallas ahead of President Kennedy's arrival on November 22. The former vice president was a corporate attorney in 1963, and his firm—Mudge, Stern, Baldwin, and Todd—represented the soft drink giant.

That left the Women's Building and the Trade Mart. Bruno liked the former, but his hosts countered that it seemed too drab for a presidential visit. Why not the modern, showy Trade Mart? It was only five years old, a beautiful venue that would show Big D at its best.[185]

Bruno hesitated to make a decision; it wouldn't be resolved for two more weeks.

October 31—Havana

Castro sends word, via ABC journalist Lisa Howard, that he is eager to negotiate with the Kennedy administration. According to Howard, Castro offers to send a plane to Mexico to pick up Kennedy's representative and fly him to a private airport near Veradero, where Castro would talk to him alone.[186]

November 1—The White House

Kennedy is woken up at 3:00 a.m. and told that a coup in South Vietnam is underway.[187]

Dealey Plaza

Oswald rents a post office box—number 6225—at the Terminal Annex Building overlooking Dealey Plaza. The rental form, filled out in handwriting that will later be judged to be his, lists "Fair Play for Cuba Committee" and "American Civil Liberties Union" in the space as recipients. And Oswald, as always, sees the need to lie, listing his address as "3610 North Beckley," as opposed to his real address of 1026 North Beckley. The form is signed in Oswald's real name, however.[188]

Texas School Book Depository

By now, Oswald has been working at the depository for two weeks. As was the case with every job he ever had, he considers the low-paying menial work beneath him. And as was the case with every job he ever had, he makes no effort to get along with anyone.

"He never would speak to anyone," coworker Bonnie Ray Williams would recall. "He was just a funny fellow."[189]

Irving

FBI agent Hosty visits the Paine residence. He learns from Ruth that Marina Oswald and her two children are living apart from Lee, who typically visits only on weekends.[190] He also learns that Oswald is working at the Texas School Book Depository. But Ruth doesn't know where Oswald was living.

While they are chatting, Marina appears. Seventeen months removed from the Soviet Union, she trembles at the sight of a US government agent. Seeing that she is frightened, Hosty makes no attempt to speak with her but tells her, via Ruth, that he'll come back another time. Ruth tells Hosty she'll try and find an address for Oswald.[191]

When Oswald later found out that Hosty had visited, he wrote in his notebook:

> Nov. 1 James Hasty [sic], RI1-1211, MV8605,
> 1114 Commerce, Dallas

RI1-1211 was the phone number for the FBI's Dallas office, and 1114 was its address. MV8605 was his license plate, though it was off by one letter. Oswald had previously told Marina that if the FBI showed up again, she was to quickly scribble it down.[192]

November 2—The White House

Kennedy is informed that South Vietnamese president Ngô Đình Diem and his brother (a close advisor) have been killed. JFK is described as "somber and shaken," with a "look of shock and dismay on his face."[193]

November 4—The Justice Department

Byron Skelton, the Democratic National Committeeman for Texas, sends Robert Kennedy a newspaper article. It's about Edwin Walker, the general who was sacked two years earlier for spreading right-wing propaganda among his troops. Skelton tells RFK: "Frankly I am worried about President Kennedy's proposed visit to Dallas. You will note that Walker says that 'Kennedy is a liability to the free world.' A man who would make this kind of statement is capable of doing harm to the President. I would feel better if the President's itinerary did not include Dallas. Please give this your earnest consideration."[194]

The White House

Recording his thoughts into a Dictaphone, Kennedy discusses the weekend's events in South Vietnam.

"I feel that we must bear a good deal of responsibility for it," he said, "beginning with our cable of early August, in which we suggested the coup."

Diem and his brother were bayoneted and shot while being transported in the back of an armored personnel carrier.

"I was shocked by the death of Diem and Nhu..." JFK said. "The way he was killed made it particularly abhorrent...."[195]

November 4—Dallas

Forrest Sorrels, the special agent in charge of the Secret Service's Dallas field office, is asked by Gerald Behn, the special agent in charge of the White House's Secret Service detail, to examine two locations for a presidential visit "around November 21st." Sorrels reports back later that day that one possibility, the Women's Building, located on a fairground in southern Dallas, would be more secure. The other location, the newer, splashier, Trade Mart, has more issues, namely multiple entrances and interior walkways on upper floors.[196]

November 5—Washington

Behn recommends the Women's Building for Kennedy's visit.

Had the Secret Service's preferred site been selected, President Kennedy's motorcade wouldn't have gone anywhere near Dealey Plaza on November 22. But Gov. Connally recommended that the event be held at the Trade Mart. The issue was bucked up the ladder to Kenneth O'Donnell, special assistant to President Kennedy. The title understated O'Donnell's power in the West Wing. He was the de facto chief of staff.[197]

November 5—Irving

Accompanied by another FBI agent, Hosty returns to Ruth Paine's house. Standing at the front door, they're told by Ruth that she doesn't know where Oswald lives. They leave, after a few minutes, catching a glimpse of Marina. They don't speak with her—not that Marina knows where her husband lives, either.

The purpose of these visits, Hosty wrote years later, was to determine if Lee and/or Marina were Soviet intelligence agents. "In November 1963," he wrote years later, "the bureau had no direct information that the Oswalds were Russian agents, but this was the height of the cold war, and for national security purposes we had to be prudent."[198]

The White House (undated)

"[Secret Service Director] Jim Rowley is most efficient. He has never lost a President."—JFK[199]

November 7—The White House

The White House announces that Jacqueline Kennedy will travel to Texas with her husband. It is big news. Jackie has never been to Texas before; in fact, she hasn't ventured west of the Kennedys' Middleburg,

Virginia, home since the 1960 election. Now, for the first time, she will make a whirlwind trip through San Antonio, Houston, and—on Friday, November 22—Fort Worth, Dallas, and Austin.

JFK was delighted—but nervous—that Jackie would visit Texas with him. "He was afraid that she would later regret having gone."[200]

Dallas

Another Secret Service advance man, Winston "Win" Lawson, is sent to Dallas to inspect the two options—the Women's Building and the Trade Mart—for President Kennedy's speech on November 22. Because the Trade Mart has sixteen hidden catwalks—a considerable security risk in the Secret Service's eyes—the Women's Building, despite its drab appearance, is considered the safest venue. Still, no final decision is made.

November 8—Irving

It's Friday, and Oswald asks Frazier for a lift to Ruth Paine's house in Irving, so he can visit Marina, June, and three-week-old Rachel.

Aside from going into Dallas the next day to pick up a driving permit for Oswald, Paine says that "Lee Oswald remained in my home from the time of his arrival, the late afternoon of November 8, 1963, until he departed for Dallas, Texas, on the morning of November 12, 1963."[201] *

New York

"I had wondered what I would do when I retired from the presidency, whenever that time might come," Kennedy says during a speech to a Protestant group at the Hilton in midtown Manhattan.[202] He then makes what is called an "OTR" (off-the-record) stop. Not even the

* Monday, November 11, was Veterans Day.

Secret Service is told ahead of time where he is going. OTRs—in 1963—usually meant "no press, no motorcades and minimal police presence."[203] It is yet another example of Kennedy's casual attitude towards his own security.

November 11—Arlington National Cemetery

President Kennedy attends Veterans Day ceremonies. He takes John Jr. with him. The boy, whose third birthday is exactly two weeks away, is fascinated with soldiers and has been practicing his salute for several weeks. He kept trying to use his left hand, but on this day, he does it properly.

At the Tomb of the Unknowns, Sergeant Keith Clark, the lead trumpet player in the United States Army Band, played taps. With the president just yards away, Clark, who had performed at hundreds of military funerals, rendered its twenty-four notes perfectly.

November 12—Dallas

Oswald, livid over Hosty's visits to the Paine home in Irving, goes to the FBI's office in downtown Dallas. He tells receptionist Nannie Lee Fenner that he wants to speak with Hosty. Told that Hosty is out, Oswald leaves an unsealed envelope for her to give him.

Fenner gave it to another agent, Kyle Clark, who read it and returned it to Fenner, who put it in Hosty's in-box.

"When I came back to the office, I read the note and saw that it was unsigned," Hosty wrote years later, "which meant it could have come from any one of the subjects whose cases I was working on at the time."[204]

Irving

"I never realized how much he [Oswald] could lie," Ruth Paine tells her estranged husband.[205]

The White House

Even as he's seeking secret, direct talks between US officials and Castro, Kennedy signs a national security memorandum outlining continued and aggressive efforts to undermine the Cuban government. The memo notes things like sabotage efforts, support for opposition groups, and a continued propaganda campaign.[206]

November 14—The White House

With President Kennedy's trip to Dallas just eight days away, a final decision on where he will speak still has not been made. Advance work by the Secret Service has narrowed it down to the Women's Building on the south side of town and the Trade Mart on Stemmons Freeway.

Citing Governor Connally's preference, Ken O'Donnell, the top aide to President Kennedy, chose the Trade Mart. Oswald had been working in the depository for a month before the decision was made.

Thus—and despite the Secret Service's preference for the Women's Building—the November 22 luncheon venue, from which the motorcade route derived, was decided by President Kennedy's top aide and Governor Connally.

O'Donnell would later say that the goal of any motorcade was to bring the president "through an area which exposes him to the greatest number of people, and vice versa."[207]

The State Department

At a news conference, Kennedy hints of a drawdown of American forces from South Vietnam. "That is our object, to bring Americans home, permit the South Vietnamese to maintain themselves as a free and independent country."

He also blasted the Soviet government for its detention of Yale professor Frederick Barghoorn. Barghoorn was in Moscow conducting research for a book when he was arrested for allegedly conducting espionage. Kennedy denied this and said the arrest "greatly damaged" relations with the US.[208]

New York

Another example of Kennedy's disdain for tight security: heading into Manhattan from LaGuardia Airport, he travels without the usual police escort clearing the highways because he doesn't want to cause a delay in the evening rush hour. At one point, another car nearly gets between JFK's car and the Secret Service follow-up car. The driver ignores shouts from the agents, until one points a rifle out the window.[209]

Minutes later, when JFK's car stopped for red light at the intersection of Madison Avenue and 72d Street, a photographer, a woman, came out of nowhere and rushed up to the president's side of the car, pushing her camera against the window and firing its flashbulb. "She might well have been an assassin," a New York police official told reporters.[210]

Two incidents in one trip, all because the president didn't want a police escort and insisted on stopping at red lights.

That night he went to a party, and ran into Ambassador Stevenson—who had been roughed up in Dallas three weeks before. He warned JFK about going. Oleg Cassini, one of Jackie's favorite designers, overheard them and asked Kennedy: "Why do you go? Your own people are saying you should not." Kennedy said nothing and shrugged.[211]

It's almost as if Kennedy, who had cheated death so many times in his forty-six years, who had suffered the loss of so many members of his family, who spoke constantly of his own demise, who didn't think he'd live past the age of forty-five, was deliberately daring fate. To revisit something he had once told Janet Travell, one of his doctors: "I will not live in fear, what will be, must be."

What will be, must be. He sometimes questioned whether it would be better to die by hanging, strangling, or drowning. Pennsylvania governor David Lawrence recalled—with good reason—a brief car ride with JFK one day, and the name of another politician came up.

> [Kennedy:] "When does that guy run, in '66?" And I said, "No, Mr. President he doesn't come up until '68." He said, "Well, probably neither you nor I will be here then." A chill went up my back. I said, "Wait, a minute, wait a minute." I said, "That might apply to me at my age, but not to you." He went on into the hotel. I've thought of that a hundred times since, you know. He must have had a premonition he wasn't going to live too long in any event."[212]

November 15—Atoka

At the Kennedys' weekend home near Middleburg, Virginia, Jacqueline Kennedy worries about Dallas and its reputation for violence. She tells a friend, the British aristocrat Robin Douglas-Home (a man), that "I'll hate every minute of it. But if he wants me there, then that's all that matters. It's a tiny sacrifice on my part for something that he feels is very important to him."[213]* Yet—and this is a clear reflection of the degree to which the Kennedys have grown closer since the death of Patrick—she tells a friend later that she is looking forward to it and going "because I want to."[214]

The White House

Presidential advance man Jerry Bruno writes in his diary that the "the White House announced that the Trade Mart had been approved."[215]

Dallas

Now that the venue for Kennedy's visit has been chosen—and reported by Dallas newspapers—Secret Service officials and Dallas police begin work on a motorcade route.

* "One week later, almost to the hour, she was a widow," Home wrote in 1967.

The White House

After working with Gov. Connally to select the Trade Mart for Kennedy's visit, Ken O'Donnell gets a confidential report from the Justice Department. The subject: political conditions in Dallas. Residents, it says, are "conservative politically and socially," which "stems from a fundamental religious training and years of conditioning." More ominously, it adds that attitudes have hardened, becoming "overtly active" and "politically militant."[216]

Irving

Marina Oswald tells Lee not to visit her or the children that weekend. Oswald replies that since he isn't wanted, he will stay away. Oswald knows his marriage is all but over.[217]

November 16—Dallas

The *Dallas Times-Herald*, the more moderate of the city's two newspapers, speculates that Kennedy's motorcade in six days "apparently will loop through the downtown area, probably on Main Street, en route from Dallas Love Field" on its way to the Trade Mart. No mention of Dealey Plaza, Houston Street, or Elm Street is made.[218]

Oak Cliff

Oswald's rude behavior continues to turn people off. He has now been renting a small room at 1026 North Beckley Street for a month, and his landlady, Earlene Roberts, has concluded that he's not exactly a nice guy. On one occasion, Roberts says "good afternoon" to him, only to get a dirty look. Nor does Oswald—who lies about himself as usual, claiming that his name was O. H. Lee—ever speak with any of the tenants, either.[219]

Miami

A letter postmarked from Miami Beach and sent to the "Chief of Police of Miami," threatens Kennedy's life. Written by a group calling itself the "Cuban Commandos," the letter is poorly written and rambling, but says bombs will be used and that an attack will be carried out at either the airport or convention hall where the president is scheduled to speak on November 18.[220]

At the same time, the apparent threat coincided with a recording that was made days earlier by a Miami police informer of a conversation with a right-wing militant named Joseph Milteer. Milteer said that a plot against JFK was in the works and that it would be done "from an office building with a high-powered rifle." *

But as Bugliosi points out, after reading the entire transcript of the tape recording (as opposed to cherry-picking it), it's clear Milteer was just a blowhard with "no advance knowledge of any plot at all and was merely engaging in loose talk."[221] Even conspiracy writers like Douglass and Newman don't bother to mention him in their books.

Oak Cliff

Since Marina told Oswald he wasn't wanted and should stay away over the weekend, he may have gone to the "Sports Drome" rifle range to practice with his Mannlicher-Carcano. Or maybe not.

Conspiracists say this couldn't be so, because, after all, neither Oswald's name nor any of the aliases he was known to have used were found in the firing range's sign-in register. Not "Oswald," not "O. H. Lee," not "Alek Hidell." Well, that solves that! But in saying that these aliases weren't found in the register, the conspiracists are acknowledging Oswald's inherent dishonesty—he used phony names—to begin with.

Conspiracists also claim that somehow there was an Oswald impersonator at the rifle range. But if there was an imposter, why not sign

---

* Kennedy himself said if he was ever going to be assassinated, that is how it would probably occur.

the register as Lee Oswald to firmly establish his presence there? And if it was an attempt to frame Oswald, why didn't the descriptions of the rifle used by "Oswald" at the rifle range match the Carcano? And if someone was trying to frame Oswald by placing him at the rifle range, shouldn't it be noted that the physical descriptions of "Oswald" —the clothing and hair—do not resemble Lee Harvey Oswald in the least? The firing range story is full of holes.[222]

November 17—Dallas

"Incident-Free Day Urged for JFK Visit"—that's the headline in a front-page article in the *Dallas Morning News.* "The good citizens of Dallas will greet the President of the United States with the warmth and pride that keep the Dallas spirit famous the world over," predicts Robert B. Cullum, president of Big D's Chamber of Commerce.

Adds J. Erik Jonsson of the Dallas Citizens Council: "I think we must extend every courtesy to our distinguished visitors regardless of individual political differences…let's show them what true Texas hospitality is. Whether we agree with our guests' political party or performance, let us have no incidents that will reflect on Dallas or Texas."[223]

At this point, it was known that President Kennedy would ride in a motorcade through the city, and that he would speak at a Trade Mart luncheon. But the exact route he would take still had not been publicized.

Dallas

"There was not time for (Secret Service officer Win) Lawson to check each building along the route," said Elizabeth Forsling Harris, a Dallas public relations executive who was helping to advance Kennedy's upcoming trip. "Nor," she wrote in 1988, "was that expected."[224]

Irving

After seeing two-year-old June playing with the rotary dial on the phone, Marina impulsively asks Ruth Paine to call Lee at his Dallas boarding house. Paine dials—the number is WHitney 8-8998—but the man who answers says no one named Lee Oswald lives there. Neither Marina nor Ruth know that Oswald is living at 1026 North Beckley under the phony name "O. H. Lee."[225]

Palm Beach

Wrapping up a "really relaxing" weekend in Palm Beach, President Kennedy says he will never forget it.[226]

November 18—Atoka

Jacqueline Kennedy draws up an itinerary and list of clothes for Texas, including:

Nov 22—Fri
8:45 Breakfast
10:45 Leave for Airport
11:35 Arrive Dallas
Motorcade

LUNCH
2:00 Leave Lunch

Next to this, she decides what she will wear:
Pink & Navy Chanel Suit
Navy Shoes
Navy Bag
White Kid gloves
Topping it all off was a pink pillbox hat.

Dallas

Meeting in a private club, Secret Service agents and local businessmen give the final approval to the motorcade route President Kennedy will take in four days. They do not consult with anyone else.[227]

Oak Cliff

Oswald calls Marina. She is furious about her husband deceiving her yet again—living under a false name at the boarding house. He's furious too, and orders her to remove his name and number from Ruth Paine's address book. He claims he has been living in the boarding house because he doesn't want his landlady to know his real name or that he lived in Russia (not that he is in the news). Oswald adds that he doesn't want the FBI to know his number, either.[228]

Dallas

Sorrells, the agent in charge of the Secret Service's Dallas office, advance man Lawson, and Police Chief Jesse Curry drive the ten-mile motorcade route. Looking for possible trouble spots, the men agree that Friday's crowds will be greatest along Main Street. Sorrells looks up at the skyline—there are more than twenty thousand windows overlooking the route—and says "Hell, we'd be sitting ducks." Minutes later, they turn into Dealey Plaza. Lawson asks: "Say, what's the Texas School Book Depository?" Curry and Sorrells reply that it's just a warehouse for textbooks.[229]

Dallas

With Kennedy's visit just days away, the Dallas office of the FBI is unaware of any physical threats to him. Meanwhile, Dallas mayor Earle Cabell tells CBS: "We undoubtedly will have a few pickets, as you have everywhere in the United States. There will probably be a few of the radical right wing. Possibly a few of the radical left wing. But, sincerely, we anticipate no trouble."

Tampa

Throughout this book, I've written about a different time, a more innocent era, in which presidents, and not just Kennedy, rode around in open cars, often with security that today seems shockingly thin. And how Kennedy, a man who had cheated death on several occasions in his still-young life, was overly casual about the prospects of his demise. November 18, 1963, was one such day.

In Tampa, he set off on the longest motorcade ride of his presidency, twenty-eight miles. It was a beautiful Florida day and the (non-bulletproof) bubbletop was left off of X-100, the famous midnight blue 1961 Lincoln Continental.

Kennedy's usual driver, fifty-four-year-old Bill Greer, was behind the wheel. Next to him was Agent Floyd Boring. Mounted on the rear bumper were two more agents: Don Lawton and Chuck Zboril.

Crowds were enormous, and when they got too thick, Greer would slow down while Lawton and Zboril jogged alongside before moving back to the bumper.

"Kennedy grew weary seeing bodyguards roosting every time he turned around," noted William Manchester, and in Tampa, he asked Boring to have Lawton and Zboril move to the follow-up car.

"It's excessive, Floyd," JFK told Boring later. "And it's giving the wrong impression. We've got an election coming up. The whole point is for me to be accessible to the people."[230]

Thus, for much of a very long ride, Kennedy was highly visible, often standing up, with agents relegated to the follow-up car.

This was remarkable, given that there was, reportedly, another threat against the president. There was also particular concern over the fact that his limo would have to make a sharp left turn in front of the eighteen-story Floridian Hotel, with dozens of unguarded windows. In a 1996 interview, former Tampa police chief J. P. Mullins claimed that his department had been told of the threat by the Secret Service. Authors Lamar Waldron and Thom Hartmann also claimed that Kennedy himself had been told of the threat.[231]

Miami Beach

In a speech at the Americana Hotel, JFK says the Cuban revolution that brought Castro to power had broad support on that island because it was "against the tyranny and corruption of the past." He adds:

> What divides Cuba from my country…is the fact that a small band of conspirators has stripped the Cuban people of their freedom and handed over the independence and sovereignty to forces beyond the hemisphere [an obvious reference to the Soviet Union]. They have made Cuba a victim of foreign imperialism… This, and this alone, divides us. As long as this is true, nothing is possible. Without it, everything is possible. Once this barrier is removed, we will be ready and anxious to work with the Cuban people."[232]

United Press International's headline from the speech was "Kennedy Virtually Invites Cuban Coup." The journalists had no way of knowing the subtle undertone of Kennedy's words: that Cuba could remain communist and have better relations with the United States—if Castro distanced himself from Moscow and ceased trying to export communism elsewhere in Latin America.[233]

To that end, earlier that very day, William Attwood, a US delegate to the United Nations, secretly called Castro aide René Vallejo to discuss a possible secret meeting in Havana between Attwood and Castro. The goal of such a meeting, Kennedy hoped, would be to improve ties between Havana and Washington, which had been severed by President Eisenhower in January 1961.

Air Force One

"God I hate to go out to Texas," Kennedy told his old friend George Smathers, the Florida senator, on the flight home from Miami. JFK added that he had "a terrible feeling about going."

His thoughts, as they winged north through the November night, were of death—his own.

"Thank God nobody wanted to kill me today," he said to aide Dave Powers. Powers had heard his boss speak of death so often, and so casually, that he shrugged it off. But then Kennedy continued, saying that the best way for someone to assassinate him would be with a high-powered rifle with a scope. There would be so much noise and commotion, he said, that no one would be able to point and say, "It came from that window!"[234]

Perhaps Kennedy privately thought, as he often did, of his favorite poem, Alan Seeger's "I Have a Rendezvous with Death."

November 19—Dallas

White House officials release the route that President Kennedy will take through Dallas on Friday. Both of Big D's papers publish it in their next editions.

From Love Field the ten-mile route would take JFK down Mockingbird Lane, Lemmon Avenue, Turtle Creek Boulevard, Cedar Springs Road, and Harwood Street. From there, a right turn onto Main Street and then all the way down Main through downtown Dallas to Houston Street, on the eastern edge of Dealey Plaza. From there, a right turn onto Houston, a sharp left onto Elm Street, under the Triple Underpass, then onto Stemmons Freeway and the Trade Mart.[235]

When he read this, FBI Agent Hosty—who had known for two weeks that Oswald worked in the Book Depository—didn't make the connection that Kennedy's motorcade would approach the seven-story building on Houston Street, then make a sharp left turn right in front of it, before continuing down Elm. Oswald still wasn't considered a threat—he hadn't threatened anyone. The Walker shooting and the fact that he owned a high-powered rifle weren't known.

"I noticed it was coming up Main Street," he said five months later. "That was the only thing I was interested in, where maybe I could watch it if I had a chance."[236]

The White House

Kennedy is at his desk when Salinger pops in. The press secretary will depart at midnight with several members of the president's cabinet for Japan, where they'll lay the groundwork for a possible Kennedy visit in early 1964.

"I'm off tonight," Salinger told the boss. "I just wanted to say goodbye."

The two men discussed a few pieces of business, then the president, removing the reading glasses that he wore in private, said, "I wish I weren't going to Texas."

"Don't worry about it," Salinger said. "It's going to be a great trip and you're going to draw the biggest crowds ever."

JFK smiled. "Hurry back."[237]

Havana

Castro meets with French journalist Jean Daniel. The Cuban president, who has been nudging along the idea of talks with the Kennedy administration for several weeks, says "He [Kennedy] still has the possibility of becoming, in the eyes of history, the greatest president of the United States, the leader who may at last understand that there can be coexistence between capitalists and socialists." And looking ahead to the 1964 presidential election in the United States, he tells Daniel—who knew Kennedy personally as well—that "If you see him again, you can tell him that I'm willing to declare Goldwater my friend if that will guarantee [his] reelection."[238]

Dallas

Vice President Johnson speaks at a convention of soft drink executives. He denounces "people who bellyache about everything America does." While he is speaking—and unbeknownst to him—Dallas newspapers print the motorcade route for Friday's presidential visit. Johnson has no say and is never consulted about the motorcade route.[239]

Austin

Connally is still trying to cancel the Dallas motorcade. Security isn't his worry—being seen with Kennedy is. Connally is more popular in Dallas than the president, and the governor, who like Kennedy is up for re-election in 1964, thinks that being seen with him in deeply conservative Dallas might cost him votes.

The governor wanted the president to be taken directly from Love Field to the luncheon site—which still hadn't been finalized yet. "If it were to be the Trade Mart," wrote Elizabeth Forsling Harris, a Dallas public relations executive and former Kennedy staffer who was helping to advance the trip, "the motorcade would follow the usual parade route from the airport through town." As noted before, she added that there wouldn't be enough time for the Secret Service to check every building on the long motorcade route, "nor was that expected."

Harris took Connally's demand to another advance man, Bill Moyers—who called Ken O'Donnell in the White House.

O'Donnell was dismissive of the governor. "The president is not coming down," he told Moyers, "to be hidden under a bushel basket. Otherwise, we can do it from here by television."

That was that.[240]

Dallas

Texas journalist Ronnie Dugger—who will be riding on Friday's Dallas motorcade—has a dark premonition about Kennedy's visit. "He will not get through this without something happening to him."[241]

The White House

Evelyn Lincoln's husband, Harold, expresses deep reservations about Kennedy going to Texas. She passes the concerns along to the president, telling them that Harold was fearful.

He didn't seem alarmed, Lincoln later said. "He merely said, as I had heard him say many times before, 'If they are going to get me, they will get me, even in church.'"[242]

The White House

Kennedy discusses his weekend plans with O'Donnell and Powers. After returning from the LBJ ranch, he'll go directly to Camp David for talks on Vietnam with Henry Cabot Lodge, his ambassador to Saigon.

"Are you sure I'll be leaving Texas in time to have lunch here with Cabot Lodge on Sunday? He's coming all the way from Vietnam to see me and I don't want to keep him waiting."

"Don't worry about it," O'Donnell reassures him. "It's all set."[243]

November 20—Texas School Book Depository

By now Oswald has been working as a clerk at the depository for five weeks. As was the case with every other job he's had, he is a loner, sticking to himself and barely communicating with anyone.

TSBD employee James Jarman:

WC investigator Joseph Ball: Did Oswald have any friends there?

Mr. Jarman: Well, not that I know of.

Mr. Ball: Did he have any close friend that he would eat lunch with every day?

Mr. Jarman: No, sir; not that I know of.[244]

The White House

Kennedy makes an off-the-cuff reference to the Texas trip. During a breakfast with Congressional leaders in the mansion, he says "Things always look so much better away from Washington."

After the meeting, a few lawmakers walked back to the West Wing with him. House Whip Hale Boggs (D-LA) told him that some Congressmen were worried about the Texas trip.

Kennedy shrugged.

Boggs: "Mr. President, you're going into quite a hornet's nest."

Kennedy: "Well, that always creates interesting crowds."[245]

Texas School Book Depository

Workers begin moving book cartons from the west side of the sixth floor to the east side, which overlooks Dealey Plaza. Once the west side is clear, they plan to lay down new flooring, and then repeat the process for the other half of the floor. The east side soon becomes a jungle, with cartons stacked high.

The White House

Jacqueline Kennedy returns from Atoka and begins packing for Texas. Meanwhile, President Kennedy—worried about the wind blowing Jackie's hair out of place during the Texas motorcades—calls her press secretary, Pamela Turnure. Turnure suggests putting the bubbletop on the limo. No, that is out of the question, JFK replies, unless it is raining. What about a shorter motorcade, Turnure asks? Another no. The purpose of a motorcade, JFK says, is to be seen by as many people as possible.[246]

Evening—The White House

President and Mrs. Kennedy host a reception for the Supreme Court, other members of the federal judiciary, and their spouses. Attorney General Robert Kennedy will later recall that his brother's mood, as it has been for more than a week, seems gloomy. He doesn't know why.

Bobby's wife, Ethel, also notices something different about her brother-in-law. "She realized that something very grave must be on his mind," William Manchester wrote in *Death of a President*. Then:

> "The Chief Justice called over jocularly that Texas would be rough. There was no reply. Kennedy had withdrawn into a private sanctuary of thought. *Why*, Ethel wondered, *is Jack so preoccupied?* Just before the group prepared to drift toward the stairs, she tossed over and greeted him herself. In the past, no matter how complex his problems, the president had always responded. Not now. For the first time in thirteen years, he was looking right through her."[247]

Treasury Secretary Douglas Dillon to JFK: "This is hello and goodbye. We're leaving for Japan." Kennedy: "*I* know [he makes a face]. *You're* off *to* Japan—and *I've* got to go to Texas." He adds: "God, how I wish we could change places!"[248]

McLean, Virginia

Returning home to their home in Virginia, Ethel Kennedy throws a birthday party for her husband. Robert Kennedy is thirty-eight years old. She remarks to Supreme Court justice Byron "Whizzer" White: "It's all going too perfectly."

At the party, RFK asked Ken O'Donnell: "Did you see that letter from Byron Skelton?" (*See Nov. 4*)

O'Donnell nodded. He had.[249]

November 21

The front pages of Dallas newspapers show maps of the motorcade route Kennedy will take the next day.

San Antonio

X-100, President Kennedy's limo, is flown to San Antonio International Airport ahead of his arrival.

Dallas

Five thousand "WANTED FOR TREASON" leaflets appear in Dallas. Below photos of President Kennedy's photo is a list of alleged offenses, from being "lax" on communism, to "appointing anti-Christians to Federal office," to lying to the American people about his personal life and more.[250]

9:00—White House

"Caroline! John!" JFK summons his children by clapping his hands. They come running. Caroline is wearing a blue leotard and dark blue velvet dress; John is wearing short plaid pants. Caroline is due in school at 9:15—her classroom is in the sunroom on the third floor of the White House—so they spend a few minutes together. Finally, it's time for her to go. She embraces her father.

"Bye, Daddy."

"Bye, Caroline."

Caroline is very excited, because tomorrow—November 22—she will go to a friend's home for her first sleepover.

There's no goodbye for John Jr. yet—the boy will accompany his parents to Andrews Air Force One base.[251]

9:30—Oval Office

Kennedy writes letters to the families of five service members who have recently died (he personally wrote the family of every American who died in uniform during his presidency). To the wife and two children of one Texan who had made the supreme sacrifice, he writes:

> "I want you to know that your father was an outstanding soldier who repeatedly demonstrated his loyalty and devotion to duty. These fine qualities won for him the respect and admiration of those with whom he served. As you grow older you will realize the full importance of the service your father rendered his country and will take pride and comfort in the knowledge that his countrymen are deeply grateful for his contribution to the security of the Nation. Mrs. Kennedy joins me in extending our heartfelt sympathy to you in the loss of your father."[252] *

Due to depart for Texas at 10:45, Kennedy then reviewed his Dallas speech. Knowing the political opposition—and potential hostility—he might face, it was toughly worded, including a long list of ways in which he had beefed up American defenses. He also included a few deliberate jabs at his critics:

> There will always be dissident voices heard in the land, expressing opposition without alternatives, finding fault but never favor, perceiving gloom on every side, and seeking influence without responsibility. Those voices are inevitable.
>
> We cannot expect that everyone, to use the phrase of a decade ago, will "talk sense to the American people." But we can hope that fewer people will listen to nonsense. And the notion that this Nation is headed for defeat through deficit, or that strength is but a matter of slogans, is nothing but just plain nonsense.[253]

* Whenever one of Kennedy's letters produced a reply, he invited the widow and children to the White House for a talk in the Rose Garden.

Dallas

A schoolteacher at W.E. Greiner Junior High School tells her students that no one will be allowed to attend the next day's presidential parade.

> "Nobody here will be let out for that parade. I don't care if your whole family shows up. You still have to be in this class. He's not a good President, and I don't say that because I'm a Republican. It don't make no matter whether it's him or his brother Bobby. One's as bad as the other. You're not going, I'm not going, period."
>
> She added:
>
> "If I did see him," she said, "I'd just spit in his face."[254]

Texas School Book Depository

A clerk runs into the building waving a copy of the Dallas Times-Herald. It is true: President Kennedy's motorcade will pass right in front of the depository tomorrow. The route is on the front page.

Oswald, too cheap to buy a newspaper for himself, typically read them after his Book Depository colleagues had discarded them on the table in the building's break room (they called it the "domino room"). At some point he looked at the paper and realized that in twenty-four hours, the president of the United States would come within yards of him.[255]

10:40—The White House

"Good-bye. Safe journey home," nanny Maude Shaw tells JFK.[256]

10:45—The White House

Kennedy, John Jr., and the boy's Secret Service agent, Bob Foster, board Army One on the White House South Lawn. Before departing—they are waiting for Jacqueline Kennedy—aide Fred Holborn hands him a memo from National Security Advisor McGeorge Bundy requesting a two-week vacation at the end of January. Kennedy approves it, scrawling in his usually indecipherable cursive, "Fine—I think it's time I left myself. JFK."[257]

10:50—The White House

As Army One disappears into the overcast sky, administration official Dean Markham remarks: "This is a trip the President can't win, no matter what happens."[258]

11:00—Andrews Air Force Base

At Andrews, JFK and Jackie hug John Jr.

"I want to come," the boy says, and begins to cry.

"You can't," his father says quietly.

The president turns to Agent Foster: "You take care of John, Mister Foster."

"Yes, sir," Foster replies. He considers JFK's remark odd, because the president has never said anything like this to him before.[259]

At 11:05, Air Force One is wheels up for San Antonio. At some point, JFK looks at his watch and moves it an hour back, to Central Time. We will do the same as our countdown continues.

1:25 p.m. Central Time—San Antonio International Airport

Air Force One arrives.

After working a rope line, the Kennedys plop down in their Lincoln Continental; it sparkles in the Texas sun. Governor and Mrs. Connally are in the jump seats ahead of them. The governor's seat is slightly to the left of Kennedy's, and also several inches lower. Because it's a nice day, the non-bulletproof bubble top is stowed away in the trunk, as JFK prefers.

Texas School Book Depository

At some point in the afternoon, Oswald goes into the Book Depository's shipping room. He uses brown shipping paper to construct a wrapper thirty-eight inches long, big enough to conceal his disassembled rifle.[260]

San Antonio

A San Antonio newspaper reporter criticizes the Secret Service, writing that agents are "nitpickers," adding that "taxpayers foot the bill while the Secret Service heroes gumshoe around thinking up different kinds of new—and ruinously expensive—duties for themselves." The article will run the next afternoon.[261]

Meanwhile, Kennedy's motorcade stopped at least twice. Once when schoolchildren ran into the street to get a better glimpse of its famous occupants; and again in front of a Catholic school, where both children and grown-ups, running and calling out, waving American flags and holding hands, broke through lines on the curbs and converged on the vehicle. Those nearest stretched out their hands to touch the president. John F. Kennedy, who wanted to be seen, who liked to be seen, was delighted.

Brooks Medical Center

Ahead of Kennedy's speech, a man dressed as a priest and carrying a black bag is ushered to the front row. It is only then that a horrified acquaintance recognizes him as a mental patient.[262]

In his address, Kennedy talked of America's future, noting that from time to time, "There will be setbacks and frustrations, disappointments," and "whatever the hazards, they must be guarded against."[263]

Houston

At Houston's Rice Hotel, final security checks are made ahead of President Kennedy's arrival. Over the prior nine days, employees have been grilled, air-conditioning units checked for poison gas, and armed guards posted.[264]

3:05—Brooks Medical Center

Touring the base's new Aerospace Medical Center, Kennedy detours to inspect an oxygen chamber. It's used for space program research but reminds the president of the recent death of his son Patrick. "Do you think your work might improve oxygen chambers for, say, premature babies?"

The doctor—B. E. Welch—said, yes, it might. He didn't know why the president was so concerned with infant mortality, or why, as JFK looked into the oxygen chamber, he appeared sad.[265]

3:52—San Antonio International Airport

Air Force One is wheels up for Houston.

4:37—Houston

The Kennedys arrive in Houston.

4:40—Texas School Book Depository

Oswald approaches Wesley Frazier, the neighbor of Ruth Paine and Marina Oswald.

"Could I ride home with you this afternoon?" Oswald asked.

"Sure," Frazier answered. "Like I told you, you can go home with me any time you want to. Any time you want to see your wife, that's all right with me." Frazier would recall later that the following conversation took place moments after both men learned, from the map on the front page of the *Dallas Times-Herald*, that Kennedy's motorcade would drive down Elm Street the next day.

He also thought Oswald's request was odd. Oswald never went to Irving on Thursdays.

"Why are you going home today?"

Oswald: "To get some curtain rods. You know—to put in an apartment."

Oswald's tiny room in his Oak Cliff boarding house already had curtain rods. But Frazier had no way of knowing this.[266]

Houston

Kennedy motorcades into the city in an open car. Along the motorcade route—which was publicized—there is a turnout of some 175,000 people. The reception, as it will be the next day in Dallas, is largely quite positive. Yet right-wing opponents make their presence known. Journalist Ronnie Dugger takes notes:

> "WATCH KENNEDY STAMP OUT YOUR BUSINESS," read one sign. Along the expressway two young boys, perhaps eleven or twelve, each held Confederate flags, and one the sign, "TEXAS BELONGS TO THE SOUTH," and the other the sign, "KHRUSHCHEV, KENNEDY, AND KING." Reporters on the other side of the bus said they saw an airplane aloft with a streamer, "COEXISTENCE IS SURRENDER."[267]

At one point, the crowds were so thick they actually swarmed onto the freeway, bringing the motorcade to a near standstill. Kennedy, in his open car, remarked: "That's why I've started going into New York without a police escort. For every vote we're winning here, there's some poor guy who can't get to his home over there—" he points to the traffic jam on the other side of the freeway—"who'll be two hours late to his dinner. *He* won't love us. He'll just be furious."[268]

Dallas Love Field

X-100, the presidential limo, is flown from San Antonio to Dallas on an Air Force C-130. It is parked in an underground garage and guarded by Dallas police.

5:25—Irving

Frazier drops Oswald off at the Paine home. Ruth is at the grocery store, but Marina is startled—and then angry—at his unannounced visit.

Oswald said he wanted to make peace. He told his wife how much he missed her, that he was lonely, and that he missed his two daughters. He begged her to leave Ruth and move back in with him.

But Marina, fed up with two and a half years of her husband's atrocious behavior, had had enough. The beatings, the lies, the living in near poverty. The Walker shooting. The bizarre airplane hijack scheme. Enough.

"He tried very hard to please me," she said, adding that Oswald grew increasingly disturbed as his begging was ignored.

The begging continued. Then, there was this:

> "He suggested that we rent an apartment in Dallas."[269]

He suggested that we rent an apartment in Dallas.

Marina continued:

> He didn't want me to remain with Ruth any longer, but wanted me to live with him in Dallas. He repeated this not once but several times, but I refused. And he said that once again I was preferring my friends to him, and that I didn't need him.

Consider Marina Oswald's situation for a moment. Twenty-two years old, she knew very little English. No job, no relatives. Two young girls to take care of. As difficult a situation as that was for her, she didn't want or need Lee Harvey Oswald in her life anymore.

No, she told him. No. She would stay with Ruth. But if you want to do something for me, she said, taking advantage of Oswald's weakness and desperation, you can buy a washing machine. It was too difficult, she said, to wash clothes for two children by hand. Oswald said he would.

But then Marina, according to her February 5, 1964, testimony to the Warren Commission, indicated that she was just toying with her estranged husband:

Mrs. Oswald: He said he would buy me a washing machine.

Mr. Rankin: [J. Lee Rankin, general counsel] What did you say to that?

Mrs. Oswald: Thank you. That it would be better if he bought something for himself—that I would manage.

Mr. Rankin: Did this seem to make him more upset, when you suggested that he wait about getting an apartment for you to live in?

Mrs. Oswald: Yes. He then stopped talking and sat down and watched television and then went to bed. I went to bed later. It was about 9 o'clock when he went to sleep. I went to sleep about 11:30. But it seemed to me that he was not really asleep. But I didn't talk to him.[270]

Earlier in the evening, when Paine returned from the grocery store, she was also startled to see Oswald.

Decades later, Paine recalled the scene with clarity. "I wasn't angry that Lee was there," she says. "It was nice to see him playing with June." She tried to converse with Oswald about Kennedy's visit to Dallas:

Mrs. Paine: And it was at that time that I said to him "Our President is coming to town." I believe I said it in Russian, our President is coming to town in Russian.

Mr. Jenner: [Albert Jenner, senior counsel] And you gave us his response yesterday but you might do it again.

Mrs. Paine: He said "Uh, yeah" and brushed on by me, walked on past.[271]

After dinner, when the Oswalds were alone for a few minutes, the groveling continued. He would get an apartment for them in Dallas, he pleaded, if she took him back. The answer, again, and for a final time, was no. Marina coldly rejects him. She would stay in Irving with Ruth.

Here is Lee Harvey Oswald on the evening of November 21, 1963. Lifelong failure. High school dropout. Twice-court-martialed marine. Unable to hold even the most menial job. Would-be assassin. Would-be hijacker. Wifebeater. Failed husband and father.

"This may have been the breaking point for Oswald," William Manchester wrote. "He had nothing left, not even pride."

"He was universally rejected and he knew it," Larry Sabato said. "He was getting close to the end of his rope."

After this final snub, Oswald gave up. He plopped down in front of the TV.

Around 9:00, Paine noticed that the garage light had been left on. She knew at once that Oswald had been in there.[272] What she didn't know was that stashed amid the clutter, wrapped in a brownish and cream-striped blanket, was a disassembled rifle, with a six-round magazine and a muzzle velocity of nearly 2,200 feet per second. This was, as Norman Mailer put it, "Marina's dirty little secret." She never told Ruth, the Quaker, that Oswald owned a rifle, much less that it had been stored under her roof.*

Washington

In the nation's capital, Minnesota Senator Hubert Humphrey gives a speech to a group called the National Association of Mental Health. The topic: "Mental Health and World Peace." Humphrey, who is worried about President Kennedy's trip to Dallas and that city's reputation for violence, says that communities as well as individuals "can be afflicted

* In a 2021 interview, I asked Paine—then ninety—what she would have done had she known. "I would have told him to remove it and store it elsewhere," she replied. It has often been asked why Marina Oswald didn't say anything to Ruth. Now remarried and living a quiet life in Rockwall, Texas, Marina Oswald Porter, eighty-one, did not respond to requests for an interview.

with emotional instability, frustrations, and irrational behavior." The senator adds "that emotional instability that afflicts a significant but small minority in our midst that some call the extreme right, some the Birchers, some the wild men of reaction....They still see the world in total black and white. They are looking for immediate and final answers. They are still substituting dogma for creative thought. They are still angry, fearful, deeply and fundamentally disturbed by the world around them." He adds this warning: "The act of an emotionally unstable person or irresponsible citizen can strike down a great leader..."[273]

Houston

Henry Brandon of the London *Sunday Times*—the only foreign correspondent on the Texas trip—has dinner with an English friend who lives in Houston. The friend alarms Brandon with his talk of just how hostile the far-right in Texas is to Kennedy.

"To Brandon, his countryman seemed almost obsessed with the subject. The radicals couldn't be more vicious, the man said over and over; the situation couldn't possibly be exaggerated."[274]

Houston–Rice Hotel

Jacqueline Kennedy, practicing for a speech in Spanish to a Latino group, is having trouble memorizing her words. "I must be cracking up," she tells her husband. She wonders if the August death of her son Patrick has damaged her ability to focus.[275]

9:10–Houston Coliseum

At a dinner in honor of Congressman Albert Thomas, President Kennedy makes jokes about not being around much longer:

"When I read the report that Congressman Thomas was thinking of resigning, I called him on the phone and asked him to stay as long as I stayed. I didn't know how long that would be...."[276]

9:45—Houston

On the ride to the airport, the president and Mrs. Kennedy are joined in their car by John Jones, publisher of the *Houston Chronicle* and his wife, Freddie. Freddie tells Jackie about Dallas: "Dallas! It's a merchant's town—really, a terrible town."

At the airport, Marty Underwood, a Democratic Party advance man, watched as JFK shook hands with his police escort—a Kennedy custom. The next day Underwood, thinking of that moment, realized how vulnerable the president was on that dark airstrip.[277]

10:00—Irving

Oswald goes to bed.[278]

10:30—Houston

Air Force One is wheels up from Houston, en route to Fort Worth.

11:07—Carswell AFB, Fort Worth

Air Force One lands in a light rain. Despite the weather and the late hour, some ten thousand people, according to the *Fort Worth Star-Telegram*, line the West Freeway from the base to downtown.

11:30—Irving

Marina, still angry, goes to bed. On this, the final night she will spend with her husband, she senses that he is still awake.

11:50—Fort Worth

The Kennedys arrive at Fort Worth's Hotel Texas. "WELCOME, MR. PRESIDENT," its marquee reads. Its best suite, the "Will Rogers Suite" on the thirteenth floor, has been deemed too difficult to protect by the Secret Service, so JFK is given a smaller suite on a corner of the eighth floor—suite 850.

Asked by reporters for a comment on how the trip was going, Jacqueline Kennedy, through her spokeswoman, issued a statement: "Thursday was a wonderful day. Texas friendliness was everything I'd heard it to be."

Before turning in for the night, JFK had a brief conversation with his wife:

"You were great today," he said.

"How do you feel?" she asks.

"Oh gosh, I'm exhausted."

They retired to separate rooms. Before getting into bed, Jackie laid out her clothes for the next day: A navy blue blouse, navy handbag, low-heeled shoes, and a stunning, line-by-line reproduction of a pink and navy Chanel suit, with matching pillbox hat.

Under a glass top in the suite was a message: "Hotel Texas. Check out time is 12:30 p.m. If you plan to stay after this time please contact Assistant Manager."[279]

* * *

Before proceeding, I'd like to share the following from Ted Sorenson, who worked for Kennedy during his years in both the Senate and White House. With the exception of Jacqueline and Robert Kennedy, probably no one knew JFK as well as Sorenson; Kennedy came to regard the bespectacled Nebraskan as "my intellectual blood bank."

> Simply accepting death as an inevitable fact of life, and simply recognizing assassination as an unavoidable hazard of the Presidency, he refused to worry about his personal safety—not with any bravado or braggadocio but with an almost fatalistic unconcern for danger. He had preferred the risks of a dangerous back operation to the frustrations of a life on crutches. He had preferred the risks of flying in poor planes and poor weather to the frustrations of holding back his campaign. And he preferred the risks of

less protection in the Presidency to the frustrations of cutting off public contact.

He mentioned more than once—but almost in passing—that no absolute protection was possible, that a determined assassin could always find a way, and that a sniper from a high window or rooftop seemed to him the least preventable. Occasionally he would read one of the dozens of written threats on his life that he received almost every week in the White House. But he regarded assassination as the Secret Service's worry, not his.

He paid little attention to warnings from racist and rightist groups that his safety could not be guaranteed in their areas. He went to Caracas where Nixon had been endangered by rioters, he stood overlooking the Berlin Wall within communist gunshot, he traveled more than 200,000 miles in a dozen foreign countries where anti-American fanatics or publicity seeking terrorists could always be found, he waded into uncontrolled crowds of hand-shakers at home and abroad, he advocated policies he knew would provoke venom in violence from their opponents, and he traveled in an open car in Dallas Texas, where the Lyndon Johnsons and Adlai Stevenson had been manhandled by extremists – not to prove his courage or to show defiance but because it was his job. "A man does what he must," he had written in *Profiles in Courage* "in spite of personal consequences, in spite of dangers—and that is the basis of all human morality." Life for him had always been dangerous and uncertain, but he was too interested in its opportunities and obligations to be intimidated by its risks.[280]

CHAPTER NINE

November 22, 1963

"Death, a necessary end, will come when it will come."
—WILLIAM SHAKESPEARE, *JULIUS CAESAR*

It remains remarkable, painfully remarkable, that fate could bring two men so completely different as John F. Kennedy and Lee Harvey Oswald into the same spot for a few terrible seconds. Notes William Manchester:

> Lee Harvey Oswald had become the most rejected man of his time. It is not too much to say that he was the diametric opposite of John Fitzgerald Kennedy.
>
> Oswald was aware of this. Significantly, he attributed the President's success to family wealth; as he saw it, Kennedy had had all the breaks. Like many delusions, this one had a kernel of truth. The President was ten times a millionaire. But that was only one of a thousand differences between them. One man had almost everything and the other almost nothing. Kennedy, for example, was spectacularly handsome. Although Oswald's voice hadn't yet lost its adolescent tone, he was already balding and had the physique of a ferret. The President had been a brave officer during the war, and while strapped to a bed of convalescence he had written a book which won a Pulitzer Prize. Oswald's record in the peacetime service was disgraceful, and he was barely literate.

> As Chief Executive and Commander in Chief, Kennedy was all-powerful. Oswald was impotent. Kennedy was cheered, Oswald ignored. Kennedy was noble, Oswald ignoble. Kennedy was beloved, Oswald despised. Kennedy was a hero; Oswald was a victim.[1]

Yet there they were, just yards apart. That Oswald—bitter, resentful, desperately hungry for a place in the history books—could erase the former so easily, so suddenly, so casually, to this day renders the magnitude of the killing nearly beyond comprehension. It is this, the simple casualness of such a vast crime, that causes the incredulity and sorrow to linger.

After all, most of history's great assassinations were either well-thought-out events or were driven by clear political motives. Some were both; the murder of John F. Kennedy was neither.

Julius Caesar was stabbed to death in 44 BC by senators who claimed that the emperor had accumulated too much power and was undermining the Roman Republic.

John Wilkes Booth stalked Abraham Lincoln for weeks—"what an excellent chance I had, if I wished, to kill the President on Inauguration day!" he scribbled in his diary, after the president was sworn in for his second term on March 4, 1865. Booth, of course, wanted to avenge the South's defeat in the Civil War.

Mentioned earlier in this book, the 1914 murder of Archduke Francis Ferdinand was the result of six assassins who fanned out on the streets of Sarajevo, planning to kill the Archduke—the presumed heir to the Austro-Hungarian Empire—in a bid to break off the empire's southern provinces so they could form a new country to be called Yugoslavia.

Nathuram Vinayak Godse, who shot Mahatma Gandhi to death in New Delhi in 1948, was angry at the Indian leader for being, in Godse's view, too accommodating towards Muslims when British India was split up into India and Pakistan the prior year.

Also mentioned earlier was the attempted assassination of President Truman in 1950, by two Puerto Rican gunman who sought independence for their island from the United States.

The last momentous assassination of the twentieth century was the 1995 gunning down of Israeli prime minister Yitzhak Rabin. A right-wing radical named Yigal Amir was angry that Rabin had signed the Oslo Accords, an attempt to resolve the ongoing Israeli-Palestinian conflict.

The history books are filled with many more examples, of course, but perhaps you get the point. President Kennedy's assassin was driven, as an examination of his youth and young adulthood have exposed, by a need for attention and fame; there was no Roman senate or Booth-like political motivation for him to kill Kennedy. Thirteen months before Dallas, Kennedy could have invaded Cuba during the missile crisis and removed Castro, but opted for a peaceful resolution instead, allowing the communist dictator—one of Oswald's heroes—to remain in power. And as we have seen, Oswald's near assassination of an enemy of Kennedy's—General Edwin Walker—in April 1963 supports the claim that Oswald was politically ambiguous. He was a violent man who simply wanted to kill; it didn't matter what side of the spectrum his prey was on.

Nor was Kennedy's murder long-planned. The motorcade route though Dallas, including Dealey Plaza, wasn't confirmed publicly until November 19, and as late as the evening of November 21, Oswald begged Marina to take him back, promising to rent an apartment in Dallas for them if she did. It was only her final rejection, one last nyet, *that made him reach for his gun. He was so unprepared for what he decided to do that his clip wasn't even full. Never in the course of human history has a crime of such earth-shaking magnitude been committed so casually, and with so little planning or preparation.*

Let us now review those final hours and final moments.

Dallas

Hours after the *Dallas Times-Herald* publishes an exact route of Kennedy's motorcade through the city, the *Dallas Morning News* does the same. "Main to Houston, Houston to Elm, Elm under the Triple Underpass," it says.

"I was quite pleased," advance person Elizabeth Forsling Harris will recall years later, because the publicity would help generate what JFK wants: big crowds.[2]

Fort Worth—Hotel Texas

Secret Service agent John "Muggsy" O'Leary, standing under the marquee of the hotel, scanning everything around him, spots a man reclining on a roof diagonally opposite President Kennedy's hotel suite. O'Leary summons a policeman and points. "Get him off that roof."*

1:10—Fort Worth

Nine off-duty Secret Service agents, in search of food and drink, ask local reporter Roy Stamps where they should go. Stamps suggests the Fort Worth Press Club. By the time they arrive, the club is out of food. But the agents, accompanied by assistant White House press secretary Malcom "Mac" Kilduff, have beer and cocktails. According to affidavits later filed by the agents, the drinking "in no case amounted to more than three glasses of beer or 1½ mixed drinks."

Affidavits show that some agents spend anywhere from thirty to ninety minutes at the press club. According to Manchester, seven go on to a nearby nightclub called "The Cellar," where some order "Salty Dicks," said to be a non-alcoholic fruit-juice specialty of the house. Another specialty is surely the waitresses, who wear nothing more than their underwear.

This makes it sound like the club, which had no liquor license, doesn't serve booze. But it does. Fort Worth newspaperman Bob Schieffer, who would go on to an illustrious career at CBS News, says the club's owner, a former stock-car racer named Pat Kirkwood, would serve friends Kool-Aid spiked with grain alcohol. This, in fact, was the real "Salty Dick."

* Jim Bishop, in his book, claims this took place around eight o'clock that morning. (Bishop, 8)

Did the off-duty agents drink this concoction? Manchester offers no evidence that they did, nor does Schieffer, who has gotten off work around 1:30 a.m. and accompanies the visiting caravan from the press club to the Cellar.

"I never saw anyone drink" [at the Cellar], he will say in 2022.

But among the agents out on the town for at least a portion of the evening are four who will ride in the president's follow-up car in Dallas just a few hours later. These include Clint Hill, who will write years later that after having a scotch at the press club, he now tries "some kind of fruit drink, which tasted horrible." He will testify that he returns to the hotel by 2:45 a.m.

Meanwhile, Paul Landis, in a December 9, 1963, affidavit, will say he has a scotch and soda at the press club and two "Salty Dicks" before returning to the hotel around 5:00 a.m.

Another agent is Don Lawton, who will say in his own affidavit that he has three glasses of beer at the press club and two more glasses of "what I can best describe as grapefruit juice" before returning to the hotel at 3:15 a.m. Lawton's assignment a few hours later is to remain at Love Field for the duration of President Kennedy's visit to Dallas.

Manchester writes: "at various times they were joined by three agents of the twelve-to-eight shift—who were officially on duty, assigned to guard the president's bedroom door—and chose to break the boredom of sentry duty in this fashion."*

In his terrific 2003 autobiography, *This Just In*, Schieffer noted that "it must have been quite an evening. I remember that we stayed long

---

* On April 14, 1865, one guard was assigned to protect Abraham Lincoln at Ford's Theater. John Parker was hardly a vigilant sentinel. As a member of the Washington, DC, police force, he had been cited for conduct unbecoming an officer, drinking (and sleeping) on the job and frequenting a whorehouse, according to *Smithsonian* magazine. He had fourteen disciplinary infractions on his record. Yet when a four-man detail was created to protect Lincoln in 1864, Parker was selected. He showed up late at Ford's on the fourteenth, arriving at 7:00 p.m. instead of four. The Lincolns and their guests arrived at nine. During the play, Parker, who had been stationed outside the door leading to the presidential box, moved down to a lower balcony to better see the performance. During intermission, he went to a saloon next door for a drink with Lincoln's coachman and footman. When John Wilkes Booth, who had been at the same saloon, arrived at Lincoln's box, the coast was clear.

enough for some of the Easterners to see their first Fort Worth sunrise." On the morning of November 22, 1963, the sun rose at 7:05 a.m.

The Cellar, by the way, has a sign that hangs on the wall. It says:

"Tomorrow is canceled."[3]

6:30—Irving

Marina Oswald stirs ahead of the alarm. Up twice during the night with one-month-old Rachel, she is exhausted and still angry with her husband. He's still asleep. Marina, who senses that he might not have fallen asleep until five o'clock, wakes him up ten minutes later.

Oswald gets dressed: a work shirt and gray pants. He begs no further for them to get a new apartment together. Instead, he tells her that he's left some money for her in the bureau. "Take it and buy everything you and Junie and Rachel need," he says. He kisses June and Rachel. He has always kissed his wife goodbye. On this morning, he doesn't. "Bye-bye," he quietly utters, and slips out. She falls back asleep.[4]

Marina will later find $170.† But Oswald has also left something else: his wedding ring. He has never removed it before, but now he has, placing it in a china teacup that belonged to Marina's grandmother. After all his beatings, his lies, his unstable behavior, Oswald knows that his wife has finally had enough. Their marriage is finished.

He fixes himself a cup of instant coffee. Sitting in silence at the kitchen table, he sips it, pondering the day ahead. The thoughts running through his mind this morning must be extraordinary.

At this point he returns to the garage and retrieves his rifle and four-power scope, which he almost certainly wrapped up the night before.

Holding his package, he quietly slips out the door, leaving Paine's home and his wife and two daughters behind for the final time. He walks half a block on West Fifth Street to number 2439, Wesley Frazier's home.

---

† Bugliosi says $170. Manchester says $187.

7:00—Hotel Texas, Suite 835

O'Donnell reviews the schedule as he shaves. It's going to be a long day: two speeches here in Fort Worth, a motorcade to Carswell AFB, the short flight to Dallas; a motorcade to the Trade Mart, another speech; a flight to Bergstrom AFB outside Austin. Then another motorcade, a series of receptions; a speech at the Austin fund-raising banquet; then one final motorcade, followed by a helicopter flight to the LBJ Ranch.

There's another matter for O'Donnell to deal with: whether to have the bubble top on top of the limousine in Dallas. He looks outside at the gray skies and sees that it is drizzling.[5]

Meanwhile, Agent Rufus Youngblood, tasked with guarding Vice President Johnson, asks another agent, "Anything new from PRS?" PRS is the Secret Service's Protective Research Section. The agent says no, but hands Youngblood page 14 of that morning's *Dallas Morning News.*

The headline from a group which called itself "The American Fact-Finding Committee"—with links to the John Birch Society and Nelson Bunker Hunt, the son of H. L. Hunt—is sarcastic, and the rest is full of hatred and vitriol.

"WELCOME MR. KENNEDY TO DALLAS..."

> **...A CITY** so disgraced by a recent Liberal smear attempt that its citizens have just elected two more Conservative Americans to public office.
>
> **...A CITY** that is an economic "boom town," not because of Federal handouts, but through conservative economic and business practices.
>
> **...A CITY** that will continue to grow and prosper despite efforts by you and your administration to penalize it for its non-conformity to New Frontierism.
>
> **...A CITY** that rejected your philosophy and policies in 1960 and will do so again in 1964—even more emphatically than before.

MR. KENNEDY, despite contentions on the part of your administration, the State Department, the Mayor of Dallas, the Dallas City Council, and members of your party, we free-thinking and America-thinking citizens of Dallas still have, through a Constitution largely ignored by you, the right to address our grievances, to question you, to disagree with you, and to criticize you.

In asserting this constitutional right, we wish to ask you publicly the following questions—indeed, questions of paramount importance and interest to all free peoples everywhere—which we trust you will answer. . .in public, without sophistry.

These questions are:

WHY is Latin America turning either anti-American or Communistic, or both, despite increased U. S. foreign aid, State Department policy, and your own Ivy-Tower pronouncements?

WHY do you say we have built a "wall of freedom" around Cuba when there is no freedom in Cuba today? Because of your policy, thousands of Cubans have been imprisoned, are starving and being persecuted—with thousands already murdered and thousands more awaiting execution and, in addition, the entire population of almost 7,000,000 Cubans are living in slavery.

WHY have you approved the sale of wheat and corn to our enemies when you know the Communist soldiers "travel on their stomachs" just as ours do? Communist soldiers are daily wounding and or killing American soldiers in South Viet Nam.

WHY did you host and entertain Tito—Moscow's Trojan Horse—just a short time after our sworn enemy, Khrushchev, embraced the Yugoslav dictator as a great hero and leader of Communism?

WHY have you urged greater aid, comfort, recognition, and understanding for Yugoslavia, Poland, Hungary, and other Communists countries, while turning your back on the pleas of Hungarian, East German, Cuban and other anti-Communists freedom fighters?

WHY did Cambodia kick the U.S. out of its country after we poured nearly $400 Million of aid into its ultra-leftist government?

WHY has Gus Hall, head of the U.S. Communist Party praised almost every one of your policies and announced that the party will endorse and support your re-election in 1964?

WHY have you banned the showing at U.S. military bases of the film "Operation Abolition"—the movie by the House Committee on Un-American Activities exposing Communism in America?

WHY have you ordered or permitted your brother Bobby, the Attorney General, to go soft on Communists, fellow-travelers, and ultra-leftists in America, while permitting him to persecute loyal Americans who criticize you, your administration, and your leadership?

WHY are you in favor of the U.S. continuing to give economic aid to Argentina, in spite of the fact that Argentina has just seized almost 400 Million Dollars of American private property?

WHY has the Foreign Policy of the United States degenerated to the point that the C.I.A. is arranging coups and having staunch Anti-Communists Allies of the U.S. bloodily exterminated.

WHY have you scrapped the Monroe Doctrine in favor of the "Spirit of Moscow"?

MR. KENNEDY, as citizens of the United States of America, we **DEMAND** answers to these questions, and we want them **NOW**.

THE AMERICAN FACT-FINDING COMMITTEE

"An unaffiliated and non-partisan group of citizens who wish truth"

BERNARD WEISSMAN,
Chairman
P.O. Box 1792 — Dallas 21, Texas

7:08—Dallas

Dallas police chief Jesse Curry goes on TV to urge citizens to extend a warm and peaceful greeting to President and Mrs. Kennedy.

"Because of the unfortunate incident which occurred here during the visit of Ambassador [Adlai] Stevenson *[see October 24]*, people everywhere in the world will be hypercritical of our behavior. Nothing must occur that is disrespectful or degrading to the president of the United States. He is entitled to the highest respect of all of our citizens, and the law enforcement agencies in this area are going to do everything within their power to ensure that no untoward accident or incident occurs. We will take immediate action if any suspicious conduct is observed. And we also urge all good citizens to be alert for such conduct. It should be reported to officers immediately. These officers will be stationed at close intervals along the route that the president will travel. Citizens themselves may take action if it becomes obvious that someone is planning to commit an act that is harmful or degrading to the president of the United States."

Curry has pulled out all the stops. All leaves are canceled. He borrows firemen, sheriffs, state police, Texas Rangers, and agents of the Texas Department of Public Safety. With the exception of a handful of squad cars and detectives, all personnel will be posted everywhere Kennedy will soon be: Love Field, along the motorcade route, and at the Trade Mart. At the Trade Mart itself, one officer stands in the rain on the roof over the entrance with a rifle. The police department's radio channel one will be kept clear for Kennedy's visit; all other activity will be on channel two.

"The city glittered with badges," William Manchester wrote. "Dallas had never seen such security."[6]

7:21—Irving

Wesley Frazier lives with his sister's family. He's finishing breakfast. His sister, Linnie Mae Randall, is standing in front of the kitchen sink. She looks out the window and sees a man crossing the street and walking up the driveway. He puts a long brown package, which she estimates to be three and a half feet long, into the back seat of Wesley's car.

Frazier will later tell the Warren Commission that it is the first time Oswald had ever showed up at his house.

He brushes his teeth, puts on a jacket, and goes outside into the damp, gray morning. He and Lee get into his car, a black, four-door, 1954 Chevy.

Frazier, noticing the large package in the backseat, asks, "What's the package, Lee?'"

"Curtain rods."

"Oh, yes, you told me you were going to bring some today."

From his 1964 testimony to the Warren Commission:

Mr. Ball *[assistant counsel Joseph Ball]*: What did the package look like?

Mr. Frazier: Well, I will be frank with you, I would just, it is right as you get out of the grocery store, just more or less out of a package, you have seen some of these brown paper sacks you can obtain from any, most of the stores, some varieties, but it was a package just roughly about two feet long.

Mr. Ball: It was, what part of the back seat was it in?

Mr. Frazier: It was over on his side in the far back.

Mr. Ball: How much of that back seat, how much space did it take up?

Mr. Frazier: I would say roughly around two feet of the seat.

Mr. Ball: From the side of the seat over to the center, is that the way you would measure it?

Mr. Frazier: If, if you were going to measure it that way from the end of the seat over toward the center, right. But I say like I said I just roughly estimate and that would be around two feet, give and take a few inches.

Mr. Ball: How wide was the package?

Mr. Frazier: Well, I would say the package was about that wide.

Mr. Ball: How wide would you say that would be?

Mr. Frazier: Oh, say, around five inches, something like that. Five, six inches or there.[7]

As noted before, Frazier's sister thought the package was three and a half feet long, while Frazier guessed it was two feet long. As shown here, and in the incredible discrepancy over the *Titanic* earlier in this book, well-meaning people can see things differently. It would hardly be the only moment when people would have different recollections about the events of November 22.

In any case, Frazier and Oswald set off on the fifteen-minute drive to work. As usual, Oswald has little to say; Frazier has to pry words out of his mouth.

"I asked him did he have fun playing with them babies and he chuckled and said he did." And that is it. As mentioned numerous times throughout this book, practically everyone who ever crosses paths with Oswald takes note of his uncommunicative demeanor; it is no different on this day.[8]

7:30—Dallas Trade Mart

The pace picks up ahead of President Kennedy's luncheon appearance, now just five hours away. Chefs have asked the Secret Service for permission to select the best marbled steak they have for the president. The request is denied. When the platters of steaks are carried from the kitchen, the Secret Service will select one at random for him.

7:30—Hotel Texas, Suite 850

President Kennedy is awakened by his valet, George Thomas. "Mr. President," Thomas says, knocking on the bedroom door of the Hotel Texas's Suite 850, "It's raining out."

"That's too bad," JFK says. He groans.[9]

7:50—Dealey Plaza

Passing Parkland Memorial Hospital on their left, Frazier and Oswald soon pull off the Stemmons Freeway; the brownish-red hulk of the depository looms in the distance. Frazier, pulling into an employee parking two blocks away from the Book Depository, stays in the car to let the engine run a bit longer, thinking it will charge the battery. Usually they walk in together, but today, Oswald is impatient. He retrieves his long brown package from the back seat and bolts ahead.*

Frazier follows, thinking it's the first time they haven't walked into the building together. He notices that Oswald has quickened his pace, and moments later enters the depository with his package, using the back entrance off the loading dock.

Mr. Ball: Is this the first time that he had ever walked ahead of you?

Mr. Frazier: Yes, sir; he did.

Mr. Ball: You say he had the package under his arm when you saw him?

Mr. Frazier: Yes, sir.

Mr. Ball: You mean one end of it under the armpit?

Mr. Frazier: Yes, sir; he had it up just like you stick it right under your arm like that.

Mr. Ball: And he had the lower part—

Mr. Frazier: The other part with his right hand.

Mr. Ball: Right hand?

Mr. Frazier: Right.

Mr. Ball: He carried it then parallel to his body?

Mr. Frazier: Right, straight up and down.

Representative [Gerald] Ford: Under his right arm?

Mr. Frazier: Yes, sir.

Mr. Ball: Did it look to you as if there was something heavy in the package?

---

* "The only package I brought to work was my lunch," Oswald would lie during his interrogations at Dallas police headquarters.

Mr. Frazier: Well, I will be frank with you, I didn't pay much attention to the package because like I say before and after he told me that it was curtain rods and I didn't pay any attention to it, and he never had lied to me before so I never did have any reason to doubt his word.

Mr. Ball: Did it appear to you there was some, more than just paper he was carrying, some kind of a weight he was carrying?

Mr. Frazier: Well, yes, sir...[10]

It's likely that Oswald, with what Frazier says was a weighted package, immediately goes to the sixth floor, perhaps taking the stairs instead of the elevator to avoid seeing anyone. He most likely hides the package among the scores of boxes that are piled up on the southern and eastern sides of the floor.

Oswald is lucky. The towering piles of boxes overlook the motorcade route, offering him the perfect sniper's perch—a dim, hidden-away spot, hard for anyone to find—and the perfect place to stash his long, brown package for a few hours. He hopes no one will be the wiser.

7:50—Hotel Texas, Suite 850

After showering, Kennedy gets dressed. Known to just a handful of people, this includes a back brace; it's a tight canvas corset.

To further secure it, "he tightly laced it and put a wide Ace bandage around in a figure eight around his trunk," said Dr. Thomas Pait, a spinal neurosurgeon who co-authored a 2017 paper about Kennedy's failed back surgeries. The tight brace stabilized the president's back and also helped him sit up straight. Pait would write that it also restricted Kennedy's movements. "If you think about it," he wrote, "if you have that brace all the way up your chest, above your nipples, and real tight, are you going to be able to bend forward?"[11]

8:00—Hotel Texas

As she dresses in her suite at the Texas Hotel, Lady Bird Johnson recalls the 1960 visit that she and Lyndon made to Dallas, when both were attacked and spit upon by an ugly mob. She notices that her hands are trembling.[12]

Hotel Texas—Suite 850

Kennedy, a voracious reader of newspapers, scans the headlines for coverage of his Texas trip. The *Chicago Sun-Times* gushes over the presence of Jacqueline Kennedy, saying she may help JFK win the Lone Star State in 1964. But other papers anger him by playing up the divisions between Governor Connally and Senator Ralph Yarborough. "Storm of Political Controversy Swirls Around Kennedy on Visit," the *Dallas Morning News* says, with the sub headline saying, "Split State Party Continues Feuds."

JFK, angry, tosses the paper aside, missing another story on the midday motorcade through Dallas, which includes this line: "the motorcade will move slowly so that crowds can get a good view of President Kennedy and his wife."[13]

8:50—Fort Worth

JFK arrives in the parking lot across the street from his hotel. It's drizzling, but he waves away a raincoat and mounts a flatbed truck to address a crowd of several thousand people. Advance man Jeb Byrne remembers that "on the roofs of nearby buildings, policemen in slickers were outlined against the gray sky."

Everyone else is wearing a raincoat, but not Kennedy. He speaks briefly, praising Fort Worth's role in the nation's defense. He ends with "We are going forward!"

Then, flanked by Secret Service agents, he works the rope line, shaking hands and reaching for grasping fingers. It's a friendly, exuberant crowd. Audio from the event records delighted shrieks from the crowd as Kennedy, smiling, slowly makes his way back to the hotel. Agents, not smiling, keep an eye on outstretched hands. Behind the president towers Roy Kellerman, the SAIC—special agent in charge—who often seems to have a scowl on his face. Instead of having both hands free to respond in a sudden emergency, Kennedy's raincoat is draped over his left arm and hand.

Eight floors up, Jacqueline Kennedy hears her husband's voice blaring through the public address system below. She looks out and is happy to see rain, which means the top will be on the Lincoln in Dallas.

As she primps and gets ready for the day, she looks into the mirror and tells her secretary, Mary Gallagher: "Oh, gosh: One day's campaigning can age a person thirty years."[14]

9:00—Dal-Tex Building

Abraham Zapruder, a fifty-eight-year-old Dallas clothing manufacturer, is having coffee with his secretary, Lillian Rogers. Zapruder's company, Jennifer Juniors, is located at 501 Elm Street, at the corner of Elm and Houston, directly across the street from the Texas School Book Depository. As everyone knows, in a little more than three hours, President and Mrs. Kennedy will drive right by on their way to the Trade Mart.

Zapruder has recently bought a snazzy new movie camera, a 414 PD Bell & Howell Zoomatic, and had thought of filming the motorcade. But he left it at home that morning, thinking that with the expected crowds, he'd never be able to see President and Mrs. Kennedy, let alone get close enough to film them.[15]

"Mister Z," Lillian asks, "how many times will you have a crack at color movies of the president?"

At some point, receptionist Marilyn Sitzman and another employee, Erwin Schwartz, join the conversation. Sitzman encourages the boss to go home and get the camera, but Schwartz says it is a waste of time.

"You're crazy," Erwin says. "When he comes around that corner, makes that run onto Elm off Houston, they'll be going over a hundred miles an hour. You won't get to see anything. I mean, the parade's over."

But Lillian persists.

"Oh, Mister Z, go home and get the camera. Don't listen to him."[16]

Zapruder: "OK, Lillian, OK! So I'm going!"[17]

9:05—Dallas Love Field

Former Vice President Nixon leaves Dallas on American Airlines flight 82, headed home to New York. A corporate attorney, he was in Big D for a Soft Drink Bottlers Association convention. The night before, he predicted to reporters that Kennedy might replace Vice President Lyndon Johnson on the Democratic ticket in 1964.

Texas School Book Depository

James Jarman, who works on the first floor of the depository as an order checker, is approached by Oswald.

"Lee Oswald asked me what all the people were doing standing on the street. I told him that the President was supposed to come this way sometime this morning. He asked me, 'Which way do you think he is coming?'. I told him that the President would probably come down Main Street and turn on Houston and then go down Elm Street. He said, 'Yes, I see.'"[18]

9:07—Hotel Texas, Grand Ballroom

Kennedy is running late for a breakfast hosted by the Fort Worth Chamber of Commerce. Filling the time, TV reporter Ed Herbert says JFK "broke one of the cardinal rules of security" by wading into the parking lot crowd that morning.

"Of course, Secret Service men find this the most nervous time of any presidential appearance," Herbert says. "As long as Secret Servicemen can keep the crowd away from the president, they have a good chance of protecting him. But once he moves into a crowd," he continues, "the Secret Servicemen are nearly immobilized in protecting him. Another rule is that anyone who approaches the president should have both hands visible and empty. And as you can tell in a crowd, there's no way to determine that. So whenever the president does move out into the crowd for handshaking and backslapping and exchanging pleasantries, he is always at the mercy of the crowd and the Secret Service is at its least effective position."

But Herbert isn't done. He then tells the story of what can happen to a president when those rules are violated—the September 6, 1901, shooting, in an exhibition hall in Buffalo, New York, of President William McKinley. He mentions how security was lax that day—and how a twenty-eight-year-old man, Leon Czolgosz, a self-described anarchist with a long history of mental illness, was able to approach the president in a receiving line with a gun hidden under a handkerchief.

"When McKinley reached out to shake Czolgosz's hand," Herbert says, the assassin "slapped McKinley's hand away and fired two quick point blank." McKinley died eight days later—the third president murdered in just thirty-six years.

Moments after Herbert finishes this eerily prophetic story, the strains of "Hail to the Chief" are heard. President Kennedy enters the ballroom to a standing ovation. It's a largely Republican crowd, but one that is proud to be in the presence of the president of the United States. But there's disappointment that Jacqueline Kennedy isn't with him.[19]

Texas School Book Depository

In the steady hum of filling book orders, coworker Bonnie Ray Williams cannot say with clarity that Oswald is on the sixth floor this morning. "But he was always around that way. In the place I think I saw him was as the east elevator come up to the sixth floor, he was on that side of the elevator."[20]

9:20—Hotel Texas, Grand Ballroom

Two thousand heads bow as Monsignor Vincent Wolf of Holy Family Church delivers the invocation. It includes this passage, adapted from Archbishop John Carroll's "Prayer for Government," written on November 10, 1791, during the presidency of George Washington:

> Oh God of might and wisdom, assist with thy spirit of counsel and fortitude the president of these United States, that his administration will be eminently useful and fruitful to thy people over whom he presides.
>
> May we, with him, be thine instruments in establishing divine harmony throughout the world so that thy sons and daughters from one end of the Earth to the other may be free to join the glorious hymn of worship, "Glory to the highest, Oh God, and peace on earth."

Fifteen minutes pass. Then, with a theatrical flourish, Chamber of Commerce president Raymond Buck sweeps his arm towards the kitchen door. "And now, an event I know all of you have been waiting for!"

Clint Hill appears; he nods back at his protectee: Jacqueline Kennedy.

The First Lady enters to thunderous applause. She looks ravishing in her pink and navy suit, the pillbox hat arranged just so. She follows Hill through the crowd, appearing to touch a few hands along the way, and mounts the dais.

"There are some very happy women here today," TV announcer Herbert says. "They made the trip down to see her and now they've seen her."

Watching the ovation for Mrs. Kennedy—making her first political trip with her husband in three years, and her first-ever trip to Texas—Robert McNeil of NBC News tells his cameraman: "Well, if nothing else happens today, we've got a story with Jackie…."[21]

Buck, in his introduction of the president, says: "May God bless you and cause his light to shine on you and on your companions, and your family."

9:30—Dallas Trade Mart

Three hours ahead of President Kennedy's scheduled arrival for a luncheon address, protestors begin to gather. "YANKEE, GO HOME," and (in red letters) "HAIL CAESAR." They are members of a group called the Indignant White Citizens Council.

9:32—Hotel Texas, Grand Ballroom

President Kennedy gives a toughly worded speech on America's national security. It is a rejection of criticism that he has been weak on national security. He reels off a string of figures:

> In the past three years we have increased the defense budget of the United States by over 20 percent; increased the program of acquisition for Polaris submarines from twenty-four to forty-one; increased our Minuteman missile purchase program by more than 75 percent; doubled the number of strategic bombers and missiles on alert; doubled the number of nuclear weapons available in the strategic alert forces; increased the tactical nuclear forces deployed in Western Europe by over 60 percent; added five combat-ready divisions to the Army of the United States, and five tactical fighter wings to the Air Force of the United States; increased our strategic airlift capability by 75 percent; and increased our special counter-insurgency forces which are engaged now in South Viet-Nam by 600 percent. I hope those who want a stronger America and place it on some signs will also place those figures next to it.[22]

The statistics are also included in the speech he is to deliver later at the Dallas Trade Mart.

Under Dwight Eisenhower, the five-star Army general, the hero of D-Day, the conservative Republican, defense spending was slashed 27 percent after the armistice ended the Korean War.[23] Kennedy reversed this, yet it was he, some in the Pentagon and national security establishment said, who was soft on defense. Kennedy, heeding Douglas MacArthur's advice, was looking to get out of Vietnam—which Eisenhower had also avoided—yet it was he who was accused of placing American security at risk by not confronting the communists. Eisenhower, dealing with some of the same bellicose advisors in the Pentagon, rejected suggestions to use nuclear weapons against China. Were it not for Kennedy's leadership and incremental management of the Cuban Missile Crisis, the world might have been plunged, and nearly was, into nuclear Armageddon, which historians estimate would have killed half of all Americans—at the time about ninety-five million people—and a similar number of Soviet citizens.

Kennedy continues:

> This is a very dangerous and uncertain world. As I said earlier, on three occasions in the last three years the United States has had a direct confrontation. No one can say when it will come again. No one expects that our life will be easy…

And:

> We would like to live as we once lived. But history will not permit it…

He wraps up with:

> I am confident, as I look to the future, that our chances for security, our chances for peace, are better than they have been in the past. And the reason is because we are stronger. And with that strength is a determination to not only maintain the peace, but also the vital interests of the United States. To that great cause, Texas and the United States are committed. Thank you.[24]

9:55—Hotel Texas, Grand Ballroom

Kennedy's speech is over, and now it's time for gifts.

"You have brought rain," Buck says, and Kennedy laughs. But it's already clearing up.

Buck bends down to pick up a box.

"We know you don't wear a hat," he says, pulling one out of the box. "But we couldn't let you leave Fort Worth without providing you with some protection against the rain."

Kennedy stands up to accept the gift, and there are shouts for him to put it on.

"I'll put it on in the White House on Monday," JFK jokes. "If you come up there, you'll have a chance to see it then."

But Buck has another gift, and it comes with words that in retrospect are ominous:

"And to protect you against local enemies, in the manner that you are protecting this nation against our foreign enemies, and to keep the rattlesnakes on Vice President Johnson's ranch from striking you, we want to present this pair of boots."

10:05—Hotel Texas, Grand Ballroom

Delivering the benediction to wrap up the Chamber of Commerce breakfast, the Reverend Granville Walker prays for the president's health and safety. An excerpt:

> The Lord bless our president and all in places of responsibility with wisdom, and with health equal to their tasks. And now the Lord bless you and keep you...the Lord cause his face to shine upon you and give you peace both now and forever. Amen.

10:10—Hotel Texas, Suite 850

Back in their suite, the Kennedys have a bit of downtime before leaving for Dallas. The First Lady marvels at how smoothly everything is going.

"Oh Jack, campaigning is so easy when you're president. I'll go anywhere with you next year...."

Her husband asks: "How about California in the next two weeks?"

"Fine. I'll be there," she says.

Kennedy turns to O'Donnell. "Did you hear *that*?"[25]

Kennedy also made two calls. One to former vice president John Nance Garner, who is marking his ninety-fifth birthday, and the other to Ruth Carter Johnson, the wife of a Fort Worth newspaper executive. In the hubbub since their late-night arrival, neither Kennedy had noticed that their hotel suite had been decorated with a staggering art display—on walls and tables were a Monet, Picasso, Van Gogh, watercolors and bronzes.

Mrs. Johnson's name is listed first in an accompanying booklet of those who arranged it. JFK speaks to her first, then Mrs. Kennedy comes on. "They're going to have a dreadful time getting me out of here, with all these wonderful works of art," she gushes. "We're both touched—thank you so much."

Mrs. Johnson will later recall that the First Lady sounds "thrilled and vivacious."

The mood turns grim, though, when O'Donnell shows Kennedy the nasty advertisement in the *Morning News*. As JFK reads it, his expression turns stony. He hands it to his wife. She skims it and feels sick.

JFK: "Can you imagine a paper doing a thing like that?"

Then: "You know we're going into nut country today."

He pauses.

"You know, last night would have been a hell of a night to assassinate a president." He pauses. "I mean it. There was rain, and the night, and we were all getting jostled. Suppose a man had a pistol in a briefcase."

Kennedy points his index finger and jerks his thumb to show the action of the hammer. "Then he could have dropped the gun and the briefcase, and melted away in the crowd...."[26]

And: "Jackie, if somebody wants to shoot me from a window with a rifle, nobody can stop it, so why worry about it?"[27]

After this disturbing episode, Jackie gazes out the window at the partly cloudy sky. "Oh, I want the bubble top...."

But in another room, O'Donnell is on the phone with Kellerman, who has agents Sorrels and Lawson on hold at Love Field. Sorrels says he thinks the rain is moving eastward, away from Dallas.

"If the weather's clear and it's not raining, have that bubble top off," the president's top aide orders.[28]

11:00—Fort Worth

As the presidential party leaves the hotel, Kennedy aides O'Donnell and O'Brien are relieved to see that the sun has emerged. It's a beautiful day.

O'Brien winks at O'Donnell. "Kennedy weather, Charlie."

There will be no bubbletop in Dallas.

The Kennedys depart Fort Worth for a seven-mile motorcade to Carswell Air Force Base. They ride in a 1963 white Lincoln Continental convertible, with the Kennedys and Governor Connally squeezed into the back seat.

The driver of O'Brien's car says: "Flying to Dallas?"

O'Brien nods.

"That's the hell hole of the world."[29]

11:20—Carswell Air Force Base

As they walk towards Air Force One, President and Mrs. Kennedy hold hands. The display of public affection, once rare, is now more common, Jackie's Secret Service agent, Hill, says.

"It became more so after the death of Patrick," he said. "It was more evident; from that point on, they caressed in public, they held hands. Prior to that time they never showed that emotion in public. But after that happened, it didn't matter any more."[30]

They board the plane at 11:23 and take off two minutes later. During the thirteen-minute flight, Kennedy is served a dish of fresh pineapple and a cup of coffee. He adds four spoonfuls of sugar. He has a brief conversation with Albert Thomas. The Houston Congressman issues one more warning about Dallas:

"If I were you, I'd be careful what I said in Dallas, It's a tough town."

Kennedy doesn't reply.

Evelyn Lincoln goes into Kennedy's private cabin to give him some papers to sign. He is in the middle of a conversation about how the trip is going so far. "I didn't think I'd get such a fine reception," he says.[31]

Just as the plane is landing, Gov. Connally, who has been resisting efforts to end a feud with Texas Senator Ralph Yarborough, gives in to pressure from the president's lieutenants. "All right," he tells O'Donnell. "I'll do anything the president says. If he wants Yarborough at the head table [at tonight's fundraising dinner in Austin], that's where Yarborough will sit."

O'Donnell informs Kennedy, who has changed into a new shirt for the Dallas motorcade.

"Terrific!" Kennedy smiles. "That makes the whole trip worthwhile."[32]

Fort Worth security was heavy. The Fort Worth Police Department assigned 300 officers, the Carswell Air Force Base Police 80, the Tarrant County Sheriff's Department 60, and the Texas State Police 5. The Secret Service, including agents who traveled with the President and those in the advance party, had 32 on hand. The Fort Worth Fire Department and the River Oaks Police Department also contributed personnel.[33]

In Dallas, it will be even heavier. There are 365 policemen at Love Field alone, and 80 at the Trade Mart alone. Chief Curry has canceled all leaves, borrowed firemen, sheriffs, state police, Texas Rangers, agents of the Texas Department of Public Safety, and the governor. All told, there are some 700 officers on duty.[34]

11:30—Dal-Tex Building

Zapruder returns to his office with his movie camera.[35]

11:38—Dallas Love Field

Taking a southern route over downtown Dallas—with Dealey Plaza visible from the left side of the plane—Air Force One lands. From the plane, heavy security is visible.

"We have a lot of blue sky showing and a bright sunshine," Bob Walker of WFAA-TV says.

The plane glistens in the midday sun, and President and Mrs. Kennedy soon emerge, with the First Lady leading the way. The crowd roars.

"It was so bright, my eyes ached in the sunlight," said NBC's Robert MacNeil. "And then when Mrs. Kennedy came out, and with this pink strawberry ice cream–colored suit, with the facings of navy blue turned inside out, and the little pillbox hat to match…her hair glossy in this bright light…the vivid color…it looked surreal. It made the eyes ache to watch."

At every other stop in Texas—San Antonio, Houston, and Fort Worth, Jacqueline Kennedy has been presented with yellow roses. Some five hundred were needed for the Trade Mart luncheon alone, and now local florists are out. All Dearie Cabell, wife of Dallas Mayor Earle Cabell, has is red roses. She presents the First Lady with a bouquet, hoping she won't notice the difference.[36]

Watching this, MacNeil said the roses were "blood red;" adding, decades later, that "their color in that bright sunlight against the pink of the suit was really startling…."[37]

As for JFK, "I can see his sun tan all the way from here," TV newsman Walker says excitedly.

"Just a beautiful break in the weather," Walker repeats. "Clear blue sky and a warm sun."[38]

Despite security concerns, the Kennedys stroll over to the crowd behind a fence and begin shaking hands. The crowd has not been screened; anyone could have a weapon, and agents do their best to watch everyone and every hand that's straining to touch the First Couple. More shrieks of delight are heard.

Walker: "The President and his wife are right up on the fence. He's done as he has done in several places—he's broken away and gone right up to the fence to shake hands with people. This is great for the people and makes the egg shells even thinner for the Secret Service, whose job it is to guard the man."

Kennedy aide Dave Powers scribbles: "They look like Mr. and Mrs. America."

It's a very friendly crowd, with signs like "WE LOVE JACK," AND HOORAY FOR JFK." But not completely friendly. A Confederate flag is seen, along with signs like: "YANKEE GO HOME" and "YOU'RE A TRAITER" [sic]. There were more: "CAN THE CLAN," "HELP KENNEDY STAMP OUT DEMOCRACY," and "LET'S BARRY KING JOHN," a reference to the expected 1964 Republican nominee Barry Goldwater. Liz Carpenter, a top aide to Vice President Johnson, will later say the hostile signs are the ugliest she has ever seen. One group of high school teenagers is hissing.[39]

"As they went along and shook hands along the fence, I was right beside Jackie when a hand reached through the chain-link fence and broke one of the roses off," MacNeil said.

As the crowd surges around them, Jacqueline Kennedy, nervous about Dallas, blurts out: "Where's my husband?" Then, relieved: "Oh, there he is."

As the Kennedys continue to work the crowd, the editor of the *Texas Observer*, Ronnie Dugger, writes that "Kennedy is showing he is not afraid."

But fear is in the air. *Time* correspondent Hugh Sidey feels tense, as does Congressman Henry González, who says, "I sure wish somebody would invent a spit-proof mask," and adds, "And I forgot my bullet-proof vest."

A local reporter tells *Newsweek*'s Chuck Roberts: "After Kennedy leaves here, they won't let anybody get within ten feet of him.[40]

Mr. Specter *[WC Assistant Counsel Arlen Specter]***:** What were the weather conditions on the arrival at Love Field in Dallas?

Mr. O'Donnell: The weather was clear, sunny, excellent weather.

Mr. Specter: What decision had been made as to whether to have an open car in Dallas?

Mr. O'Donnell: The decision had been made to have an open—if the weather was good, he would ride in an open car.

Mr. Specter: And do you recall who made that decision?

> **Mr. O'Donnell:** Well, I would make that decision under normal circumstances. But it was almost an automatic decision, that whenever the weather was clear, he preferred to ride in an open car.[41]

Texas School Book Depository

Employee Jarman, who encountered Oswald earlier this morning, sees him again.

It was "between 11:30 a.m. and 12:00 noon when he was taking the elevator upstairs to go get some boxes."

Jarman: "At about 11:45 a.m. all of the employees who were working on the 6th floor came downstairs and we were all out on the street at about 12:00 o'clock noon. These employees were: Bill Shelley, Charles Givens, Billy Lovelady, Bonnie Ray [Williams] and a Spanish boy (his name I cannot remember). To my knowledge Lee Oswald was not with us while we were watching the parade."[42]

In what will soon become perhaps the most famous still photo taken of the assassination, the twenty-six-year-old Lovelady can be seen standing in the doorway of the depository.

Numerous conspiracists would later claim that it was Oswald, not Lovelady in the photo. Lovelady testified under oath that no, it was him. He ate his lunch and then stayed to wait for the president:

> **Mr. Ball:** [Warren Commission lawyer Joseph Ball] Did you stay on the steps?
> **Mr. Lovelady:** Yes.
> **Mr. Ball:** Were you there when the President's motorcade went by?
> **Mr. Lovelady:** Right.[43]

11:45—Dal-Tex Building

Jennifer Juniors staffers begin leaving to secure good spots to watch the motorcade. Zapruder, realizing that someone needs to stay behind, offers to do so and suggests that Lillian, his secretary, take the movie camera and film the motorcade.

"Mr. Z was telling me to take the camera and I could go and he would stay, but he really didn't mean it," she recalled. "So he went on but I stayed there and I could see. I had left the window open. It was a warm day, beautiful day, the sun was shining."[44]

11:55—Love Field

The Kennedys finally walk to their limousine. The president plops down in the right rear seat as usual. Mrs. Kennedy is to his left. In the jump seats in front of them are Governor and Mrs. Connally. The governor's seat isn't directly in front of JFK. It's slightly to the left and also lower.

The motorcade moves out, with two motorcycle cops leading the way, followed by an unmarked white Ford, which is driven by police chief Curry. Agents Win Lawson, Forrest Sorrels, and Sheriff Bill Decker are with him. Three more motorcycle cops are directly behind them.[45]

Some five car lengths behind this is the president's limo. Behind the wheel as usual is fifty-four-year-old William Greer. Next to him is forty-eight-year-old Roy Kellerman. "At forty, JFK's agents liked to say among themselves, a man in this detail is *old*." But Secret Service tradition is that positions close to the president should be reserved for senior agents. "Younger, more agile agents were relegated to advance assignments or, at best, to the follow-up car."[46]

Behind this is the "Queen Mary," the Secret Service follow-up car, code-named Halfback. It carries eight Secret Service agents. In the rear, two of them, George Hickey and Glen Bennett, sit with a powerful AR-15 .223 automatic rifle between them. Kennedy aides O'Donnell and Powers are also aboard, sitting on jump seats.

A convertible carrying Vice President and Mrs. Johnson and Senator Yarborough was next. With Johnson is Secret Service agent Rufus Youngblood.

Behind LBJ is a hardtop, driven by a Texas state policeman. Johnson aide Cliff Carter and three more agents are aboard.

Following this is the pool car of reporters, including the dean of the White House press corps, UPI's Merriman Smith, and the Associated Press's Jack Bell. They sit in front next to the driver, with Smith in the middle closest to the car's radiophone. ABC's Bob Clark and Robert Baskin of the *Dallas Morning News* are in back.

The bulk of the motorcade is behind all this, including a bus carrying the president's personal physician, Dr. (and Navy Rear Admiral) George Burkley. He's disturbed at his place in the motorcade.

"The President's personal physician should be much closer to him," Burkley tells Evelyn Lincoln, JFK's personal secretary.[47]

As the motorcade slowly heads out, a film shows one agent—twenty-nine-year-old Don Lawton—jogging alongside X100, then throwing up his arms three times, but appearing to smile, as he stops escorting the limo. The film, indeed, appears to show Agent Emory Roberts, in the follow-up car, ordering Lawton away.

Conspiracy buffs have made much of this, saying that agents always surrounded the limousine but were pulled away in Dallas. The inference is certainly slanderous, that somehow the Secret Service was involved in something nefarious.

But again—and as shown in numerous descriptions of the travels of Presidents Roosevelt, Truman, and Eisenhower—the claim that agents always surrounded presidential vehicles simply wasn't so, nor was it so during the Kennedy era. There has always been the suggestion that a thick security blanket always enveloped presidents in this pre-Dallas era, and therefore the fact that this wasn't the case on November 22 is odd. It wasn't. It was the product, as chapter three notes, of a more innocent era. To be fair, it must be acknowledged that sometimes guards were around their protectees, and sometimes they were on the car itself. But quite often—and for all presidents—they were not. The suggestion that Dallas was a security outlier simply isn't so.

Back to Lawton and the departure from Love Field. Eight days after the assassination Lawton wrote that his assignment was to "remain at the airport to effect security for the President's departure." Years later, he told Clint Hill that as the president's car drove away, he was saying "See you, I'm going to lunch. Have a good trip."[48]

11:55–Texas School Book Depository

Workers wash up before lunch.

"I believe this day we quit about maybe five or ten minutes [before noon]," said Bonnie Ray Williams, "because all of us were so anxious to see the President—we quit a little ahead of time, so that we could wash up and we wanted to be sure we would not miss anything."[49]

Before heading down, there's a rare occurrence: Oswald spoke. "And I am not sure whether he was on the fifth or the sixth floor," Williams recalled. "He hollered 'Guys, how about an elevator?' I don't know whether those are his exact words. But he said something about the elevator. And Charles said, 'Come on, boy,' just like that."

Oswald then said, "Close the gate on the elevator and send the elevator back up. I don't know what happened after that," Williams said, referring to his uncertainty as to whether Givens sent the elevator back up as Oswald requested. Asked if he was sure it was Oswald, Williams said, "I am sure it was Oswald."[50]*

But while Williams isn't sure which floor Oswald was on, Givens knows. After going downstairs, he realizes that he left his cigarettes in his jacket on the sixth floor. Returning there, he encounters Oswald. "Boy, aren't you coming downstairs? It's near lunchtime."

"No sir," Oswald replies.[51] After being spotted on the sixth floor, no one else in the entire depository will see Oswald again until some ninety seconds after the assassination.

---

* Givens couldn't send the elevator back up; it was stuck upstairs somewhere. "He strolled away, thinking no more about it." He recalled the time was five minutes before noon. (Manchester, *Death of a President*, 133)

12:00—Dealey Plaza

After walking around Dealey Plaza looking for the best place to take a home movie of the Kennedys, Abraham Zapruder finds the perfect vantage point.

"I found the spot, one of these concrete blocks they have down there near the park near the underpass," he would tell a TV reporter later that day. "And I got on top there, there was another girl from my office, she was right behind me."[52]

12:05—Lemmon Ave. and Lomo Alto Drive

"Let's stop here, Bill," Kennedy tells Greer, after spotting a group of schoolchildren with a sign reading, "MR. PRESIDENT, PLEASE STOP AND SHAKE OUR HANDS." The children erupt in glee.

A local couple watches the frenzy around JFK. The woman tells her husband that she just heard, that very morning, a radio program on the Lincoln assassination. The woman says, "President Kennedy ought to be awarded the Purple Heart just for coming to Dallas."[53]

Texas School Book Depository—Sixth Floor

After retrieving his lunch—a chicken sandwich, bag of Fritos, and a bottle of Dr. Pepper—Williams returns to the sixth floor to eat. Why the sixth floor? "Well, at the time everybody was talking like they was going to watch [the motorcade] from the sixth floor. I think Billy Lovelady said he wanted to watch from up there. And also my friend; this Spanish boy, by the name of Danny Arce, we had agreed at first to come back up to the sixth floor. So I thought everybody was going to be on the sixth floor."

Williams sat by the third or fourth set of windows looking out over Dealey Plaza. Could he see the southeast corner of the sixth floor? "I couldn't see too much," he said later, "because the books at the time were stacked so high…I could not possibly see anything to the east side of the building."[54]

As we'll see in a few minutes, Williams's sixth-floor lunch coincides with witnesses in Dealey Plaza who happen to look up at the corner window—just steps from where Williams eats his modest lunch—to see a man sitting still "like a statue." And holding a rifle. Lee Harvey Oswald, not moving, not making a sound, is afraid of being discovered by a coworker.

12:10—Lemmon Ave. and Reagan Street

Jumping up and down to get a glimpse of the motorcade, Father Oscar Huber sees JFK's head, which is turned away from him. Suddenly Kennedy spins around, looks directly, him and smiles. "Hurray!" Huber says with delight—the sixty-eight-year-old priest has now seen his first president.[55]*

12:10—White House Press Bus

As the motorcade rolls on, NBC's Robert MacNeil gets drowsy and has a daydream: "In my daydream, somebody took a shot, fired a shot. And I got out of the bus and I chased the person who fired the shot. And then I woke up and said 'Come on, get real.'"[56]

12:14—Houston Street

Arnold Rowland, eighteen, and his wife, Barbara, seventeen, are standing on the east side of Houston Street, about 150 feet from the Book Depository. Looking around, Rowland's eyes drift up towards the building (he will remember the exact time from the huge Hertz sign on the roof), where he sees the silhouette of a man in the window. The

* Huber would see Kennedy again some forty minutes later at Parkland Hospital—where he would administer the last rites to the president.

man is very still and holding a high-powered rifle mounted with a telescopic sight at about a forty-five-degree angle. One of the man's hands is on the stock, the other on the barrel.

How much of the weapon could Rowland see? "All of it."

The Rowlands consider telling someone before deciding that the man in the window was a security agent.[57]

Rowland assumes the man is there to protect the president.

"Do you want to see a Secret Service agent?" he asks his wife.

"Where?"

"In that building there," he points.[58]

By the time Mrs. Rowland figured out which window her husband was pointing at, "the man had apparently stepped back, because I didn't see him," she said. She might have had difficulty anyway, she said; she was near-sighted and wasn't wearing glasses that day.[59]

Arnold Rowland looks at the window every thirty seconds or so, never sees anyone else in the window where he saw the man with the gun. But he does see, further down (to the right of the window where the gunman was seen), another man. "It was a colored man, I think," he says, which—again—lines up with Bonnie Ray Williams's testimony about eating his lunch on the sixth floor.[60]

In the wake of what was to follow, Rowland will tell a deputy sheriff that he saw two men pacing back and forth on the west side of the sixth floor, on the opposite end of where three shell casings will be found (and heard from three men directly below on the fifth floor). But in later tellings of the story, he will only mention seeing the man with the gun. It's possible that the men Rowland saw were on the fifth floor, where we know three workers gathered to watch the motorcade. We'll come back to the Rowlands in a few minutes.

12:15—Oak Lawn Park

In the motorcade's lead car, Agent Sorrels frets about all the open windows along the motorcade route.[61]

As the motorcade enters downtown Dallas, the crowds thicken, standing up to twelve deep on the sidewalks and spilling out into the street. Surging crowds force Greer to slow the presidential limo to fifteen miles an hour from twenty, and for policeman B. W. Hargis—who has been riding two feet from the left fender of the president's car—to drop back. Agent Hill periodically runs from the follow-up car to the back of the Lincoln and grasps the handles on the trunk. Each time Mrs. Kennedy raises her white-gloved hand to wave, she is met with excited cries of "Jackiiieeee!"[62]

NBC's MacNeil: "The street ahead looked like a river whose banks were constantly shifting, because people would swell out in the crowd and then swell back. And you wondered how the motorcade could get through because they were weaving sinuously through this crowd. Amazing to see. And the reception was euphoric, unbelievable. We all kept commenting on all the nice things people were saying and shouting."[63]

In this more innocent era, bystanders could get uncomfortably close; X-100 slowed down from time to time, and there were photos of Greer with his car door ajar—his way of keeping crowds away.

12:18—Dealey Plaza

Construction worker Howard Brennan finishes his lunch at a cafeteria and decides that he has enough time to see President Kennedy. He walks to the corner of Houston and Elm, directly across from the southeast corner of the Book Depository. "And I walked over to this retainer wall of this little park pool and jumped up on the top ledge."[64]

12:20—Texas School Book Depository, Fifth Floor

James Jarman and a colleague, Harold Norman, decide that they'll have a better view of the motorcade from one of the depository's upper floors. Knowing that the east side of the sixth floor is a thick jungle of cartons, they go to the fifth floor.

"We walked around to the windows facing Elm Street," Norman recalled, "and I can't recall if any were open or not but I remember we opened some, two or three windows ourselves."

Mr. Ball: [WC senior counselor James Ball] How long did you stand there? [On the sidewalk]

Mr. Jarman: Well, until about 12:20, between 12:20 and 12:25.

Mr. Ball: Who do you remember was standing near you that worked with you in the Book Depository?

Mr. Jarman: Harold Norman and Charles Givens and Daniel Arce.

[The men then decided to go upstairs to watch the motorcade.]

Mr. Ball: Where did you go?

Mr. Jarman: To the fifth floor.

Mr. Ball: Why did you go to the fifth floor?

Mr. Jarman: We just decided to go to the fifth floor.

Mr. Ball: Was there any reason why you should go to the fifth floor any more than the fourth or the sixth?

Mr. Jarman: No.

Mr. Ball: Did you know who made the suggestion you go to the fifth floor?

Mr. Jarman: Well, I don't know if it was myself or Hank.

Mr. Ball: When you got there was there anybody on the fifth floor?

Mr. Jarman: No, sir.

Mr. Ball: What did you do when you got to the fifth floor?

Mr. Jarman: We got out the elevator and pulled the gate down. That was in case somebody wanted to use it. Then we went to the front of the building, which is on the south side, and raised the windows.

Mr. Ball: Which windows did you raise?

Mr. Jarman: Well, Harold raised the first window to the east side of the building, and I went to the second rear windows and raised, counting the windows, it would be the fourth one.

Mr. Ball: It would be the fourth window?

Mr. Jarman: Yes.

Mr. Ball: Did somebody join you then?

Mr. Jarman: Yes, sir; a few minutes later.

Mr. Ball: Who joined you?

Mr. Jarman: Bonnie Ray Williams.

Mr. Ball: And where did he stand or sit?

Mr. Jarman: He took the window next to Harold Norman.[65]

12:20—Texas School Book Depository, Sixth Floor

Williams says it takes him "maybe 12 minutes to finish his lunch."[66] Since none of his coworkers have joined him to watch the motorcade go by, he leaves the sixth floor, going down one floor—to the fifth—where he finds Norman and Jarman in front of the windows overlooking Dealey Plaza. Williams acknowledges that he doesn't know the exact time he went to the fifth floor. In any case, his story lines up with Jarman's, and it also dovetails, approximately, with the Rowland testimony about seeing a "colored man" on the sixth floor.

It's unknown whether Oswald, concealed and hushed, hears Williams depart.

12:20—Houston and Elm Streets

Two men, Robert Edwards and Ronald Fischer, are standing on the southwest corner of Houston and Elm Streets. Edwards, looking around, happens to look up at the depository's sixth floor. "Look at that guy," he says, pointing at the window. "He looks like he's uncomfortable," (or words to that effect).[67]

The rifle, seen earlier by Rowland, isn't visible. But what's odd, both Fischer and Edwards agree, is the man himself.

"The man held my attention for 10 or 15 seconds," Fischer said, "because he appeared uncomfortable for one, and, secondly, he wasn't watching-uh—he didn't look like he was watching for the parade. He looked like he was looking down toward the Trinity River and the triple underpass down at the end—toward the end of Ell Street. And—uh—all the time I watched him, he never moved his head, he never—he never moved anything. Just was there transfixed."[68]

Back to the Rowlands. It never occurs to the young teenage couple to say anything to a policeman who is standing just a dozen feet away, and why should they? This is 1963 after all, and the young, thin man with the long gun—they are sure—is there to protect the approaching president. The other man Rowland saw was surely Bonnie Ray Williams eating his chicken sandwich, by, according to Williams, "the third or the fourth set of windows, I believe."[69]

Which in turn explains Oswald sitting, as Fischer says, "like a statue." The remains of Williams's lunch—a greasy bag and empty Dr. Pepper bottle—are later found by a sixth-floor window, just steps from where Oswald hides, frozen and silent.* History can turn on the tiniest things.

* * *

In contrast to the heavy security at Love Field and the Trade Mart, the number of law enforcement officers in Dealey Plaza is minimal. It was believed that crowds here—away from the downtown business area—would be smaller, and they are. There are clusters of people around the intersection of Houston and Elm Streets, where the motorcade will make a sharp left turn onto Elm, and people are lined up on the western side of Elm, but certainly not a dozen deep as is the case on Main Street. Further down Elm, as the curving street leads to the triple underpass, the number of bystanders is even fewer.

Among these are Charles Brehm and his five-year old son, Joe. A veteran of World War II and Korea—as an Army Ranger he landed in Normandy on D-Day and was wounded three months later—the thirty-eight-year-old Brehm and Joe are standing on the south side of Elm Street.

* The bottle and bag were so close to the corner window that some news reports later said, erroneously, that Oswald had dined on fried chicken and soda pop while waiting to shoot the president.

Brehm tells his son, "Be sure and wave at the President and maybe he'll wave back."[70]

Just across Elm, perched atop a white concrete pergola at the top of a sloping patch of grass, is Abraham Zapruder. He's waiting with his movie camera.

12:21—Harwood and Main

The president is now just eight blocks from Dealey Plaza. To his left he likely gets a glimpse of the Municipal Building, headquarters of the Dallas Police Department.

12:21—Texas Route 71, between Houston and Austin

Dean Gorham, director of the Texas Municipal Retirement System, is in his blue Buick, racing to deliver programs for that night's gala fund-raising dinner in Austin. The programs have a welcome message from Governor Connally to the Kennedys which ends: "This is a day to be remembered in Texas."[71]

Texas School Book Depository—Fifth Floor

Perched in front of windows overlooking Elm Street, Williams, Norman, and Jarman wait for the motorcade. Norman is sitting directly under the sixth-floor window, where just feet above him, Oswald sits, silent and, according to eyewitnesses on the street, unmoving. "And I think I was a window over," Williams says. "And I think James Jarman was two or three windows over."[72]

The building is so shabby that "you could see daylight" between the fifth and sixth floors," Norman said later, "because during the times they put the plywood down you can see the plywood, some portion of the plywood, so I would say you could see a little daylight during that time." Asked if he happened to look up at the fifth-floor ceiling on November 22, he said he did. "There was one place I could see the plywood and then another place you could still see a little daylight, I mean peering through the crack."[73]

Which again helps explain why eyewitnesses in the plaza who happen to look up see that the man in the sixth-floor window is so still—and why, in a few minutes, the sound of spent cartridges hitting the sixth floor will be heard on the fifth.

12:22—Main and Reverie

Clint Hill, running from the follow-up car to be closer to Jacqueline Kennedy, jogs alongside the left side of X-100. Another agent, Jack Ready, also jumps off to thwart an overly enthusiastic photographer.

Two cars back, agent Lem Johns opens his car door a few inches, ready to spring out if anyone rushes Vice President Johnson.[74]

Elm and Houston

As he sits on the three-and-a-half-foot white cement wall, Howard Brennan dries his forehead with the sleeve of his shirt. Craning his neck, he looks upward at the Hertz sign on the depository's roof, hoping to see it flash the temperature. But he's so close to the building that he can't see the sign, which is set back from the roof. As he lowers his head, he sees a man in the southeast corner of its sixth floor. He will later say:

> "I was more or less observing the crowd and the people in different building windows, including the fire escape across from the Texas Book Store on the east side of the Texas Book Store, and also the Texas Book Store Building windows. I observed quite a few people in different windows. In particular, I saw this one man on the sixth floor which left the window to my knowledge a couple of times."

Brennan, about ninety-three feet away, would add "There was no other person on that floor that ever came to the window that I noticed. There were people on the next floor down, which is the fifth floor, colored guys."[75]

12:23—Main and Akard

The crowds are thick, and they are roaring as the president's limo slowly makes its way down Main Street. In the lead car, Forrest Sorrels looks up. "My God, look at the people hanging out the windows!" Just feet from the Kennedys, Clint Hill is also scanning them. In Johnson's car, Yarborough, between shouts of "Howdy, thar!" to the crowd, is also looking up. In contrast to the cheers on the street, he sees that no one is smiling.

"To him it seemed that their expressions were hard and disapproving; he had the impression that they were outraged by the display of Kennedy support on the sidewalks."[76]

12:24—Main and Field

The presidential limousine glides by FBI agent Hosty. From the curb, packed with cheering people, he sees Kennedy from behind up close as the car passes by. Hosty later recalls that he is "shocked to see how poorly protected he was."[77]

12:25—Irving

While Ruth Paine prepares lunch, Marina Oswald tends to her children and watches coverage of the Kennedy visit. Marina doesn't understand what's being said but enjoys the images of the glamorous First Couple.

Michael Paine, meanwhile, Ruth's estranged husband, is eating lunch with a friend, Dave Noel, at a restaurant. Paine has been hearing assassination jokes for the last few days and is sick of it. Yet he and Noel begin discussing the emotional makeup of assassins. They stop, after realizing they don't know enough about assassins and what makes them tick.[78]

Elm and Houston

Brennan sees the man in the window again. "He came to the window and he sat sideways on the window sill. That was previous to President

Kennedy getting there. And I could see practically his whole body, from his hips up." He will later describe the man as "in his early thirties, fair complexion, slender but neat, neat slender, possibly 5-foot 10," and weighing "from 160 to 170 pounds."[79] *

12:26—Main and Poydras

"Jackiieeee!" the crowd yells. "Jackie, over here! Jackiieee!" JFK, meantime, beaming, keeps saying "Thank you, thank you, thank you." In the jump seat, Nellie Connally knows there's no way anyone can hear him. "Why does he bother?" she thinks to herself, and decides that the president was raised to be polite.

Clint Hill keeps running back and forth between the follow-up car and X-100. He begins to breathe heavily.[80]

12:28—Main and Market

The green of Dealey Plaza is now a block away; the sky looms big and blue on the horizon. Yarborough continues to worry. "It will be good to have the President out of this," he thinks. Two cars ahead of him, the presidential limo goes by what's known as the Old Red Courthouse, a castle-like structure on the left. From a third-floor tower, a clerk, twenty-six-year-old Patsy Paschall, films Kennedy with her Bell and Howell 8mm color movie camera. "I had a view with a camera that no one else had," she will say thirty-two years later, though the film she shoots is jumpy and somewhat blurry.[81] †

In the plaza itself, spectators wait. From the rising crescendo on Main Street, they know that the president is near.

---

* Brennan's estimate was quite good, considering that Oswald's Selective Service card said he was 5'11" and weighed 150 pounds.

† Paschall gave the film to the FBI a few days later. After it was returned, she put it in a safe deposit box, away from public view for thirty-two years, with the exception of one frame, which appeared in the Nov. 24, 1967 issue of *Life* magazine. "I used to think that someone would blow my head off," she told the Associated Press in a 1995 interview.

12:29—Entering Dealey Plaza

As the lead motorcycles in the motorcade proceed down Houston Street, the eastern edge of the plaza, they are followed by the white Ford sedan driven by Chief Curry. Further back, Yarborough sees the lead car turn right and is confused. *What's over there?* he wonders.

Secret Service agent Sorrels, sitting next to Curry, continues to scan windows. Many are open, including many in the depository. But the veteran agent, in his fortieth year on the job, sees nothing that would construe a threat. Behind them are three more motorcycles.

Suddenly, the sight that everyone in the plaza has been waiting for bursts into view: X-100, the presidential limousine, gleaming in the midday sun. All eyes automatically gravitate towards the Kennedys. The Lincoln Continental rolls on, disappearing from Paschall's viewfinder, but into that of two other amateur photographers.

The sun is blinding. In one home movie taken by Mark Bell, a US mail carrier, Kennedy appears to be squinting as he faces Mrs. Kennedy. "It was terribly hot," she would say in 1964. "Just blinding all of us."[82]

Watching from just a few yards behind them on the follow-up car, Clint Hill thinks the First Lady's pink suit and hat seem "to be illuminated" by the midday sun.[83]

Bell doesn't look through his viewfinder the whole time and thus portions of his film miss its occupants entirely—a great loss. But a nearby photographer, Robert Hughes, standing on the southwest corner of Houston and Main, is more skilled. As X-100 proceeds down Houston—the Book Depository is dead ahead—Kennedy appears to lean slightly forward and to his left. He is trying to hear Nellie Connally, who later says she told him, "Mr. President, you can't say Dallas doesn't love you."[84]

Kennedy's exact response is a matter of conjecture. William Manchester says the president smiled and told Mrs. Connally, "No, you can't." Jacqueline Kennedy says her husband said, "'No, you certainly can't,' or something."[85]

There is also a remarkable, albeit somewhat washed-out photo of this moment that was taken from another angle. As the limo turns onto Houston, JFK pats the right rear of his head, apparently smoothing out his hair. The Book Depository looms in the distance, approximately three hundred feet away. No one is visible in the open sixth floor window. It's likely that Oswald, seen just moments before, is satisfied that his prey is drawing near, and sits to the left of the window, hiding himself and his rifle from approaching cars and vigilant eyes until the very last second.

Back to the Hughes film. While another home movie buff—Zapruder—is about to shoot a far more famous film, Hughes shows us something that Zapruder does not: images of the president and the sixth-floor window in the same frame. This time, there clearly is a figure in the open window. Directly beneath this, figures are also visible on the wide-open fifth-floor windows. They are Bonnie Ray Williams, Harold Norman, and James Jarman Jr.*

12:29—Main and Houston

There's no question that the six occupants of X-100 see the Book Depository before them. The Hughes film captures this moment, and again, one can see in his 8mm film a figure in the southeast corner window—the sixth-floor window. Hughes films the car making the sharp left turn onto Elm.

By now, Oswald has been seen holding a rifle by numerous witnesses. In subsequent decades, armchair critics studying photographs, films, light and shadow, will convince themselves that there is someone else with a gun in Dealey Plaza—in some cases several people with guns. Yet the only gun actually spotted this day—and spotted repeatedly—is

* In a matter of seconds they would hear a series of sharp, loud bursts of noise right above them, just feet away, and something that "sounded like cartridges hitting the floor" and "the action of the rifle, I mean the bolt, as it were pulled back, or something like that." The sound was so near and so loud, "it even shook the building, the side we were on (and) cement fell on my head." "Cement, gravel, dirt, or something from the old building." (Williams, WC, Vol. III, 175)

the gun in the southeast corner of the sixth floor, the one held by Lee Harvey Oswald.

What did it look like from his vantage point? A lesser-known home movie gives us a tantalizing look. It was taken by Elise Dorman, a fifty-seven-year-old employee of publishing firm Scot Foresman in no less a spot than the fourth floor of the depository, just two floors below and two windows to the right of Oswald.

Like Zapruder, Dorman had also brought a camera from home that morning. It was her husband's, and for that reason she wasn't too familiar with it. And yet, in her shaky hand, we're able to see Kennedy's car moving down Houston Street. There's the president, exposed and vulnerable, as he draws closer.

Why didn't Oswald shoot at this point? We'll never know. But after reading of the exact motorcade route in the newspaper, he had more than enough time to contemplate murder. Some writers have said that Oswald had never seen a presidential motorcade before. He certainly had never seen one in person but had probably seem images on TV—Kennedy in West Berlin or Ireland five months earlier, or in Tampa just four days before, or even in Houston the night before, for example—and knew that the president might be quite exposed, and that Secret Service agents might not be close enough to rush to his aid when the moment came.

It has been speculated that had Oswald—the Marine-trained sharpshooter/marksman who was an "excellent shot," according to the noncommissioned officer who helped train him[86]—fired while Kennedy approached him on Houston Street, the president's driver, William Greer, could have hit the gas, swerved, and continued down Houston Street, past the sniper's lair. Why not let his target turn onto Elm Street? If Greer tried to flee, the safety of the Triple Underpass was some 425 feet away. The president would be exposed for a much longer period of time, and his guards would be turned away from the sixth-floor window, not facing it.

Indeed, Zahm—who in 1964 was in charge of the Marksmanship Training Unit Armory at the Marksmanship Training Unit in the

Weapons Training Battalion Marine Corps in Quantico, Virginia—said Elm Street offered the better shot:

> **Sergeant ZAHM.** It would make it easier because Oswald was in an elevated position, and therefore if the car was traveling on a level terrain, it would apparently—he would have to keep adjusting by holding up a little bit as the car traveled. But by going downgrade this just straightened out his line of sight that much better.

Yes, better to be patient, Oswald may have reasoned.

And as he waits—just a few moments more, he must have told himself—does this cold, heartless, selfish, and delusional man ever think, even briefly, that the life he is about to take is a father of two adoring children? Or the impact of what he is about to do will ruin the lives of his own two children? That they will live the rest of their lives in the monstrous shadow that will forever be cast upon them? It is doubtful, for even a second of such contemplation might have given him pause.

What *is* Oswald thinking in these final moments? Perhaps what places him in the sixth-floor window of the Texas School Book Depository this day, taking a bead on John F. Kennedy through the scope of his cheap rifle, isn't so much because of a hatred of Kennedy, but of himself. He is a twenty-four-year-old man who has known nothing but disappointment, failure, and in the end—just hours before—one final, penultimate rejection from his wife, the mother of his two girls. Lee Harvey Oswald—unwanted, unloved, unneeded—has nothing and no one left.

His own words speak for themselves:

> "You know my terrible character…you know I can't hold myself in very long…"
>
> He was violent, a wifebeater, he told Marina, "Because I love you. I can't stand it when you make me mad."

Perhaps there was one final thing remaining: his visions of fame and grandeur. Perhaps that one aria from *The Queen of Spades*—that he played over and over again, as many as twenty times a night, on his record player in Minsk—runs through his mind:

I love you. I love you beyond measure.
I cannot conceive of life without you.
I would perform a heroic deed of unheard-of-prowess for your sake…

The analyses of the American doctor, Hartogs, the KGB, various employers, his wife—they were right. He was a violent man, a desperate man. A man who considered himself brilliant, who hungered for attention, determined to make his mark on the world. He was quite mad, of course.

I would perform a heroic deed of unheard-of-prowess for your sake…

12:30

The gleaming Lincoln Continental makes the sharp left turn onto Elm Street and passes beneath the window.

Bibliography

Interviews

Edward Kosner
Jefferson Morley
John Newman
Ruth Paine
Gerald Posner
David Priess
Larry Sabato
Bob Schieffer
Philip Shenon
Mark Zaid

Books

Bagley, Tennent H. *Spymaster: Startling Cold War Revelations of a Soviet KGB Chief.* (New York, Delaware: Skyhorse Publishing, 2013).

_____. *Spy Wars: Moles, Mysteries, and Deadly Games.* (Yale University Press, 2007).

Bamford, James. *Body of Secrets: Anatomy of the Ultra-Secret National Security Agency.* (New York: Anchor Books, 2002).

Bill, James A. *George Ball: Behind the Scenes in U.S. Foreign Policy.* (Yale University Press, 1998).

Bishop, Jim. *The Day Kennedy Was Shot.* (New York: Greenwich House, 1968).

Blaine, Gerald with Lisa McCubbin. *The Kennedy Detail: JFK's Secret Service Agents Break their Silence.* (New York: Gallery Books, 2010).

Bohrer, John R. *The Revolution of Robert Kennedy: From Power to Protest After JFK.* (New York: Bloomsbury Press, 2017).

Bourne, Peter G. *Fidel: A Biography of Fidel Castro*. (New York City: Dodd, Mead & Company, 1986).

Bugliosi, Vincent. *Four Days in November*. (New York: W.W. Norton & Company, 2007).

_____. *Parkland*. (New York: W.W. Norton & Company, 2007).

_____. *Reclaiming History: The Assassination of President John F. Kennedy*. (New York: W.W. Norton & Company, 2007).

Callanan, James. *Covert Action in the Cold War: US Policy, Intelligence and CIA Operations*. (London: I. B. Tauris, 2009).

Caro, Robert. *The Years of Lyndon Johnson—Means of Ascent*. (New York: Alfred A. Knopf, 1990).

_____. *The Years of Lyndon Johnson—The Passage of Power*. (New York: Alfred A. Knopf, 2012).

Clarke, Thurston. *JFK's Last Hundred Days*. (New York: Penguin Press, 2013).

Coltman, Leycester. *The Real Fidel Castro*. (New Haven and London: Yale University Press, 2003).

Corsi, Dr. Jerome R. *Who Really Killed Kennedy?* (Washington, D.C., WND Books, 2013).

Cullather, Nicholas. *Secret History: The CIA's Classified Account of its Operations in Guatemala, 1952–1954*. (Palo Alto, CA: Stanford University Press, 1999).

Cush, Denise, Catherine Robinson, and Michael York. *Encyclopedia of Hinduism*. (London and New York: Routledge, 2008). p. 544.

Crenshaw, Charles. *Trauma Room One: The JFK Medical Coverup Exposed*. (New York: Cosimo Books, 2001).

Dallek, Robert. *An Unfinished Life: John F. Kennedy, 1917–1963*. (New York: Little, Brown and Company, 2003).

_____. *Flawed Giant: Lyndon Johnson and His Times*, 1961–1973. (New York: Oxford University Press, 1998).

Douglass, James W. *JFK and the Unspeakable*. (New York: Touchstone, 2008).

Epstein, Edward Jay. *Legend: The Secret World of Lee Harvey Oswald*. (New York: Reader's Digest Press/McGraw-Hill, 1978).

Farber, David and Eric Foner. *The Age of Great Dreams: America in the 1960s.* (New York: Farrar, Straus and Giroux, 1994).

Fay, Paul B. *The Pleasure of His Company.* (Ann Arbor: The University of Michigan, 1966).

Forster, Cindy. *The Time of Freedom: Campesino Workers in Guatemala's October Revolution.* (Pittsburgh: University of Pittsburgh Press, 2001).

Gallagher, Mary. *My Life with Jacqueline Kennedy.* (New York: David McKay Company, Inc., 1969).

Gibbons, William Conrad. *The U.S. Government and the Vietnam War: Executive and Legislative Roles and Relationships, Part II: 1961–1964.* (Princeton University Press, 2014).

Gillon, Steven. *The Kennedy Assassination—24 Hours After: Lyndon B. Johnson's Pivotal First Day as President.* (New York: Basic Books, 2010).

Golway, Terry and Les Krantz. *JFK: Day by Day: A Chronicle of 1,036 Days of John F. Kennedy's Presidency.* (Philadelphia: Running Press, 2010).

Goodwin, Doris Kearns. *Lyndon Johnson and the American Dream.* (New York: St. Martin's Griffin, 1976).

Guthman, Edwin. *We Band of Brothers.* (New York: Harper & Row, 1971).

Guthrie, Lee. *Jackie: The Price of the Pedestal.* (New York: Drake Publishers, 1978).

Halberstam, David. *The Best and the Brightest.* (New York: Ballantine Books, 1969).

_____. *The Powers That Be.* (Champaign: University of Illinois Press, 2000).

Hill, Clint with Lisa McCubbin. *Five Days in November.* (New York: Gallery Books, 2013).

_____. *Five Presidents: My Extraordinary Journey with Eisenhower, Kennedy, Johnson, Nixon, and Ford.* (New York: Gallery Books, 2016).

_____. *Mrs. Kennedy and Me.* (New York: Gallery Books, 2012).

Hilty, James W. *Robert Kennedy: Brother Protector.* (Philadelphia: Temple University Press, 1997).

Hosty, James P. *Assignment: Oswald.* (New York: Arcade Press, 1996).

Hunt, Michael. *The World Transformed: 1945 to the Present.* (Oxford University Press, 2003).

Immerman, Richard H. *The CIA in Guatemala: The Foreign Policy of Intervention*. (Austin, Texas: University of Texas Press, 1982).

Karnow, Stanley. *Vietnam: A History*. (New York: Penguin Books, 1997).

Kessler, Ronald. *In the President's Secret Service*. (New York: Crown Publishers, 2009).

Langguth, A.J. *Our Vietnam: The War 1954–1975*. (New York: Simon & Schuster, 2000).

Leaming, Barbara. *Jacqueline Bouvier Kennedy Onassis: The Untold Story*. (New York: Thomas Dunne Books, 2014).

Lee, R. Alton. *Eisenhower & Landrum-Griffin: A Study in Labor-Management Politics*. (Lexington, KY: University Press of Kentucky, 1990).

Leffler, Melvyn P. *For the Soul of Mankind: The United States, the Soviet Union, and the Cold War*. (New York: Macmillan, 2007).

Lincoln, Evelyn. *My Twelve Years with John F. Kennedy*. (David McKay Co., 2000).

Lord, Walter. *A Night to Remember*. (New York: Henry Holt and Company LLC, 1955).

Manchester, William. *American Caesar: Douglas MacArthur 1880–1964*. (New York: Back Bay Books, 1978).

_____. *Death of a President*. (New York: Harper and Row, 1967).

_____. *Portrait of a President*. (New York: Rosetta Books, 2017).

Mailer, Norman. *Oswald's Tale: An American Mystery*. (New York: Random House, 1995).

Mayo, Jonathan. *The Assassination of JFK: Minute by Minute*. (London: Short

Books, 2013).

McCullough, David. *Truman*. (New York: Simon & Schuster, 1992).

McMillan, Priscilla Johnson. *Marina and Lee*. (New York City: Harper and Row, 1977).

Meagher, Sylvia. *Accessories After the Fact: The Warren Commission, the*

Authorities & the Report on the JFK Assassination. (New York: Skyhorse Publishing, 2013).

Melanson, Philip H. with Peter F. Stevens. *The Secret Service: The Hidden*

History of an Enigmatic Agency. (New York: Carroll & Graf Publishers, 2002).

Melanson, Philip H. *Spy Saga: Lee Harvey Oswald and U.S. Intelligence.* (Ann Arbor: The University of Michigan Press, 1990).

Myers, Dale K. *With Malice: Lee Harvey Oswald and the Murder of Officer J.D. Tippit.* (United States: Open Road Media, 2013).

National Academy of Sciences. *Identifying the Culprit: Assessing Eyewitness Identification.* (Washington, DC: The National Academies Press, 2014).

O'Donnell, Kenneth P. and David Powers with Joe McCarthy. *Johnny, We Hardly Knew Ye: Memories of John Fitzgerald Kennedy.* (New York: Little, Brown, 1972).

Oswald, Robert L. with Myrick Land and Barbara Land. *Lee: A Portrait of Lee Harvey Oswald by His Brother.* (New York: Coward-McCann, Inc., 1967).

Parmet, Herbert S. *Jack: The Struggles of John F. Kennedy.* (New York: The Dial Press, 1980).

Penkovsky, Oleg. *The Penkovsky Papers.* (Collins, 1966).

Perlstein, Rick. *Nixonland.* (New York: Scribner, 2008).

Parr, Jerry with Carolyn Parr. *In the Secret Service: The True Story of the Man Who Saved President Reagan's Life.* (Carol Stream, IL: Tyndale House Publishers, Inc.. 2013).

Posner, Gerald. *Case Closed: Lee Harvey Oswald and the Assassination of JFK.* (New York: Random House, 1993).

Powaski, Ronald E. *March to Armageddon: The United States and the Nuclear Arms Race, 1939 to the Present.* (Oxford University Press, 1987).

Reeves, Richard. *President Kennedy: Profile of Power.* (New York: Simon and Schuster, 2011).

Roeper, Richard. *Debunked!: Conspiracy Theories, Urban Legends, and Evil Plots of the 21st Century.* (Chicago: Chicago Review Press, 2008).

Rubenstein, David M. *The American Story: Conversations with Master Historians.* (New York: Simon and Schuster, 2019).

Russo, Gus. *Live by the Sword: The Secret War Against Castro and the Death of JFK.* (Baltimore: Bancroft Press, 1998).

Sabato, Larry. *The Kennedy Half-Century: The Presidency, Assassination, and Lasting Legacy of John F. Kennedy*. (New York: Bloomsbury, 2013).

Schlesinger, Arthur. *Journals 1952–2000*. (New York: Penguin, 2007).

_____. *Robert Kennedy and His Times*. (New York: First Mariner Books, 1978).

_____. *A Thousand Days: John F. Kennedy in the White House*. (New York: Mariner Books, 2002).

Schlesinger, Stephen and Stephen Kinzer. *Bitter Fruit: The Story of the American Coup in Guatemala*. (Cambridge, MA: David Rockefeller Center series on Latin American studies, Harvard University, 1999).

Scott, Peter Dale. *The American Deep State: Wall Street, Big Oil, and the Attack on U.S. Democracy*. (Rowman & Littlefield, 2014).

Shaw, Maude. *White House Nannie*. (New York: Signet Books, 1965).

Shenon, Philip. *A Cruel and Shocking Act: The Secret History of the Kennedy Assassination*. (New York: Henry Holt and Co. LLC., 2013).

Shesol, Jeff. *Mutual Contempt: Lyndon Johnson, Robert Kennedy, and the Feud That Defined a Decade*. (New York: W.W. Norton & Company, 1997).

Shono, L.D. Jr. *He Died for Peace: The Assassination of John F. Kennedy*. (Bloomington, IN, iUniverse, Inc., 2012).

Smith, Ira with Joe Alex Morris. *Dear Mr. President*. (New York: Julian Messner Inc., 1947).

Smith, Jeffrey K. *Bad Blood: Lyndon B. Johnson, Robert F. Kennedy, and the Tumultuous 1960s*. (Bloomington, Indiana: Author House, 2010).

Sorenson, Ted. *Kennedy: The Classic Biography*. (New York: HarperPerennial, 2009).

Stockton, Bayard. *Flawed Patriot: The Rise and Fall of CIA Legend Bill Harvey*. (Virginia: Potomac Books, 2006).

Summers, Anthony. *Not in Your Lifetime: The Defining Book on the J.F.K. Assassination*. (New York: Open Road Media, 2013).

Swanson, James. *End of Days: The Assassination of John F. Kennedy*. (New York: William Morrow, 2013).

Talbot, David. *The Devil's Chessboard: Allen Dulles, the CIA, and the Rise of America's Secret Government.* (New York: Harper Collins Publishers, 2015).

Thomas, Evan. *Robert Kennedy: His Life.* (New York: Simon & Schuster, 2000).

_____. *The Man to See.* (New York: Simon & Schuster, 1992).

Thompson, Jenny and Sherry Thompson. *The Kremlinologist: Llewellyn E Thompson, America's Man in Cold War Moscow.* (Baltimore: Johns Hopkins University Press, 2018).

Travell, Janet. *Office Hours: Day and Night.* (Ann Arbor: World Publishing Co., 1968).

Truman, Margaret. *Harry S. Truman.* (New York: Morrow, 1973).

Waldron, Lamar. *The Hidden History of the JFK Assassination.* (Berkeley, CA: Counterpoint, 2013).

Weiner, Tim. *Legacy of Ashes: The History of the CIA.* (Random House Digital, 2008).

White, Theodore. *In Search of History: A Personal Adventure.* (New York: Warner Books, 1978).

Woolsey, James and Ion Mihai Pacepa. *Operation Dragon: Inside the Kremlin's Secret War on America.* (New York: Encounter Books, 2021).

Zapruder, Alexandra. *Twenty-Six Seconds: A Personal History of the Zapruder Film.* (New York: Twelve, 2016).

Articles

"A History of the Secret Service." CBS News. July 5, 2015.

Ambrose, Stephen. "The Ike Age." *New Republic*, May 9, 1981.

"An Oswald Alias Seen As Anagram." *New York Times*, November 1, 1964.

"Baby Talk In White House…" *Miami News*, April 12, 1963.

Baskin, Robert. "Kennedy To Visit Texas Nov. 21–22 Dallas Included." *Dallas Morning News*, September 26, 1963.

Bernstein, Sharon. "Recollections: The JFK Assassination." *Los Angeles Times*, April 12, 1992.

Beschloss, Michael. "When J.F.K. Secretly Reached Out to Castro." *New York Times*, December 17, 2014.

Brandus, Paul. "Did JFK Predict His Own Death?" *The Week*, November 13, 2013.

Breo, D.L. "JFK's death, Part II—Dallas MDs recall their memories." *Journal of the American Medical Association* 267, no. 20 (May 1992): 2804–2807.

Carter, Terry. "Spence's No-Loss Record Stands with Fieger Acquittal." *American Bar Association*, June 2, 2008.

Constantino, Renato Redentor. "Nothing New in the World." *Mother Jones*, September 13, 2004.

Coren, Robert W., Mary Repel, David Kepley, and Charles South. "Records of Senate Select Committees, 1789–1988." *Guide to the Records of the United States Senate at the National Archives, 1789–1989: Bicentennial Edition*. (Doct. No. 100–42.) Washington, D.C.: National Archives and Records Administration, 1989 (1912 hearings into the *Titanic* disaster).

Corley, Felix. "The KGB Wanted List 1979: Death Penalty for Defectors?" Academia.edu, 2021.

Cowell, Alan. "Ireland Knew of Threats to Kennedy in 1963 Trip." *New York Times*, December 29, 2006.

Dershowitz, Alan. "Suppression of the Facts Grants Stone a Broad Brush." *Los Angeles Times*, December 25, 1991.

Douglas-Home, Robin. "Jacqueline Kennedy." *Washington Post*, February 13, 1967.

"Driver Sees Red, Crashes White House." *Pittsburgh Press*, September 26, 1963.

Dugger, Ronnie. "Dateline Dallas." *Texas Observer*, November 21, 2003.

_____. "Reverberations of Dallas." *New York Times*, January 29, 1989.

_____. "The Last Voyage of Mr. Kennedy." November 29, 1963, as reprinted in the *Texas Observer*, November 22, 2013.

"Eyewitness Tales of Kennedy Slaying Among Most Telling Evidence." Associated Press, September 28, 1964.

Fakhimi, Ghobad. *Thirty Years Iran Oil: From Nationalization to Islamic Revolution*. (CreateSpace, 2016).

Falkenberg-Hull, Eileen. "U.S. Presidents and their cars: These vehicles carried the most powerful men in the world." AutomotiveMap.com, February 16, 2020.

"Fanatics Aimed to Kill Ike." *Brooklyn Eagle*, March 3, 1954.

"FBI Removed Oswald from List of Risks." *New York Times-Chicago Tribune* News Service, December 10, 1963.

"Former Kennedy speechwriter Sorensen dies at 82." Associated Press, October 31, 2010.

Frankel, Max. "President Denies that U.S. Pledged 2d Cuba Invasion." *New York Times*, April 20, 1963.

Freedman, Lawrence. "Lessons in Disaster: McGeorge Bundy and the Path to War in Vietnam." Foreign Affairs, March/April 2009.

"Full Titanic Site Mapped for First Time." *USA Today*, March 8, 2012.

Haines, Gerald. "CIA and Guatemala Assassination Proposals, 1952–1954." CIA Historical Review Program, 1997.

Galbraith, James K. "Exit Strategy: In 1963, JFK Ordered a Complete Withdrawal From Vietnam." *Boston Review*, September 1, 2003.

Gallagher, James. "Literati probing Oswald's days in Minsk." *Chicago Tribune*, January 27, 1993.

Gidman, Jenn. "Verdict is in on whether Lee Harvey Oswald photo is a fake, thanks to 3D tech." *USA Today*, October 20, 2015.

Glass, Andrew. "U.S. launches spraying of Agent Orange, January 18, 1962." *Politico*, January 18, 2019.

Goldstein, Richard. "Keith Clark, Bugler for Kennedy, Dies at 74." *New York Times*, January 17, 2002.

Gregory, Paul. "Lee Harvey Oswald Was My Friend." *New York Times Magazine*, November 7, 2013.

Harris, Elizabeth Forsling. "Looking Back in Sorrow." *Washington Post*, November 20, 1988.

"JFK Death Threat Note From Nov. 1963 In Miami Revealed For 1st Time." CBS Miami, November 21, 2013.

"JFK Files: Highlights from 2,800 previously classified records." *USA Today*, October 26, 2017.

"JFK Proposes Joint Moon Shot." *Pittsburgh Post-Gazette*, September 21, 1963.

"J.F.K. Files Released, Highlighting Hoover, L.B.J. Among Others." *New York Times*, October 26, 2017.

"JFK files, some never seen before, released by National Archives." CBS News, November 3, 2017.

Kalb, Madeleine G. "The C.I.A. and Lumumba." *New York Times*, August 2, 1981.

Kaplan, Fred. "Killing Conspiracy." *Slate*, November 14, 2013

Keating, Peter. "New JFK Files Highlight the Kennedy Administration's Dark Side." *New York*, October 28, 2017.

Kelley, Jeremy P. "John Hinckley stalked Carter in Dayton before shooting Reagan." *Dayton Daily News*, July 27, 2016.

"Kennedy Played His 'Death' for Home Movie." Associated Press, August 14, 1983.

Kettle, Martin. "President 'ordered murder' of Congo leader." *The Guardian*, August 9, 2000.

"Khrushchev calls Kennedy death 'a heavy blow.'" United Press International, November 23, 1963.

Knott, Stephen F. "JFK. A Motorcade. A Rifle. But this Wasn't Dallas." History News Network, April 24, 2016.

Kosner, Edward. "'Kennedy's Avenger' Review: The Assassin's Assassin." *Wall Street Journal*, July 30, 2021.

LaMotte, Sandee. "JFK's assassination aided by his bad back, records show." CNN, November 30, 2017.

Lewis, James G. "Smokey Bear in Vietnam." *University of Chicago Press Journals* 11, no. 3 (July 2006): 598-603.

Malkin, Elisabeth. "An Apology for a Guatemalan Coup, 57 Years Later." *New York Times*, October 20, 2011.

Manchester, William. "1963." *New York Times Magazine*, November 4, 1973.

Mangan, James. "Doctor Recalls JFK Assassination." Associated Press, November 19, 1973.

McPherson, Alan. "Misled by Himself: What the Johnson Tapes Reveal about the Dominican Intervention of 1965." *Latin American Research Review 38, no. 2* (June 2003).

Migdal, Wendy. "Retro Reads: Eisenhower visits Fredericksburg in 1954; local man reports assassination plot." *Free Lance-Star*, May 20, 2019.

Morley, Jefferson. "Beyond the smoking gun: The new JFK files fill in two holes in the assassination story." JFK Facts, July 31, 2017.

Noah, Timothy. "The Day Before JFK Was Assassinated." MSNBC, November 21, 2013.

Norwood, James. "Edmund Gullion, JFK, and the Shaping of a Foreign Policy in Vietnam." Kennedys and King, May 8, 2018.

Onion, Rebecca. "The 'Wanted For Treason' Flyer Distributed in Dallas Before JFK's Visit." *Slate*, November 15, 2013.

Pait, T. Glenn and Justin T. Dowdy. "John F. Kennedy's back: chronic pain, failed surgeries, and the story of its effects on his life and death." *Journal of Neurosurgery*, July 11, 2017.

Perry, Mark. "MacArthur's Last Stand Against A Winless War." *American Conservative*, October 3, 2018.

"Peter Deriabin, Defector from KGB." *Chicago Tribune*, September 1, 1992.

"Poll: JFK conspiracy belief slipping slightly." Associated Press, November 18, 2013.

"President Starts Countdown for Fair." *Gettysburg Times*, April 23, 1963.

"President Visits City Today." *Chicago Tribune*, November 2, 1963.

Reimann, Matt. "When Ian Fleming Met John F. Kennedy." *Books Tell You Why*, May 27, 2015.

"Robert Maheu Able Opponent in Hughes Row." *Los Angeles Times*, December 10, 1970.

"Russian Says Oswald Was A Bad Shot." *Buffalo News*, July 21, 1992.

Salinas, Sara and Martin Finucane. "Thousands of records on JFK Assassination released online." *Boston Globe*, July 25, 2017.

Savodnik, Peter. "Could a Jewish Beauty Have Saved Kennedy by Marrying Lee Harvey Oswald in Minsk?" *Tablet*, October 10, 2013.

"Secret Service Drives Hard to Protect the President." *Voice of America*, April 7, 2019.

Shapira, Ian. "Foul Traitor: New JFK assassination records reveal KGB defector's 3-year interrogation." *Washington Post*, August 16, 2017.

Smith, Alexander. "Fidel Castro: The CIA's 7 Most Bizarre Assassination Attempts." NBC News, November 28, 2016.

Stout, David. "Yuri Nosenko, Soviet Spy Who Defected, Dies at 81." *New York Times*, August 27, 2008.

Szulc, Tad. "Nixon is Stoned by Rioters Headed by Reds." *New York Times*, May 9, 1958.

"The Sinking of the Titanic, 1912." Eyewitness to History, 2000.

Wang, Amy. "Biden postpones release of JFK assassination files, citing pandemic-related delays." *Washington Post*, October 23, 2021.

Weinraub, Bernard. "Hollywood Wonders if Warner Brothers Let 'J.F.K.' Go Too Far." *New York Times*, December 24, 1991.

"White House Silent on Stoning of Nixon." *Pensacola Journal*, May 9, 1958.

Wise, David. "When the FBI Spent Decades Hunting for a Soviet Spy on Its Staff." *Smithsonian Magazine*, October 2013.

Wright, Lawrence. "Was Dallas A City of Hate?" *D Magazine*, November 1, 1988.

"Woman believes film may offer new angle on Kennedy assassination." Associated Press, October 31, 1995.

"21 Yanks Fly Home." *Miami News*, April 22, 1963.

Other

"50 years of conspiracy theory polling: What you may have missed in the polls." American Enterprise Institute, November 7, 2013.

"Public Opinion on Conspiracy Theories." American Enterprise Institute, November 2013.

Kennedy, John F. "Proclamation 3447: Embargo on All Trade with Cuba." American Presidency Project, University of California at Santa Barbara, February 3, 1962.

_____. "Remarks at the Breakfast of the Fort Worth Chamber of Commerce." American Presidency Project, November 22, 1963.

"RS#01: Background on the Guatemalan Coup of 1954." Baltimore County History Labs Program.

Bartlett, Charles. "Oral History Interview—JFK #2." John F. Kennedy Presidential Library, February 20, 1965.

Bugliosi, Vincent, author's web page.

Cloherty, Peter. "Oral History Interview—JFK #1." John F. Kennedy Presidential Library, September 29, 1967.

"The Complete Pentagon Papers." *New York Times* online, 1945-67.

Henry Ford Museum, "Kennedy Presidential Limousine."

"Investigation of the Assassination of President John F. Kennedy," Appendix to Hearings Before the Select Committee on Assassinations, Vol. X, March 1979, p. 61.

Jarman, James. Affidavit to Dallas County Notary Public, November 23, 1963.

"JFK Visits Ireland." RTE Archives, June 26–19, 1963.

"Korean War." Summary at Dwight D. Eisenhower Presidential Library.

Priess, David with Gerald Posner and Mark Zaid. "The JFK Assassination Documents." Lawfare Podcast, December 22, 2021.

Lovelady, Billy Nolan. Affidavit to Dallas County Notary Public, November 22, 1963.

"Memorandum for the Heads of Executive Departments and Agencies on the Temporary Certification Regarding Disclosure of Information in Certain Records Related to the Assassination of President John F. Kennedy." White

House, October 22, 2021.

National Security Archives Nuclear Documentation Project, via George Washington University.

"Odio Incident." House Select Committee on Assassinations Hearings Vol. X, p. 18–35.

Oswald family home movie, Thanksgiving, November 22, 1962.

Oswald, Robert, interview with ABC News, 1993 (Bugliosi, 602).

"MacArthur, Douglas, April 1961–January 1963." (Record of correspondence between President Kennedy and General Douglas) John F. Kennedy Presidential Library.

"Report of the President's Commission on the Assassination of President John F. Kennedy [with 26 volumes of testimony and exhibits]." United States Government Printing Office, September 24, 1964.

"Report of the Select Committee on Assassinations of the U.S. House of Representatives." United States Government Printing Office, 1979.

"Senate Committee on Commerce, Subcommittee on the 'Titanic' Disaster." United States Senate. Hearings held April 19–May 25, 1912.

"The Situation in South Vietnam." Central Intelligence Agency, September 16, 1963.

"The President's Bond Girl." Ian Fleming, November 2, 2016.

Titanic Disaster, United States Senate Inquiry, 62d Congress, 2d Session, Report No. 806.

U.S. Department of State. *Foreign Relations of the United States 1961–1963*, Volume X, Cuba, 1961–1962.

_____. *Foreign Relations of the United States, 1961–1963*. Volume II, Vietnam, 1962, Report by the Senate Majority Leader.

_____. "Office of the Historian: Foreign Travel of President Dwight D. Eisenhower."

"Who Was Lee Harvey Oswald?" *Frontline*, PBS, November 16, 1993.

"Who Was Mohammad Mossadegh?" Edited by Ghobad Fakhimi, Northeastern Illinois University.

Zapruder, Abraham, interview with Jay Watson, WFAA-TV, November 22, 1963.

Endnotes

Chapter 1

1 Richard Roeper, "Of Soylent Green and Men in Black: The Best and Worst Conspiracy Movies Ever Made," *Debunked!: Conspiracy Theories, Urban Legends, and Evil Plots of the 21st Century* (Chicago: Chicago Review Press, 2008), 229–230
2 "Poll: JFK conspiracy belief slipping slightly," Associated Press, November 18, 2013
3 "50 years of conspiracy theory polling: What you may have missed in the polls," American Enterprise Institute, November 7, 2013
4 Vincent Bugliosi, *Reclaiming History: The Assassination of President John F. Kennedy.* (New York: W. W. Norton & Company), xiv, 1273
5 Ibid., 1011
6 Terry Carter, "Spence's No-Loss Record Stands with Fieger Acquittal," American Bar Association, June 2, 2008
7 Quoted on Bugliosi's website for his book *The Prosecution of George W Bush for Murder*

Chapter 2

1 Posner and Zaid were interviewed on December 2021 on the "Lawfare" podcast by David Priess, a former CIA officer who is publisher of *Lawfare* and chief operating officer of the Lawfare Institute.
2 Tim Weiner, *Legacy of Ashes: The History of the CIA* (Random House Digital, 2008), 268.
3 "J.F.K. Files Released, Highlighting Hoover, L.B.J. Among Others," *New York Times*, October 26, 2017
4 "New JFK Files Highlight the Kennedy Administration's Dark Side," Peter Keating, *New York*, October 28, 2017
5 "J.F.K. Files Released, Highlighting Hoover, L.B.J. Among Others," *New York Times*, October 26, 2017
6 Ibid.
7 Ibid.
8 "JFK files: Highlights from 2,800 previously classified records," *USA TODAY*, October 26, 2017
9 "J.F.K. Files Released, Highlighting Hoover, L.B.J. Among Others," *New York Times*, October 26, 2017

10 "Khrushchev calls Kennedy death 'a heavy blow,'" United Press International, November 23, 1963
11 "JFK files: Highlights from 2,800 previously classified records," *USA TODAY,* October 26, 2017
12 Whitten, CIA memo, December 13, 1963, https://www.archives.gov/files/research/jfk/releases/104-10052-10119.pdf
13 David Wise, "When the FBI Spent Decades Hunting for a Soviet Spy on Its Staff," *Smithsonian Magazine,* October 2013
14 "New JFK files reveal Oswald was on CIA's mail 'watch list,' FBI misplaced his fingerprints," *Dallas Morning News,* December 15, 2017
15 Ibid.
16 James Hosty, *Assignment Oswald* (New York: Arcade Publishing, 1996), 42–3
17 "Trump delays full release of some JFK assassination files until 2021, bowing to national security concerns," Ian Shapira, *Washington Post,* April 26, 2018
18 Manny Legrand, "U.S. Releases 1,500 Documents on JFK Assassination," *The Dallas Express,* December 21, 2021

Chapter 3

1 Bugliosi, 1,051
2 Katie Zezima, "People used to be able to walk into the White House. Legally." *Washington Post,* September 23, 2014
3 Paul Brandus, *Under This Roof* (Guilford, CT: Lyons Press, 2015), 119
4 Ibid.
5 Ibid., 186
6 David McCullough, *Truman* (New York: Simon & Schuster, 1992), 109
7 Wendy Migdal, "Retro Reads: Eisenhower visits Fredericksburg in 1954; local man reports assassination plot," *Free Lance-Star,* May 20, 2019
8 Hill, *Five Presidents,* 44
9 Ibid., 27
10 Ibid., 27–28
11 Ibid., 28–29
12 Ibid., 30–31
13 Ibid., 33–34
14 Ibid., 39–40
15 Ibid., 41–42
16 Ibid., 46
17 Ibid., 47–48
18 Stephen F. Knott, "JFK. A Motorcade. A Rifle. But this Wasn't Dallas," *History News Network,* April 24, 2016

Chapter 4

1 Robert Oswald with Myrick and Barbara Land, *Lee: A Portrait of Lee Harvey Oswald by His Brother* (New York: Coward-McCann, Inc., 1967), 52
2 Priscilla Johnson McMillan, *Marina and Lee* (New York City: Harper and Row, 1977), 195

3 Gerald Posner, *Case Closed: Lee Harvey Oswald and the Assassination of JFK* (New York: Random House, 1993), 9
4 Ibid., 9
5 Ibid., 8
6 McMillan, 196–97
7 Posner, 10, FBI Report of June 4, 1964, of interview with Mrs. Clyde Livingston, WC Vol. XXV, 1199
8 Testimony of Philip Eugene Vinson, WC Vol. VIII, 77, 79
9 Testimony of Lillian Murret, WC, Vol. VIII, 122
10 Posner, 9, WC testimony of Hiram Conway, Vol. VIII, 86
11 Posner, 10, FBI report, April 3, 1964, of investigation into Lee Harvey Oswald's possible attendance at a day nursery in Dallas in 1944–45
12 Robert Oswald, 49; Posner, 10
13 Posner, 10, testimony of John Pic, WC Vol. XI, 38–39
14 Ibid., Pic testimony, 40–41
15 Posner, 11
16 McMillan, 199
17 Posner, 13
18 Bugliosi, 532
19 Ibid.
20 Posner, 13
21 Robert Oswald, 47
22 Myrtle Evans testimony, WC, Vol. VIII, 57
23 Julian Evans testimony, WC, Vol. VIII, 69–70
24 Ibid., 71
25 Ibid.
26 McMillan, 204–205
27 Posner 16, WC testimony of Edward Voebel, WC Vol. VIII, 10
28 William E. Wulf testimony, WC Vol. VIII, 18
29 Posner, 17
30 Ibid.
31 Ibid., 18

Chapter 5

1 Ibid, 20, testimony of James Zahm, WC, Vol. XI, 308
2 McMillan, 67
3 FBI report, June 26, 1964, of interview with Allen R. Felde (CD 1229), CE 1962, WC Vol. VIII, 268
4 FBI report, June 26, 1964, of an interview with Allen R. Felde (CD 1229), CE 1962, WC Vol. VIII, 268
5 Daniel Powers testimony, WC, Vol, VIII, 270
6 Posner, 21
7 David Christie Murray Jr. affidavit to WC, May 15, 1964
8 John Donovan testimony, WC, Vol. VIII, 290
9 Bugliosi, 552
10 Donovan, 298

11 Bugliosi, 552
12 Ibid., 554
13 De Mohrenschildt testimony, WC, Vol. IX, 242
14 Posner, 23
15 Ibid., 24
16 Affidavit of Peter Francis Connor, May 22, 1964, WC, Vol. VIII, 317
17 Affidavit of John Rene Heindel, May 19, 1964, WC Vol. VIII, 318
18 Bugliosi, 556
19 Powers, WC, Vol. VIII, 270
20 Posner, 28
21 Affidavit of Mack Osborne, May 18, 1964, WC Vol. VIII, 321
22 Affidavit of Kerry Wendell Thornley, WC, May 18, 1964, 97
23 Testimony of Nelson Delgado, April 16, 1964, WC Vol. VIII, 233
24 Ibid., 265
25 Thornley, 96
26 Posner, 32
27 Ibid., 33, CE 1114, WC Vol. XXII, 77–79

Chapter 6

1 Affidavit of Billy Joe Lord, WC, Vol. XI, 118
2 Bugliosi, 570
3 Ibid., xxvi
4 Ibid., 596
5 Mailer, 41
6 Ibid., 44–45
7 Oswald's "Historic Diary," CE 24, entry for October 21, 1959 (Original spelling, Posner, 50)
8 Ibid., Posner, 51
9 Mostovshchikov, "KGB Case No. 31451 on Lee Harvey Oswald," August 8, 1992, 7 (Posner, 51)
10 Mailer, 52
11 Ibid.
12 Ibid., 54–55
13 Posner, 52
14 William Manchester, *Death of a President* (New York: Harper and Row, 1967), 30–31
15 Oswald diary, October 31, 1959 entry
16 Testimony of Richard Edward Snyder, WC, Vol. V, 263
17 Oswald letter, written on Metropole Hotel stationery. November 8, 1959; WC Appendix 15, 749
18 Snyder, 272
19 Ibid., 263
20 Oswald diary; WC exhibit 24, 4
21 Bugliosi, 585–586
22 Hosty, 42–43
23 Mosby, www.youtube.com/watch?v=31CLFT6BlBk
24 Mailer, 60

25 McMillan, 74–77
26 Oswald letter to Robert Oswald, WC, Vol. XVI, CE 295
27 Mailer, 63
28 Oswald diary, January 4, 1960 entry, CE 985, WC, Vol. XVIII
29 Bugliosi, 596
30 Edward Nash, "Purchasing power of workers in the Soviet Union," *Monthly Labor Review*, Vol. 94, No. 5 (May 1971), 39
31 Oswald diary, January 7, 1960 entry
32 Ibid., January 13–16, 1960
33 Bugliosi, 642
34 Oswald diary, January 13–16, 1960 entry
35 McMillan, 108
36 Transcript of November 16, 1993, *Frontline* (PBS) broadcast
37 Fain, WC, Vol. IV, 405
38 Ibid., 406
39 Bugliosi, 600
40 Ibid.
41 Ibid., 597
42 Posner, 49
43 Ibid., 60
44 Bugliosi, 602
45 Ibid.
46 Ibid.
47 "Russian Recalls JFK Assassin As Weak Man And A Poor Shot," Associated Press, July 21, 1992
48 Oswald diary, October 18, 1960 entry
49 Peter Savodnik, "Could a Jewish Beauty Have Saved Kennedy by Marrying Lee Harvey Oswald in Minsk?," *TabletMag*, October 11, 2013
50 Mailer, 109
51 Ibid., 126
52 Bugliosi, 607–8
53 Paul B. Fay, *The Pleasure of His Company* (Ann Arbor: The University of Michigan, 1966), 114
54 Testimony of Francis L. Martello, WC, April 7–8, 1964, Vol. X, 56
55 Oswald letter to Robert Oswald, Nov 26, 1959
56 Snyder, WC, Vol. V, 278
57 Mark Perry, "MacArthur's Last Stand Against A Winless War," *The American Conservative,* October 3, 2018
58 William Manchester, *American Caesar* (New York: Back Bay Books, 1978), 696
59 Kenneth O'Donnell and David Powers, *Johnny, We Hardly Knew Ye* (New York: Little, Brown, 1972), 13
60 Arthur Schlesinger, *A Thousand Days: John F. Kennedy in the White House* (New York: Mariner Books, 2002), 339
61 Oswald diary
62 Bugliosi, 613
63 Ibid., 614

64 Ibid., 203
65 Guy Russo, Live by the Sword: The Secret War Against Castro and the Death of JFK (Baltimore: Bancroft Press, 1998), 106
66 Ibid., 105
67 Mailer, 248
68 Robert Dallek, *An Unfinished Life: John F. Kennedy, 1917–1963* (New York: Little, Brown and Company, 2003), 78
69 Henry Ford Museum, "Kennedy Presidential Limousine"
70 Clint Hill, *Mrs. Kennedy and Me,* (New York: Gallery Books, 2012), 267
71 McMillan, 173–4
72 Mailer, 188–9
73 Ibid., 190–91
74 McMillan, 107
75 Ibid., 108
76 Bugliosi, 616
77 Snyder memorandum, WC, Appendix 15, 755
78 McMillan, 124
79 Ibid., 126
80 Bugliosi, 619
81 McMillan, 133
82 Ibid., 151
83 Bugliosi, 620
84 McMillan, 133–4
85 Bugliosi, 621–2
86 Mailer, 279
87 WC, Appendix 15, 757
88 McMillan, 572
89 Thurston Clarke, *JFK's Last Hundred Days* (New York: Penguin Press, 2013), 37
90 McMillan, 148
91 Oswald diary
92 WC, Appendix 13, 709
93 John F. Kennedy Presidential Library and Museum
94 McMillan, 163
95 Andrew Glass, "U.S. launches spraying of Agent Orange," *Politico,* January 18, 1962
96 Oswald letter to Connally, WC, Appendix XIII, 710
97 Bugliosi, 628
98 McMillan, 170
99 Bugliosi, 629
100 Ibid., 630
101 Ibid.
102 McMillan, 173
103 Ibid., 176
104 Ibid., 176–7
105 Bugliosi, 642
106 McMillan, 178–9
107 McMillan, 181

108 Bugliosi, 578
109 Posner, 56
110 Ibid.
111 McMillan, 184–5
112 WC, Appendix 13, 713
113 Bugliosi, 639

Chapter 7

1 Ibid., 642
2 McMillan, 213–4
3 Ibid., 215
4 Ibid.
5 Bugliosi, 642
6 Ibid., 642–3
7 Testimony of Max Clark, WC, Vol. VIII, 346
8 Ibid.
9 Posner, 78
10 McMillan, 224
11 Ibid., 223
12 Ibid., 225
13 Ibid.
14 Ibid., 226
15 Bugliosi, 644
16 Ibid.
17 Ibid., 646
18 McMillan, 229
19 Perry, "MacArthur's Last Stand Against A Winless War," *The American Conservative,* October 3, 2018
20 Paul Gregory, "Lee Harvey Oswald Was My Friend," *The New York Times Magazine,* November 7, 2013
21 WC, Paul Gregory testimony, Vol. IX, 141
22 McMillan, 241
23 Bugliosi, 648–9
24 Ibid.
25 McMillan, 244
26 Bugliosi, 645
27 McMillan, 231
28 "Minutes of Meeting of the Special Group (Augmented) on Operation MONGOOSE, 6 September, 1962," National Archives, JFK Assassination, Records, Document No. 178–10003–10090 and 157–10002–10102
29 McMillan, 247
30 Bugliosi, 652
31 Ibid., 651
32 Ibid.
33 Ibid.
34 Ibid., 652–3

35 Elizabeth Forsling Harris, "Looking Back in Sorrow," *Washington Post,* November 20, 1988
36 Based on the Warren Commission's reconstruction of his income and expenses (Bugliosi, 652)
37 Bugliosi, 653
38 Ibid.
39 Ibid., 654
40 Gregory, *The New York Times Magazine,* November 7, 2013
41 Bugliosi, 661
42 Ibid.
43 Ibid., 662
44 Ibid.
45 Ibid., 663

Chapter 8

1 Gregory, *The New York Times Magazine,* November 7, 2013
2 John F. Kennedy Presidential Library and Museum, RFKAG-217-002-p0001, Folder Title:6-5: Cuba: Cuban Crisis, 1962: Cuban Prisoner Exchange (James B. Donovan)
3 McMillan, 305
4 Marina Oswald. WC, Vol. I, 11
5 WC, Appendix 13, 723
6 Bugliosi, 669
7 McMillan, 229
8 Ibid., 319
9 Bugliosi, 676
10 McMillan, 319–20
11 Ibid., 324–7
12 Testimony of Mahlon Tobias Sr., WC Vol. X, 256
13 McMillan, 328
14 Manchester, *Death of a President,* 17
15 Bugliosi, 680
16 Ibid.
17 Ibid.
18 McMillan, 329
19 Bugliosi, 680
20 Posner, 105
21 Alan McPherson, "Misled by himself: What the Johnson tapes reveal about the Dominican intervention of 1965," *Latin American Research Review* (2003) 38#2: 127–146.
22 Testimony of Marina Oswald, WC Vol. I, 13
23 Bugliosi, 682
24 Posner, 105–6
25 Testimony of Robert Stovall, WC, Vol. X, 172
26 Testimony of Dennis Ofstein, WC, Vol. X, 204–5
27 Posner, 110
28 Testimony of John Graef, WC, Vol X, 188

29 Ibid., 187
30 Ibid., 190
31 McMillan, 339
32 McMillan, 343
33 Ibid., 345
34 Testimony of Jeanne de Mohrenschildt, WC, Vol. IX, 317
35 McMillan, 346
36 Ibid., 349
37 Testimony of Edwin Walker, WC, Vol. XI, 405
38 Testimony of Marina Oswald, WV, Vol. I, 16–17
39 McMillan, 351
40 Ibid., 356
41 Ibid.
42 Manchester, *Death of a President*, 447
43 McMillan, 359
44 Testimony of George de Mohrenschildt, WC, Vol. IX, 249–250
45 McMillan, 363–4
46 "Baby Talk In White House…," Miami News, April 12, 1963, 1
47 McMillan, 367
48 Max Frankel, "President Denies that U.S. Pledged 2d Cuba Invasion," New York Times, April 20, 1963
49 McMillan, 366
50 Ibid., 366–70
51 Ibid., 603
52 Jerry and Carolyn Parr, *In the Secret Service* (Carol Stream, IL: Tyndale House Publishers, Inc.. 2013), 59–60
53 Manchester, *Death of a President*, 97
54 WC, Appendix 14, 744
55 Posner, 123
56 Ibid., 525
57 Ibid., 124
58 James W. Douglass, *JFK and the Unspeakable* (New York: Touchstone, 2008), 328
59 Ibid., xxv
60 Posner, 124
61 Testimony of Lillian Murret, WC, Vol. VIII, 136
62 Testimony of Julian Evans, WC, Vol. VIII, 45
63 McMillan, 388
64 JFK Library, JFKPOF-060-001-p0002
65 McMillan, 253
66 Ibid., 331
67 Manchester, *Death of a President*, 97
68 McMillan, 400
69 JFK Library
70 McMillan, 400
71 Manchester, *Death of a President*, 97
72 McMillan, 400

73 WC, Chapter 4, 121
74 McMillan, 402
75 National Archives, *JFK Assassination Records*, Chapter Two, 28
76 Bugliosi, 946, footnote 63
77 McMillan, 413
78 Melvyn P. Leffler, *For the Soul of Mankind: The United States, the Soviet Union, and the Cold War* (New York: Macmillan, 2007), 182–183
79 McMillan, 408–9
80 Douglass, 66
81 Clarke, 150
82 McMillan, 417
83 Ibid., 418
84 Manchester, *Portrait of a President* (New York: Rosetta Books, 2017), 146
85 McMillan, 425
86 Manchester, *Death of a President*, 98
87 Ibid.
88 McMillan, 422
89 Bugliosi, 714
90 Testimony of Charles Le Blanc, WC, Vol. X, 216
91 McMillan, 422
92 Bugliosi, 719–20
93 Clarke, 4
94 Evelyn Lincoln, *My Twelve Years with John F. Kennedy* (David McKay Co., 2000), 349–55
95 Clark, 17
96 WC Affidavit of John Quigley, February 7, 1964
97 McMillan, 435
98 Manchester, *Death of a President*, 8
99 Clarke, 68
100 Clark, 39
101 Posner, 161
102 McMillan, 450
103 National Security Archive, George Washington University
104 Bugliosi, 738–9
105 Ibid.
106 Ibid.
107 Tim Weiner, *Legacy of Ashes: The History of the CIA* (Random House Digital, 2008), 699–700
108 Ibid.
109 Larry Sabato, *The Kennedy Half-Century* (New York: Bloomsbury, 2013), 123
110 Posner, 166
111 Bugliosi, 738
112 Clarke, 137
113 Douglass, 93
114 Stephen Ambrose, "The Ike Age," The New Republic, May 9, 1981
115 Schlesinger, 339

116 Clarke, 145
117 Douglass, 69
118 Bugliosi, 1284
119 Charles Bartlett Oral History Interview – JFK #2, 2/20/1965
120 Janet Travell, *Office Hours: Day and Night* (Ann Arbor: World Publishing Co., 1968), 361
121 Clarke, 160
122 David Rubenstein, *The American Story,* (New York: Simon and Schuster, 2019), 211
123 Ibid., 212
124 L.D. Shono, Jr., *He Died for Peace: The Assassination of John F. Kennedy* (Bloomington, IN: iUniverse, Inc, 2012), 222
125 Clarke, 171
126 "JFK Plans Whirlwind Texas Trip," AP report in Victoria (TX) *Advocate*, September 14, 1963, 3
127 Clarke, 176–77
128 Ibid., 182
129 "JFK Proposes Joint Moon Shot," *Pittsburgh Post-Gazette*, September 21, 1963
130 Clarke, 70
131 Jesse Garner testimony, WC, Vol. X, 276
132 Ruth Paine testimony, WC, Vol. III, 10
133 Posner, 169
134 Ronald E. Powaski, *March to Armageddon: The United States and the Nuclear Arms Race*, 1939 to the Present (Oxford University Press, 1987), 111–112
135 Bugliosi, 1,310
136 Douglass, 158
137 Newman, 349
138 Mailer, 623
139 Larry Sabato, *The Kennedy Half*-Century (New York: Bloomsbury, 2013), 176–7
140 Posner, 171
141 Affidavit Of John Bryan McFarland And Meryl McFarland, WC, May 28, 1964
142 Robert E. Baskin, "Kennedy To Visit Texas November 21–22 Dallas Included," *Dallas Morning News*, September 26, 1963
143 "Driver Sees Red, Crashes White House," *Pittsburgh Press*, September 26, 1963
144 Testimony of Pamela Mumford, WC, Vol. IX, 217–18; Sixth Floor Museum, Oral History
145 Posner, 174
146 Sabato, 176
147 Bugliosi, 1,045
148 Ibid., 1,044
149 Sabato, 177
150 Bugliosi, 1,046
151 Sabato, 177–8
152 Posner, 185
153 Lyndon B. Johnson Presidential Library, LBJ-Hoover phone call, November 23, 1963
154 Sabato, 178
155 Newman, 353

156 Bugliosi, 1,050
157 Sabato, 180
158 House Select Committee on Assassinations, p. 123, https://www.archives.gov/research/jfk/select-committee-report/part-1c.html
159 Sabato, 181
160 Interview with the author
161 Posner, 189–90
162 Hill, *Mrs. Kennedy and Me*, 254
163 Posner, 197
164 Manchester, *Death of a President*, 22
165 Ibid., 39
166 Ibid.
167 Posner, 197
168 McMillan, 469
169 William Conrad Gibbons, *The U.S. Government and the Vietnam War: Executive and Legislative Roles and Relationships, Part II: 1961–1964* (Princeton University Press, 2014). Also: JFK Library, Tape 114/A50, Meeting on Vietnam.
170 "A-Test Ban Pact Hailed by President," *Chicago Tribune,* October 8, 1963
171 Whitten memo, December 13, 1963
172 "Kennedy Told U.S. Can End Viet Job in '65," *Chicago Tribune*, October 3, 1963
173 Paul Brandus, "JFK's murder was not a conspiracy," *The Week,* November 2013
174 Posner, 201
175 Roy Truly testimony, WC, Vol. III, 213–14
176 Bugliosi, 1,455
177 Clarke, 241
178 Buell Wesley Frazier testimony, WC, Vol II, 216
179 *USA Today*, October 26, 2017
180 Manchester, *Death of a President*, 9
181 Lawrence Wright, "Why Do They Hate Us So Much?" *Texas Monthly,* November 1983
182 Manchester, *Death of a President*, 38
183 Parr, 71–2
184 Manchester, *Death of a President,* 39–40
185 Manchester, *Death of a President*, 23–4
186 Clarke, 283
187 Ibid., 279
188 Bugliosi, *Parkland*, 190
189 Bonnie Ray Williams testimony, WC, Vol. III, 164
190 Hosty, 21
191 Bugliosi, 775
192 Hosty, 27
193 Clarke, 279
194 Ibid., 283
195 JFK Library
196 Bugliosi, 1,240
197 Ibid.

198 Hosty, 21
199 Philip H. Melanson, PhD with Peter F. Stevens. *The Secret Service* (New York: Carroll & Graf Publishers, 2002), 58
200 Manchester, *Death of a President*, 10
201 Bugliosi, 1,035
202 JFK Library, "Remarks Before the Protestant Council, New York," November 8, 1963
203 Gerald Blaine and Lisa McCubbin, *The Kennedy Detail* (New York: Gallery Books, 2010), 10
204 Hosty, 30
205 Michael Paine testimony, WC, Vol. II, 406
206 U.S. State Department Office of the Historian. Memorandum for the Record, November 12, 1963. https://history.state.gov/historicaldocuments/frus1961-63v11/d376
207 Kenneth O'Donnell testimony, WC, Vol. III, 443
208 JFK Library, News Conference 64, November 14, 1963
209 Clarke, 300
210 O'Donnell and Powers, 19; Manchester, "1963," *New York Times Magazine*, November 4, 1973
211 Clarke, 301
212 JFK Library, Oral History, 40
213 WC, Chapter 2, 29
214 Clarke, 303–4
215 Bugliosi, 1,240
216 Manchester, *Death of a President*, 42
217 Ibid., 102
218 WC, Chapter 2, 39
219 Bugliosi, *Parkland*, 110
220 "JFK Death Threat Note From Nov. 1963 In Miami Revealed For 1st Time," CBS Miami
221 Bugliosi, 1,268
222 Ibid., 1,036
223 *Dallas Morning News*, November 17, 1963
224 Elizabeth Forsling Harris, "Looking Back in Sorrow," *Washington Post*, November 20, 1988
225 Bugliosi, 4
226 Clarke, 310
227 Manchester, *Death of a President*, 6
228 Ibid., 102
229 Ibid., 33
230 Clarke, 313–14
231 Corsi, 179–80
232 JFK Library
233 Clarke, 316
234 Ibid.
235 *Dallas Morning News*, November, 19, 1963
236 Manchester, *Death of a President*, 32

237 Ibid., 12
238 Clarke, 321–2
239 Ibid., 6
240 Harris.
241 Ronnie Dugger, "Dateline Dallas," *The Texas Observer*, November, 21, 2003
242 Lincoln, 365
243 O'Donnell and Powers, 451
244 James Jarman testimony, WC, Vol. III, 199–200
245 Manchester, *Death of a President*, 14
246 Ibid., 10
247 Ibid., 18–19
248 Ibid., 28
249 Ibid., 33–4
250 Rebecca Onion, "The 'Wanted For Treason' Flyer Distributed in Dallas Before JFK's Visit," Slate, November 11, 2013
251 Manchester, *Death of a President*, 56
252 Ibid., 56–7
253 JFK Library, "Remarks Prepared For Delivery At The Trade Mart in Dallas, TX, November 22, 1963 [undelivered]"
254 Manchester, *Death of a President*, 64–5
255 Ibid., 65
256 Maude Shaw, *White House Nanny*, 100
257 Manchester, *Death of a President*, 60
258 Ibid., 61
259 Ibid., 64
260 Ibid., 94
261 Ibid., 74
262 Ibid., 75–6
263 JFK Library, "Remarks At The Dedication Of The Aerospace Medical Health Center, San Antonio, Texas, November 21, 1963"
264 Manchester, *Death of a President*, 83
265 Ibid., 77
266 Ibid., 94
267 Dugger.
268 Manchester, *Death of a President*, 80
269 Marina Oswald testimony, WC, Vol. I, 65
270 Ibid., 66.
271 Ruth Paine testimony, WC, Vol. III, 58
272 Ibid., 49
273 Manchester, *Death of a President*, 90
274 Ibid., 81
275 Ibid., 83
276 JFK Library, "Remarks At Representative Albert Thomas Dinner, Houston Coliseum, Texas, 21 November 1963"
277 Bugliosi, *Parkland*, 3
278 Manchester, *Death of a President*, 86

279 Jim Bishop, *The Day Kennedy Was Shot* (New York: Greenwich House, 1968)
280 Ted Sorenson, *Kennedy* (New York: HarperPerennial, 2009), 749

Chapter 9

1 Manchester, *Death of a President*, 93
2 Harris.
3 Jim Bishop, *The Day Kennedy Was Shot* (New York: Greenwich House, 1968), 30.
4 Bugliosi, 5
5 Manchester, *Death of a President*, 107–8
6 Ibid., 41
7 Frazier testimony, WC, Vol. II, 226
8 Ibid., 227
9 Manchester, *Death of a President*, 112
10 Frazier, WC, Vol. II, 229
11 Sandee LaMotte, "JFK's assassination aided by his bad back, records show," CNN, November 30, 2017.
12 Manchester, *Death of a President*, 108
13 Ibid., 113
14 Ibid., 114
15 Alexandra Zapruder, *Twenty-Six Seconds* (New York: Twelve, 2016), 29
16 Ibid., 30
17 Manchester, *Death of a President*, 116
18 Jarman affidavit given to Dallas County Notary Public, November 23, 1963
19 David Von Pein's JFK Archives, "President Kennedy in Fort Worth, Texas, on November 22, 1963"
20 Bonnie Ray Williams testimony, WC, Vol. III, 166
21 Robert MacNeil on John F. Kennedy's assassination—Television Academy Foundation
22 Remarks at the Breakfast of the Fort Worth Chamber of Commerce, University of California at Santa Barbara, The American Presidency Project
23 Lawrence J. Korb, Laura Conley, and Alex Rothman, "A Historical Perspective on Defense Budgets," *American Progress*, July 6, 2011
24 UCSB, The American Presidency Project
25 O'Donnell and Powers, 25
26 Manchester, *Death of a President*, 120-21
27 O'Donnell and Powers, 26.
28 Ibid., 26
29 Ibid., 125
30 Clint Hill interview with the author
31 Lincoln, 369
32 Manchester, *Death of a President*, 126–7
33 Jeb Byrne, "The Hours before Dallas," *Prologue Magazine*, Summer 2000, Vol. 32, No. 2
34 Manchester, *Death of a President*, 41, 149
35 Zapruder, 33
36 Manchester, *Death of a President*, 130
37 MacNeil, Television Academy

38 WFAA-TV Archives
39 Manchester, *Death of a President*, 128, WFAA archives
40 Ibid., 130
41 O'Donnell testimony, WC, Vol. III, 443
42 Jarman affidavit
43 Billy Lovelady testimony, WC, Vol. VI, 338.
44 Zapruder, 34
45 Manchester, *Death of a President*, 133
46 Ibid., 37
47 Ibid., 131
48 Clint Hill interview
49 Bonnie Ray Williams testimony, WC, Vol. III, 167
50 Ibid., 168
51 Manchester, *Death of a President*, 133
52 Zapruder interview with WFAA-TV's Jay Watson, November 22, 1963
53 Manchester, *Death of a President*, 135
54 Williams, WC, Vol, III, 169
55 Manchester, *Death of a President*, 136
56 MacNeil, Television Academy Foundation
57 Arnold Rowland testimony, WC, Vol. II, 169
58 Manchester, *Death of a President*, 150
59 Barbara Rowland testimony, WC, Vol. VI, 181
60 Arnold Rowland, WC, Vol, II, 174
61 Manchester, *Death of a President*, 136
62 Ibid., 137
63 MacNeil, Television Academy Foundation
64 Howard Brennan testimony, WC, Vol. 3, 141–2
65 Jarman, Vol. III, 200–03.
66 Williams, Vol. III, 170.
67 Ronald Fischer testimony, WC, Vol. VI, 193
68 Ibid.
69 Williams, Vol. III, 169.
70 Manchester, *Death of a President*, 150
71 Ibid., 147–8.
72 Williams, Vol. III, 173.
73 Harold Norman testimony, WC, Vol. III, 195
74 Manchester, *Death of a President*, 151
75 Brennan, Vol. III, 143
76 Manchester, *Death of a President*, 151
77 Hosty, 9
78 Manchester, 148–9
79 Brennan, WC, Vol. III, 143
80 Manchester, *Death of a President*, 152
81 Associated Press interview, October 31, 1995
82 Jacqueline Kennedy testimony, WC, Vol. V, 179
83 Clint Hill interview with the author

84 Nellie Connally testimony, WC, Vol. IV, 147
85 Jacqueline Kennedy, WC, Vol. V, 180
86 James Zahm testimony, WC, Vol. XI, 306